the Shenzhen
insider's guide

DISCOVERY PUBLISHER
探索出版社
NEVER SEEN BEFORE • NEVER BEEN BEFORE

New edition. Even better.

In 2008 we wrote the first Shenzhen guide ever written in English, *Shopping in Shenzhen*. The guidebook was published by *The Shenzhen Press Group*, Shenzhen's largest publishing house, and largely promoted by Shenzhen's largest English newspaper, *The Shenzhen Daily*. It was overall a large success.

A year later, in 2009, *Living in Shenzhen* was published under our company. This guide was *Shopping in Shenzhen's* companion. It covered all important areas a traveller that stays in Shenzhen more than a few days would need. To our surprise, *Living in Shenzhen* encountered an even greater success than *Shopping in Shenzhen*.

These two guides were at all time sponsored by one of Shenzhen's largest websites, *WikiShenzhen.com*.

In 2010 we published *Enjoy Shenzhen*, a new version of *Shopping in Shenzhen*, with new additions such as nightlife, restaurants, hotels and such.

In 2011 we published *The Comprehensive Shenzhen Pocket Guide*, a tiny guidebook that comprehends most of the content of *Shopping in Shenzhen, Enjoy Shenzhen* and *Living in Shenzhen*.

This 2014/2015 edition of *The Shenzhen Insider's Guide* has largely been revised and augmented.

Table of Contents

Landing in Shenzhen

From Expats to Expats
Landing in Shenzhen

DO YOU REMEMBER the moment your spouse or employer asked the question, "So, how would you feel about moving to Shenzhen, China?" Prior to this question, I had not even heard of Shenzhen. How could a city so large be so completely unknown to me? This question prompted many others, ranging from the minute to the monumental. What is it like to live overseas, let alone in China? How would I get around? And where can I buy sour cream – you know - the essentials of life.

As this was our first expat assignment, and being the adventurous sort that I am, I was so excited. But before I even stepped foot on Chinese soil, I was confronted with a battery of questions from friends and family. Their reactions ran from curious to outright questioning of my sanity. Isn't it funny how people who had never been to China, or even knew a person of Chinese descent for that matter, had all kinds of advice on what to expect?

After doing loads of research on the internet, I headed to Shenzhen for an information-gathering visit. This was no small feat as I traveled alone through time zones and immigration requirements. Making it from Hong Kong to Shenzhen by the airport ferry was reason to celebrate. I was later told that seasoned travelers often end up in the immigration lines and literally miss the boat. Such was the beginning of this unique expatriate adventure we call "Living in Shenzhen."

After the logistics of where to live and school choices were settled, thoughts of all that I would do in China were dancing in my head. I began to allow myself to dream about studying the language, learning my way around and experiencing authentic Chinese medicine. I really didn't know what to expect. So, I made some generally wrong assumptions about what it is like to live here.

When I first got here, I didn't have a clue as to what I needed to know. So even asking pertinent questions was difficult. That is why interacting with other expats was very helpful. The Shekou Women's International Club members were a good resource. They have all been through it and provided a wealth of information. From day trips to shopping, hanging out with other people in my situation made my transition easier. I appreciated the closeness of the community of expats and always enjoyed walking around, because I was bound to meet someone I knew. But the truly fun part was interacting with the locals.

The biggest challenge for me was the language. The background noise of conversations was at once very distracting, but interesting at the same time. One of the best things I did early on was take language lessons. Not only did it make things easier, but it also gave me a sense of being a part of my surroundings. I found that the Chinese people appreciated my attempts to speak their language and get to know them. Also, being able to communicate with my housekeeper was helpful and a lot of fun. Having a conversation with a beggar about her family was quite touching, although it required a lot of charades.

Language also played a big role in learning my way around the city. I remember the first time I got in a cab by myself and told the driver where I lived, and actually arriving there. I think I called everyone I knew to declare my success. At home, I always drove everywhere, so public transport, cabs and private drivers were a mystery to me. The best way to learn was to just do it. I asked someone to take me on a bus to get familiar with the routine. After that, I checked out the bus routes myself. After a time, I didn't even notice people looking at me because I was different. In fact, I felt welcomed. Walking also became a huge part of my life. I found new neighborhoods and had children shouting, "Hello." I was surprised at how many markets and parks were tucked away here.

I have done things here that I never had imagined. Chinese medicine was a big one. I had expected a grizzled, old Chinese man in the dark, back room of an interesting-smelling storefront. In reality, I have a lovely woman that comes to my house to give me massages and make me weird food that is "good for the health." (A side note- if it is good for the health, it means it is bad for the taste.) Having 100 needles sticking out of my face to help with the wrinkles is particularly interesting. I also get to practice my Chinese with her.

There are so many unexpected pleasures that I have run across. I particularly enjoy going to parks, and to Garden City in the mornings to watch the groups of people doing Tai Chi. I have friends that have been included in card games with the locals. They were invited to just pull up a chair and have tea and a game. Never mind that they hadn't a clue as to what they were playing. The people here are so friendly.

Some other activities that people do here are lessons of all sorts, including Chinese calligraphy and painting. Trying cheap Chinese food at the food court or night barbecue and climbing Nanshan Mountain are other highlights. There are clubs for interests as varied as rugby to cultural societies. The volunteer opportunities, while not as plentiful here as elsewhere, provide meaningful experiences, like the group of women who work in local orphanages. There really is something for everyone.

Time here is very different than where I am from. In some ways it, feels like the day goes on and on, never ending. But I feel I am forever "losing" a week. No day is ever the same. There are so many things to do, but some of them require digging. For those that have recently worked full-time, it can be a challenge at first to shift into this expat lifestyle.

There is such a wide range of experiences of individual expats. I have met people that have gone farther into the language and culture than I dare. I also have met people that never really leave their apartment. In all, the experience is definitely what you make of it.

■ by Virlane Torbit

 For more information about the above-mentioned places visit WikiShenzhen.com

Basic Information on Shenzhen

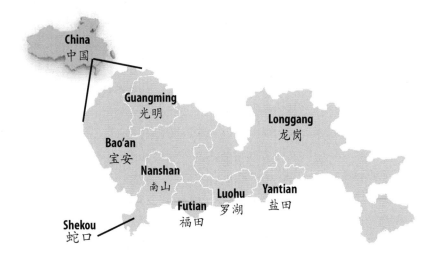

China/Shenzhen Map

Shenzhen (simplified Chinese: 深圳市; pinyin: Shēn zhèn shì]) is a city of sub-provincial administrative status in southern China's Guangdong province, situated immediately north of Hong Kong. Owing to China's economic liberalization under the policies of reformist leader Deng Xiaoping, the area became China's first, and ultimately most successful, Special Economic Zone.

The boomtown of Shenzhen is located in the Pearl River Delta.

The municipality covers an area of 2,050 km² (790 sq. miles) including urban and rural areas, with a total population of 12 million. Shenzhen is a sub-tropical maritime region, with frequent tropical cyclones in summer and early autumn, with an average temperature of 22.4°C year-round (72°F) although daytime temperatures can exceed 35°C.

Shenzhen has some of the largest public projects in China. The International Trade Center (国贸),

built in 1985, was the tallest building in China when built, and the Shun Hing building was also the tallest in Asia when it was built (still the tallest steel building in the world).

Shenzhen is also the site for many other tall building projects. Some of the supertalls that have been either proposed or approved are well over 400 meters. The current tallest building under construction is the 439 metre tall Kingkey Finance Tower, which will be finished in 2010. Other proposed buildings would surpass the Kingkey Finance Tower's height by 2015.

Modern Shenzhen
and its Rediscovered Past

'Deep Drains', calligraphy by Zhang Pingsheng 张平生

From Experts to Expats
Modern Shenzhen and its Rediscovered Past

SHENZHEN IS WELL-KNOWN as an "overnight city," which best describes its rapid development from a tiny border town to a modern city with a population of 12 million in less than three decades.

What is now Shenzhen was a tiny border town of 30,000 people, called Bao'an County, before 1979. Many people regard Shenzhen, established in 1979, as a city with a short history, or no history at all. However, relics unearthed in Shenzhen in recent years indicated human activities 6,700 years ago in the Neolithic Age. Shenzhen, as a settlement, has a history of 1,673 years.

Earliest known ancient records that carried the name of Shenzhen date from 1410 during the Ming Dynasty. Local people called the drains in paddy fields 圳 "zhen." Shenzhen, 深圳 literally means "deep drains," because the area used to be crisscrossed with rivers and streams, and there were deep drains in the paddy fields. Shenzhen became a township at the beginning of the Qing Dynasty, and was renamed Xin'an and Bao'an later.

When the Guangdong Provincial Government decided to upgrade Bao'an County to a city in 1978, the plan was aimed at establishing an export base that would boost the province's foreign trade, following Chinese leaders' decision to embrace the market economy and open up the country to the outside world. According to Zhang Xunpu, Shenzhen's first Party chief from 1979-1980, city leaders decided to name the city Shenzhen instead of Bao'an because the former was better known overseas and local people preferred a name implying "getting rich." In Guangdong and Hong Kong, "water" is synonymous with "money," so "zhen," either referring to a river, stream or drain, underlined the wishes for fortunes and wealth.

Shortly after the establishment of Shenzhen City, China's paramount leader Deng Xiaoping came up with the brilliant idea of Special Economic Zone, with the first such experimental zone to be established in Shenzhen in 1980. Deng believed Shenzhen would attract overseas investment because of its proximity to Hong Kong and the fact that both cities share language, dialect and culture.

Deng Xiaoping, who is given much credit for Shenzhen's boom, visited the city twice. During his first visit in January 1984, Deng acknowledged the rapid development in Shenzhen and especially Shekou. He wrote in a scroll in Guangzhou after visiting Shenzhen, which says "The development and experience of Shenzhen proves our decision to establish special economic zones is correct," a statement reformists have used to fend off attacks by those who at times bemoaned Shenzhen as a potential fall of socialism's frontline.

In January 1992, when debates heated up on whether the special economic zones were practicing socialism or capitalism, Deng paid his second visit to Shenzhen where he reaffirmed special economic zones were socialist in nature. After his visit, China's reforms and opening up drive was back on track, and gathered more momentum.

The history of modern Shenzhen would not be complete without mentioning Shekou. In 1979, Hong Kong-based China Merchants Group was given the task of developing and managing the Shekou industrial zone in Shenzhen. The barren land in Shekou then attracted overseas investors, notably from Hong Kong, and then foreign oil drilling and rig service companies, which formed joint ventures with China to tap oil resources in the South China Sea. Engineers from as far away as Texas, Scotland and Scandinavia, settled in Shekou, which became home to the largest number of expatriates in Shenzhen. The development of Shekou marked one of the beginnings of the economic reforms and opening up of Shenzhen, and China at large.

Deng's experiment in Shenzhen has proved to be a great success, propelling the further opening up of China and continuous economic reform. Shenzhen eventually became one of the largest cities in the Pearl River Delta region, which has become one of the economic powerhouses of China as well as the largest manufacturing base in the world. Since 1980, the city's economy has surged about 28 percent annually on average, making the city the best-ever example of rapid growth in the world history of city development.

As the country's first special economic zone, Shenzhen shouldered the mission to spearhead China's reform and opening up. It took the lead in the country in piloting reforms. China's first joint-stock company Bao'an County United Investment Co. (now known as China Bao'an Group) was established here in 1983. The company issued China's first stock certificates after 1949, drawing criticism from many people who regarded stock certificates as a symbol of corrupt capitalism at that time. Shenzhen also introduced China's first land auction system in 1987 that has made sale of land use rights more transparent, a move considered bold at that time.

Shenzhen is now a high-tech manufacturing base, logistics hub and regional financial center in South China. The high-tech, logistics, financial and cultural industries are officially listed as the four pillar industries of the city.

Shenzhen is undoubtedly a world factory, with multinational companies operating a wide array of factories here manufacturing almost everything ranging from electronic products, clothes and furniture to toys. Shenzhen is said to manufacture at least 80 percent of artificial Christmas trees and three-fourths of toys sold worldwide. The city is undergoing an industrial upgrade, with its economy becoming less labor-intensive but more service-based, and technology-intensive.

Shenzhen is city of migrants, with the population growing from about 30,000 to 12 million in less

than 30 years. Here you can find migrants from almost every part of the country, and of all the country's 56 ethnic groups. This is why restaurants in Shenzhen offer a wide range of local cuisines from other parts of the country.

Unlike other Chinese cities with a more "civilized" past, Shenzhen does not have perfectly kept historical records. The interpretation of unearthed relics is still a matter of academic discussion. Fortunately, amid the sleek skyscrapers, some legendary historical sites can be found, offering a glimpse to Shenzhen's past. Here are several examples:

1. Dapeng Fortress

Listed under State protection, the 10,000-sqm Dapeng Fortress is located in Pengcheng Village overlooking Daya Bay, Longgang District. It was first built in 1394 in the Ming Dynasty as a military fortress against Chinese and Japanese pirates, and later developed into a town in the Ming and Qing dynasties. It also served as a key fortress fighting British colonists. There are three well-preserved fortress gates, sections of ancient walls, alleys paved with stone slates, century-old temples and shrines, as well as a few mansions for some admirals of the Qing Dynasty. The best example of the mansions is that of former Admiral Lai Enjue, a residence with a history of over 150 years.

2. Nantou Ancient City

First built in 1394, the 27th year of Emperor Hongwu's rule in the Ming Dynasty, Nantou Ancient City, then called Dongguan Military Base, was home to

2,200 imperial soldiers. Located in Jiujietou Village in Nanshan District, the remains of the ancient city is a testimony to Shenzhen's ancient civilization. The cultural heritage still boasts a well-preserved gate, 10 meters in width and 4.5 meters in height. Near the gate there is a museum showing dozens of excavated artifacts. A few other traditional buildings, including a memorial hall for Wen Tianxiang, the last resisting prime minister of the Southern Song Dynasty, are also preserved.

3. Chiwan Tianhou Temple

The temple sits beside Chiwan Village at the foot of the beautiful Xiaonanshan Hill, in Nanshan District. The temple worshiping Tianhou (Matsu, the Goddess of Sea) was first built in the early Northern Song Dynasty (960-1127), which was later developed

and expanded over the course of the Ming and Qing dynasties, with support from the emperors. The temple's prime was during the Ming and Qing dynasties, when it served as an important stop on the Ocean Silk Road between China and Southeast Asia.

Legend has it that Tianhou saved the famous Ming Dynasty navigator, eunuch Zheng He, from the eye of a typhoon off Shekou. After that, the temple was renovated with official funding and all imperial delegations going to Southeast Asia had to worship at the temple before setting sail.

4. Shaodi Emperor's Mausoleum

The only imperial mausoleum found in Guangdong Province, it was built west of Chiwan Village centuries ago in memory of Zhao Ribing (known as Shaodi Emperor in history). Zhao was the last emperor of the Song Dynasty, who died in 1279 at the age of nine.

After Yuan (1271-1368) emperor Kublai Khan conquered the Southern Song capital of Lin'an

(today's Hangzhou) in 1276, Song ministers Lu Xiufu and Zhang Shijie escorted Shaodi to Xinhui, Guangdong Province, and backed him to become emperor in 1278. However, the Yuan army surrounded their base in Xinhui in 1279 and defeated the remaining Song troops.

When resistance finally crumbled, Prime Minister Lu jumped into the sea, with Shaodi on his back, and drowned, in order to avoid being humiliated. Many generals and soldiers followed them. The boy emperor's body floated to Chiwan and landed on the beach. Almost at the same time, a ridge beam in the Tianhou Temple dropped to the ground. Locals believed the goddess was sympathetic with the boy emperor and wanted them to turn the beam into a coffin for him, so they buried him near the temple.

For more information about the above-mentioned places visit WikiShenzhen.com

5. Hehu New Residence

The residence, also known as Hakka Folk Custom Museum, is one of the best-preserved Hakka-style residential buildings. It sits in Luoruihe Village in Longgang District, 28 kilometers from downtown Shenzhen. The residence, covering an area of 24,816 square meters and housing 179 rooms, was built in 1817. It is said the construction took the family 22 years to finish. The residence, with 179 "apartments" each consisting of one to three rooms, housed some 1,000 clan members at its peak. It is the largest ancient Hakka housing compound in Shenzhen, Dongguan and Huizhou.

■ by Robert Lin Min

Appendix

The following is an official account of Shenzhen's history before modern Shenzhen City was established.

Ancient Baiyue Tribe (Prehistory -214 B.C.)

In the Xia and Shang dynasties, Shenzhen was a base for the ancient sea-faring Baiyue Tribe. Those who lived here were called the Nanyue Tribe, a southern branch of the Baiyue Tribe. They lived mainly by fishing with little farming.

Qin Prefecture (214 B.C.-A.D.331)

After Qinshihuang united China to become its first emperor, he set up, in 214 B.C., three prefectures, namely Nanhai, Guilin and Xiangjun, in the area later to be known as Guangdong and Guangxi, to be developed by 500,000 people who were banished by the emperor to the southern outposts. Shenzhen was under the administration of Nanhai Prefecture at the time and was formally brought under Qinshihuang's rule.

Establishment of County (331-1573)

In 331, in the Eastern Jin Dynasty, Dongguan Prefecture was established to administer the six counties that now cover today's Shenzhen, Dongguan and Hong Kong. The capital of the prefecture was located in Nantou, Bao'an County.

During the Song Dynasty, Shenzhen became an important hub for maritime trade in South China, famous for its salt and spices. In the Yuan Dynasty, pearls were another famous product of the area. In 1394 in the Ming Dynasty, Dongguan and Dapeng military bases were set up in what is now Shenzhen.

Nantou Ancient City, with a history of at least 600 years, was once a political center of the Shenzhen, Hong Kong and Macao area in the Qing Dynasty.

Xin'an Ancient Town (1573-1841)

In 1573, a new county named Xin'an was established in the territory of today's Shenzhen and Hong Kong, with the county seat located in Nantou. Salt, tea, spices and rice were the backbone of the new county's economy.

Cession of territory (1842-1898)

Following the signing of The Treaty of Nanjing, the Convention of Peking and the Convention for the Extension of Hong Kong between China and Great Britain between 1842 and 1989, China handed Hong Kong Island, the Kowloon Peninsula and New Territories to British rule. This meant Xin'an County lost an area of 1,055.6 square kilometers to British rule.

Name resumption (1913-1979)

In 1913, Xin'an County was renamed Bao'an County with the county seat remaining in Nantou.

County seat relocation (1938-1953)

Nantou was occupied by Japanese troops and so the county government was relocated to Dongguan County.

In 1953, the Bao'an county seat moved eastward to Shenzhen Township, 10 kilometers from Nantou. As the Guangzhou-Kowloon Railway ran through Shenzhen, more people lived there and industry and trade prospered.

For more information about the above-mentioned places visit WikiShenzhen.com

Arts in Shenzhen

From Experts to Expats
Arts in Shenzhen, an Overview

I F YOU ARE visiting Shenzhen for the first time, you may be impressed with numerous high-rises along Shennan Thoroughfare 深南大道, the main avenue running from west to east.

In fact, wide-ranging diversity of architecture in Shenzhen is only a showcase of arts in general, featuring a mishmash of different genres and styles; traditional and avant-garde, parochial and exotic, Chinese and Western.

Compared with the established cities of Beijing and Shanghai, the art scene in Shenzhen is best known for its open and pioneering spirit.

If you want to know how commercial paintings are produced in China, Dafen Painting Village 大芬油画村 in Longgang District is a must see. Even if you don't want to buy anything, a half-day tour of the village will be intriguing and unforgettable.

The village is a reputed gathering place for painters from all over the country mass-manufacturing and wholesaling many imitations of European or Chinese master paintings, as well as their own original works.

Back in the early 1990s, a Hong Kong businessman, Huang Jiang, took five painters with him to the village and rented a farmer's house to live in. Then he took orders to the painters and asked them to finish them according to his requirements. Finally, he shipped their works to the rest of the world via Hong Kong.

After a complete renovation funded by the government in 2004, the village has now become an attraction for tourists as well as art dealers from all over the world.

If you have a keen interest in original avant-garde art, Shenzhen Free Art House (SFAH) 深圳艺术创库 in F518 Idea Land in Bao'an District 宝安区F518 创意园 is also a must.

Established in a disused factory

Dafen Painting Vilage - Credits Newman Huo

building in Nanshan District at the end of 2006, the SFAH had become increasingly influential in South China, and had drawn more than 40 freelance artists from all over the country by the end of 2007.

The SFAH was relocated to Bao'an District in February 2008, one month after a fire closed its previous location in Nanshan District.

F518 Idea Land - Credits Newman Huo

The 35 workshops for the SFAH artists in F518 Idea Land are open to the public every day, with a major joint exhibition staged on the first day of every month.

If you are interested in Chinese antiques, Shenzhen Curio City 深圳古玩城 in Huangbeiling, Luohu District should be a first stop.

In the Curio City, you can find antique Chinese paintings and calligraphic works, chinaware, bronzeware, furniture and a variety of other artifacts.

If you particularly love antique Chinese porcelain, you should not miss the private Xibaolou Museum of Celadon 玺宝楼青瓷博物馆 in Luohu District, which houses more than 2,000 celadon products from the Shang Dynasty (1600 BC - 1046 BC) through the Qing Dynasty (1644-1911).

Established in 1997, the museum was the first private museum in Shenzhen as well as one of China's top 10 private museums.

If you love sculpture, two city

sculptures are highly recommended.

The sculpture, "Pioneering Bull," which was completed in 1984, is located at the entrance to the government compounds on Shennan Road Central 深南中路 in Futian District.

The city sculpture is believed to symbolize the significance of establishing China's first economic special zone in Shenzhen.

The other is composed of 18 life-size bronze statues, the sculpture, "One Day in Shenzhen," was finished in 2000, and installed at the southern side of Yuanling 园岭 Residence Block in Futian District.

On Nov. 22, 1999, a total of 18 Shenzheners with different backgrounds were randomly chosen to be the models that were cast into bronze statues.

The two sculptures are regarded as the most important artistic milestones in Shenzhen's history.

Art exhibitions and cultural events are staged in the city's museums and exhibition venues, public or private, throughout the year.

The International Ink Painting Biennial of Shenzhen has been one of the most influential art events in the city since it was initiated by Shenzhen Fine Arts Institute (SFAI) 深圳画院 in 1998.

Located in the Yinhu Lake 银湖 area, the SFAI was the first in

Elements Show - Credits Newman Huo

China to popularize the concept "metropolis ink painting," calling on artists from home and abroad to paint contemporary urban landscapes and life with the traditional medium of ink painting.

The SFAI is known for hosting experimental Chinese ink painting or new medium art shows.

Located inside the scenic East Lake Park 东湖公园, Shenzhen Art Museum (SAM) 深圳美术馆 has witnessed the art development in the city over the past three decades.

The SAM has been focusing on contemporary urban art and encouraging local art by hosting exhibitions for homegrown artists.

Located in Overseas Chinese Town (OCT), He Xiangning Art Museum 何香凝美术馆 is the only national modern art museum in Shenzhen, as well as the second national modern art museum. The first was National Art Museum of China in Beijing.

Administered by the national museum, OCT Contemporary Art Terminal OCAT 当代艺术中心 is located in the eastern industrial zone of the Konka Group in the OCT.

Since it was opened in early 2005, the OCAT has become an important place in South China for avant-garde artists from home and abroad to display their works.

Besides the OCAT, you can spend half a day touring the neighboring art park of the OCT-LOFT 华侨城创意文化园, which houses more than 20 companies and organizations, including designers, architects and avant-garde artists.

The OCT-LOFT is an excellent place to relax or meet friends over a cup of tea or coffee.

Located on Hongli Road 红荔路 at the foot of Lotus Hill in Futian Distinct, Guan Shanyue Art Museum 关山月美术馆 was built in the name of the Chinese master painter Guan Shanyue in 1995 when he donated 813 works to Shenzhen.

The museum not only has Guan's works on display throughout the year, but also holds exhibitions for artists from China and abroad.

If you want to watch modern shows, you should not miss "Elements," the first Las Vegas-style show on the Chinese mainland.

Different from all the theme park performances the OCT Group has produced since 1990, the "Elements" show is the first to have been put on in a theater outside the cluster of theme parks in the OCT.

Arts in general in Shenzhen, a city of immigrants with a history of only around 30 years, are still in the making.

The Shenzhen International Cultural Industry Fair has become an extravaganza since it was started in March 2004.

The fair showcases the city's latest achievements in the "cultural industry," which actually includes art, literature, printing, animation and entertainment.

As the most powerful and wealthy sponsor of art and cultural events, the Shenzhen Municipal Government is increasing its annual investment in stepping up the development of the city's "cultural industry" in order to realize its ambitious goal of building Shenzhen into "a city of culture."

Despite its strong commercial atmosphere, Shenzhen is expected to become an important gathering place in South China for young, promising avant-garde artists in the coming years, which will be distinct in style from art communities in Beijing and Shanghai.

More importantly, with contemporary Chinese art becoming increasingly popular in auction houses worldwide nowadays, original high quality artworks produced by young, promising avant-garde artists in Shenzhen will be keenly sought after by art dealers and investors from home and abroad.

■ by Newman Huo

For more information about the above-mentioned places visit WikiShenzhen.com

Shenzhen's Arts Places

Museums

NANSHAN DISTRICT

1 He Xiangning Art Gallery 何香凝美术馆
Address: Shennan Road, Overseas Chinese Town, Nanshan District
地址: 南山区华侨城
Phone: 2660-4540
Website: www.hxnart.com (Chinese and some English)
Hours: Daily 10am -6pm (closed Monday)
Fee: 20RMB; free admission on Friday
Busses: 26, 101, 105, 113, 204
Metro: Hua Qiao Cheng Station 华侨城站

2 Nanshan Fine Art Institute 南山画院
Address: Li Yuan Road, Nanshan District
地址: 南山区荔园路南山文体中心
Phone: 2656-1080
Website: None
Hours: Daily 9h30am -9pm (closed Monday)
Fee: Free
Busses: 204, 234, etc.

FUTIAN DISTRICT

3 Guan Shanyue Art Museum 关山月美术馆
Address: 6026 Hongli Road, Futian District
地址: 福田区红荔路6026号

Phone: 8306-3086
Website: www.gsyart.com (English & Chinese)
Hours: Daily 9am -5pm (closed Monday)
Fee: 10RMB; free admission on Friday
Busses: 10, 25, 34, 105, 215, 111, 350, 228, etc.
Metro: Shao Nian Gong Station Exit B 少年宫站B出口

4 Shenzhen Museum 深圳市博物馆
Address: 1008 Shennan Road Central, across from CITIC Plaza, Futian District
地址: 福田区深南中路1008号
Phone: 8210-1706
Website: www.shenzhenmuseum.com.cn (English)
Hours: Daily 9am -5pm (closed Monday)
Fee: 10RMB, 5RMB for students; free admission on Friday
Busses: 3, 8, 12, 101, 215
Metro: Da Ju Yuan Station, Exit A 大剧院站A出口

5 Shenzhen Academy of Sculpture 深圳雕塑院当代艺术馆
Address: No.8 Zhongkang Road, Shangmeilin, Futian District
地址: 福田区上梅林中康路8号
Phone: 8395-3116

Website: None
Hours: 9am -5pm
Fee: Unknown
Busses: 44, 45, 60, 102, 216, 218, 222, 324, 374, 388

LUOHU DISTRICT

6 Shenzhen Art Museum 深圳美术馆
Address: East Lake Park, Aiguo Road, Luohu District
地址：罗湖区爱国路东湖公园内
Phone: 2542-6069
Website: www.szam.org (Chinese)
Hours: Daily 9am -5pm (closed Monday)
Fee: 5RMB; free admission on Friday
Busses: 3, 17, 365, 351, 336, 29, etc.
Metro: Get off at Lao Jie (Dongmen) and take a taxi

7 Museum of Chinese Outstanding Figures 华夏英杰墨宝园博物馆
Address: 105 Beidou Road, Luohu District
地址：罗湖区北斗路105号
Phone: 8212-9688
Website: None
Hours: Daily 9am -6pm (closed Monday)
Fee: Free
Busses: 223, 10, 14, 27, etc.

8 The Site of the Merits 元勋旧址
Address: Sungang Village, Luohu District
地址：罗湖区笋岗村内
Website: None
Fee: Free
Busses: 218

9 Shenzhen Fine Art Institute 深圳画院
Address: Jinhu Road, Luohu District
地址：罗湖区银湖路金湖路
Phone: 8243-8392
Website: www.inkpainting.org (Chinese with some English)
Hours: Daily 9am -5pm
Fee: Free
Busses: 4, 5, 7, 201, 218, 222, 301, 360, 315 , 405, etc

10 Shenzhen Paleontological Museum 深圳古生物博物馆
Address: Inside the Shenzhen Fairy Lake Botanical Garden, Luohu District
地址：罗湖区仙湖植物园内
Phone: 2570-2716
Website: www.szbg.org/English%20web/main.htm (English)
Hours: Monday-Friday 9am -5pm Saturday-Sunday 9am -6pm
Fee: 20RMB (for Fairy Lake Park)
Busses: 220, 218, 450, 468, 505, etc.

11 Shenzhen Xibao Mansion Successive Dynasties' Celadon Museum 深圳玺宝楼青瓷博物馆
Address: 2095 Bao an Road South, Luohu District
地址：罗湖区宝安南路
Phone: 2556-3935
Website: None
Hours: 9am -11pm
Fee: 30RMB
Busses: 366, 413, 404, 18, 313, 418
Metro: Da Ju Yuan Station 大剧院站

BAO'AN DISTRICT

12 Bao'an Fine Art Institute 宝安画院
Address: Fourth Xin'an Road, Bao'an District
地址： 宝安区新安四路
Phone: 2778-2645
Website: www.sbart.cn (Chinese)
Hours: Monday-Friday 9-10am , 2-6pm
Fee: Free
Busses: 603, 606, 629, 610, etc.

LONGGANG DISTRICT

13 Museum of Ancient Dapeng City 龙岗区大鹏古城博物馆
Address: Pengcheng Community, Dapeng Street, Longgang District
地址： 龙岗区大鹏街道鹏城社区
Phone: 8431-9269
Website: www.szdpsc.com (Chinese)
Hours: Daily 8h30am -6pm
Fee: 20RMB
Busses: 364, 360, 833, 818 change to 818
Note: The Museum is located inside the Dapeng Fortress

14 Longgang Hakkas Custom Museum 深圳龙岗客家民俗博物馆
Address: 1 Luoruihe North Street, Longgang Street, Longgang District
地址： 龙岗区龙岗街道罗瑞合北街一号
Phone: 8429-6108
Website: Unknown
Hours: Daily 8-11h30am , 2-5pm
Fee: 10RMB

Busses: 365, 351, 329, etc.
Note: The Museum is itself an old Hakka house compound

15 Dong Jiang Army Museum 东江纵队纪念馆
Address: Shihuipi Village Dongzhong Road, Pingshan Town, Longgang District
地址： 龙岗区坪山镇东纵路石灰陂村
Phone: 8464-2252
Website: None
Hours: Daily 8am -5pm
Fee: Free
Busses: 365, 818, etc.

YANTIAN DISTRICT

16 Zhong-Ying Street Historical Museum 中英街历史博物馆
Address: 9 Huancheng Road, Sha Tou Jiao, Yantian District
地址： 盐田区沙头角镇内环城路口9号
Phone: 2525-1104
Website: Unknown
Hours: Daily 9am -4h30pm (closed Monday)
Fee: 10RMB
Busses: 202, 205, etc.
Note: This street is part of the boundary between the PRC and Hong Kong,
          you will need to apply for a passport from the local public security department.

Galleries and Cultural Institutes

NANSHAN DISTRICT

17A Shenzhen Poly Theater 深圳保利剧院
Address: Shenzhen Poly Theater, at the intersection of Wenxin Road 5 and Houhai Bin Road, Nanshan District
地址：南山区后海滨路与文心五路交界处深圳保利剧院
Phone: 8637-1698
Website: www.szpoly.com.cn (Chinese)
Busses: 121, N1, 79, 122, 337. 350, 355, 369, 390

17 Nanshan Cultural Center 南山区文化馆
Address: Li Yuan Road, Nanshan District
地址：南山区荔园路南山文体中心
Phone: 2666-5145
Hours: Open Daily, 9h30am - 9pm
Busses: 204, 234, etc.

18 Hua Xia Arts Center 深圳华夏艺术中心
Address: 1, Guangqiao Street, Overseas Chinese Town, Nanshan District
地址：华侨城光侨街1号
Phone: 2660-2342
Busses: 222, 105, 111, 311
Metro: 华侨城站 (Hua Qiao Cheng Station)

FUTIAN DISTRICT

19 Shenzhen Children's Palace 少年宫
Address: First Fuzhong Road, Central Area of Shenzhen Futian District
地址：福田区（市中心区）福中一路
Phone: 8351-3012
Website: www.szcp.com (Chinese)
Hours: T-F 8h30 - 5pm, S-S 8am - 10h30pm
Fee: See "Activities for Children" on page 135 for details.
Busses: 10, 25, 105, 215, 111, etc.
Metro: Line 4, Shao Nian Gong 少年宫站

20 Shenzhen Citizens' Art Gallery 深圳市群众艺术馆影剧院
Address: 95 Yannan Road, Futian District
地址：福田区燕南路95号
Phone: 8335-1377
Website: www.szmassart.com (Chinese)
Hours: Daily 9am -5h30pm
Fee: Free
Busses: 10, 12, 25, 104, 225, etc.
Metro: Ke Xue Guan Station 科学官站

21 Shenzhen Citizen Center 民中心
Address: 3, Fuzhong Road Third, Futian District
地址：福田区福中三路
Phone: 8210-7992
Metro: Shi Min Zhong Xin Station 市民中心站

22 Shenzhen Hall 深圳会堂
Address: 5, Shangbu Road Central, Futian District
地址：福田区上步中路5号（总工会大厦对面）

Phone: 8210-3563, 8210-3619
Busses: 4, 13, 8, 12, 202, etc.

23 Futian Hall 福田会堂
Address: 123, Fuming Road, Gorverment of
Futian District
地址：福田区福民路123号福
田区委
Phone: 8291-8333

24 Futian Culture Center 福田区文化
馆
Address: 86, Jingtian Road North, Futian
District
地址：福田区景田北路86号
Phone: 8391-9148

LUOHU DISTRICT

25 Shenzhen Grand Theater 深圳大剧
院
Address: 5018, Shennan Road East, Luohu
District
地址：罗湖区深南东路5018
号
Phone: 2559-6043
Metro: 大剧院站 (Da Ju Yuan Station
Exit A)

26 Shenzhen Cinema 深圳戏院
Address: 1, Xinyuan Road, Luohu District
地址：罗湖区新园路1号（东
门老街西口）
Phone: 8217-5808
Website: Unknown
Busses: 454, 483, etc.
Metro: 老街站A出口 (Lao Jie
Station Exit A)

27 Shenzhen Symphony Orchestra 深圳
交响乐团
Address: 2025, Huangbei Road, Luohu
District
地址：罗湖区黄贝路2025号
Phone: 2540-5183
Phone: Hotline Booking: 2540-5183,
8211-3333, 2556-3333
Website: www.sso.org.cn (English and
Chinese)
Busses: 13, 104, 104, 208, etc.

28 Luohu Cultural Park 罗湖文化公园
Address: 2012, Leyuan Road, Luohu District
地址：罗湖区乐园路2012号
Phone: 8223-5922, 8225-9800

29 Luohu Cultural Center 罗湖区文化
馆
Address: 93, Leyuan Road, Luohu District
地址：罗湖区乐园路93号
Phone: 8229-0259
Busses: 10, 104, 17, 2, 205, 220, 223, 29,
etc.

30 Shenzhen Cantonese Opera Troupe 粤
剧团
Address: 177, Fenghuang Road, Luohu
District
地址：罗湖区凤凰路177号
Phone: 2540-2984

LONGGANG DISTRICT

31 Longgang Cultural Center
Address: Longcheng Square East, Longgang
District

地址: 龙岗区龙城广场东侧
Phone: 8955-8888

YANTIAN DISTRICT

32 Yantian Cultural Centre 盐田区文化中心
Address: 2086, Yantian Road, Yantian District
地址: 盐田区深盐路2086号
Phone: 2522-7658

Culture and Leisure

NANSHAN DISTRICT

33 Splendid China & Folk Culture Village 锦绣中华 • 中国民俗文化村
Address: Overseas Chinese Town, Nanshan District
地址: 南山区华侨城
Phone: 2660-6526
Website: www.cn5000.com.cn/english/about/index.asp (English)
Hours: 9am - 9pm
Fee: 120RMB
Busses: 101, 204, 209, 223, 301
Metro: Huaqiao Cheng Station - 华侨城站

LONGGANG DISTRICT

34 Dafen Painting Village 大芬油画村
Address: Shen Hui Road, Bu Ji Street, Longgang District
地址: 龙岗区深惠路布吉大芬立交桥东南侧

Phone: 8473-2622
Website: www.szdafen.com (Englishand Chinese)
Hours: All day, every day
Fee: None
Busses: 512, 863, 616, 537, 315, 66

YANTIAN DISTRICT

35 Minsk World 明思克航母世界
Address: Minsk Building, Seashore, Sha Tou Jiao, Yan Tian District
地址: 盐田区沙头角海滨明思克广场 ￥110
Phone: 2535-5333
Website: www.minskworld.com (Chinese)
Hours: Open Daily: 9am - 7h30pm
Fee: 110RMB for adults, 55RMB for children, under 110cm is free
Busses: 202, 205, 103, etc.

Temples

NANSHAN DISTRICT

36 Nanshan Tian Hou Museum 南山区天后博物馆
Address: 9 Chiwan Road Tian Hou Temple, Nanshan District
地址: 南山区赤湾路9号天后宫
Phone: 2685-3133
Website: None
Hours: Daily 8am -5h30pm
Fee: 15RMB (for the temple)
Busses: 226, 433, etc.

37 Guan Di Temple 南山关帝庙

Address: Guan Gong Temple, Nantou, Nanshan District

地址： 南山区赤湾路9号天后宫

Phone: 2685-3133

Website: None

Hours: Daily 8am -5h30pm

Fee: 15RMB (for the temple)

Busses: 204, etc.

Note: The Temple is located at the Western end of Shennan Road. Many busses, notably #204, stop at the Nantou stop. From there, walk 20 meters; the gate will be on your right, just before the larger gate of the Xinan old town area.

38 Lamasery Replica

Address: Folk Cultural Villages (Splendid China), Nanshan District

地址： 南山区锦绣中华华侨城

Website: None

Hours: Daily 8am -5h30pm

Fee: 120RMB (Spendid China entrance fee)

Busses: 113, 70, etc.

Metro: Hua Qiao Cheng Station 华侨城站

Note: The "Lamasery" is located in the "Tibet" area of the park; there are prayer cairns and pennants, and a Tibetan-style "house" nearby.

Futian District

39 San Sheng Gong 三圣宫

Address: Meilin, Futian District (Part of Meilin Park)

地址： 福田区三圣宫

Website: None

Hours: Unknown

Fee: None

Busses: 218, 222, 240, 242, 30, 324, 334, 35, 361, 374, 44, 45, 60, 67, N9

Note: Walk toward the reservoir, find the entry to the park on a side street to the right, and follow the left-hand path up the hill. The temple is at the top of the path.

Luohu District

40 Hong Fa Temple 弘法寺/仙湖植物园

Address: Shenzhen Fairy Lake Botanical Garden, No. 160, Xianhu Lu, Luohu

地址： 罗湖区仙湖路160号仙湖植物园

Phone: 2573-8430

Website: www.szbg.org/English%20web/main.htm (English)

Hours: 6am - 11pm

Fee: 20RMB, children 1.1 ~ 1.4m tall:10RMB

Busses: 57, 65, 218, 220, 382

Note: Mini-bus 468 (from the Hua Qiang Bei area) ends at the gates of Xian Hu (Fairy Lake) Park. From there, buy a ticket and walk inside the gates. Take the shuttle bus (2 RMB) to the temple gate.

Bao'an District

41 Fenghuang Temple 宝安区福永凤凰山

Address: Fenghuang Cun, Fuyong Zhen, Bao'an

地址： 宝安区福永镇凤凰村

Fee: Free

Busses: Bus: 310-315 Circle Line 环线 from Window of the World Station 世界之窗站 to Tongfuyu Gongyequ 同富裕工业区, then change bus to No.754

For more information about the above-mentioned places visit WikiShenzhen.com

Four Arts of the Chinese Scholar   琴棋书画

I N ANCIENT CHINA, to be a scholar was to be an artist. Chinese culture insisted that an educated and 'proper' individual's classical training had components of what in Chinese are called Qín 琴, Qí 棋, Shū 书, and Huà 画. These can be translated into "Instrumentation, Board Game, Calligraphy, and Painting". For one to be considered scholarly, or a man of the arts, the Four Arts were the arts in which to immerse oneself.

The Chinese ideal of an educated man was his strength in reason, creation, expression and dexterity.

All of these arts combined made for a platform by which scholars could compete against each others' creativity, expression, ideas and thinking power.

The Chinese created a means by which men would judge each other beyond the value of their possessions.

A Chinese pauper who excelled in the arts was as respected as the noble who equaled him. These four arts created a culture in which art flourished freely among the populace.

琴

Qín refers to the musical instrument of the literati, the gǔqín (古琴, '古' means 'old', '琴' means 'musical instrument'). Although it exclusively meant this instrument in ancient times, it has now come to mean all musical instruments.

The gǔqín is a seven-stringed zither that owes its invention to the Chinese society of some 3,000 years ago. During the reign of the imperial China, a scholar was expected to play the gǔqín. Gǔqín was explored as an art-form as well as a science, and scholars strove to both play it well and to create texts on its manipulation. Gǔqín notation was invented some 1,500 years ago, and to this day it has not been drastically changed. Some books contain musical pieces written and mastered more than 500 years ago. Gǔqín is so influential that it even made its way into space; the spacecraft *Voyager* launched by the U.S. in 1977 contained a vinyl style record of a gǔqín piece named 'Flowing Water'.

棋

Qí refers to a board game, which is now called Go (wéiqí 围棋), literally meaning 'surrounding game'. Current definitions of qí cover a wide range of board games. Qí is considered more a popular "game of the people" than Go, which was a game with aristocratic connotations. Many theories exist regarding the origin of Go in Chinese history. One of these holds that Go was an ancient fortune telling device used by Chinese cosmologists to simulate the universe's relationship to an individual. Another suggests that the legendary emperor Yao invented it to enlighten his son. Certainly Go had begun to take hold around the 6th century BCE when Confucius mentioned

Go in his masterpiece, Analects 17:22, sometimes erroneously translated as "chess."

Wéiqí is a game in which two players alternate placing black and white stones on a playing surface consisting of a grid of 19x19 lines. Stones are placed on the intersections of the grid, rather than inside the squares as in chess. Stones surrounded on four sides by those of the opposing color are removed from play, and the overall arrangement of stones must never be repeated twice in one game. The game concludes when both players agree that there are no moves left to play, and so pass. The game is then scored by way of counting the empty playable points that each player has encircled, with captured pieces filling in territory of the same color.

书

Shū refers to Chinese calligraphy, which dates to the origins of recorded Chinese history, in essence ever since written characters have existed. Chinese calligraphy is said to be an expression of a practitioners poetic nature, as well as a significant test of manual dexterity. Chinese calligraphy has evolved for thousands of years, and its state of flux stopped only when Chinese characters were unified across the empire. Chinese calligraphy differs from Western calligraphic script in the sense that it was done with a brush instead of metal implements or a quill. Calligraphy was the art by which a scholar could compose his thoughts to be immortalized. It was the scholar's means of creating expressive poetry and sharing his or her own learnedness.

Calligraphic process is also structured in the same way as Go. A minimalist set of rules conveys a system of incredible complexity and grandeur. Every character from the Chinese scripts is built into a uniform shape by means of assigning it a geometric area in which the character must occur. Only three basic forms are used in the creation of the character, those being square, triangle and circle. Each character has a set number of brushstrokes, none must be added or taken away from the character to enhance it visually, lest the meaning be lost. Finally, strict regularity is not required, meaning the strokes may be accentuated for dramatic effect of individual style. Calligraphy was the means by which scholars could mark their thoughts and teachings, and as such, represent some of the more precious treasures that can be found from ancient China.

Huà refers to Chinese painting. Brush painting is the final of the arts that a scholar is expected to learn, and is unarguably the greatest measure of individual creativity. Through painting, a Chinese noble would demonstrate his mastery over the art of line. Often Chinese paintings would be produced on a sheet of plain white rice-paper or silk using nothing but black ink and a single brush. These paintings were made to demonstrate the power of a single line, and in them was reflected a skill that valued in-

tentional and calculated strokes over instinctual erratic creation. Chinese painting can be traced back even farther than calligraphy. Some examples date back to the decorative paintings that were emblazoned on Neolithic pottery. To add tonal quality to paintings, the artists would often paint portions of the subject then wash the cloth before continuing. This made for beautiful landscapes and depictions of ritual. Painting was the art by which a scholar could separate him or herself from the others and take a name.

From Experts to Expats
The Art of Calligraphy

THE ART OF calligraphy 书法 is widely practiced and revered in the East Asian civilizations that use or used Chinese characters. These include China, Japan, Korea, and to a lesser extent, Vietnam. In addition to being an artform in its own right, calligraphy has also influenced ink and wash painting, which is accomplished using similar tools and techniques.

Professional Calligrapher - 張平生

The East Asian tradition of calligraphy originated and developed from China, specifically the ink and brush writing of Chinese characters. There is a general standardization of the various styles of calligraphy in the East Asian tradition. Calligraphy has also led to the development of many other forms of art in East Asia, including seal carving, ornate paperweights, and inkstones.

Paper

In China, Xuanzhi, tradition-ally made in Anhui province, is the preferred type of paper. It is made from the Tartar wingceltis (Pteroceltis tartarianovii), as well as other materials including rice, the paper mulberry (Broussonetia papyrifera), bamboo, hemp, etc.

Ink

The ink is made from lampblack (soot) and binders. It comes in sticks which must be rubbed with water on an inkstone until the right consistency is achieved. Much cheaper, pre-mixed bottled inks are now available, but these are used primarily for practice.

Stick inks are considered higher quality and chemical inks are more prone to bleeding over time, making them less suitable for use in hanging scrolls. Learning to rub the ink is an essential part of calligraphy study.

Traditionally, East Asian calligraphy is written only in black ink, but modern calligraphers sometimes use other colors. Calligraphy teachers use a bright orange or red ink with which they write practice characters for students and correct students' work.

Brush

The brush is the traditional writing implement in East Asian calligraphy. The body of the brush can be made from either bamboo, or rarer materials like red sandalwood, glass, ivory, silver and gold. The head of the brush can be made from the hair (or feather) of a wide variety of animals, including the wolf, rabbit, deer, chicken, duck, goat, pig, tiger, etc. There is also a tradition in both China and Japan of making a brush using the hair of a newborn, as a once-in-a-lifetime souvenir for the child. This practice is associated with the legend of an ancient Chinese scholar who scored first in the Imperial examinations by using such a personalized brush.

Today, calligraphy may also be done using a pen, but pen calligraphy does not enjoy the same prestige as traditional brush calligraphy.

Inkstone

A stone or ceramic inkstone is used to rub the solid ink stick into liquid ink and to contain the ink once it is liquid. Chinese Inkstones are highly prized as art objects, and an extensive bibliography is dedicated to their history and appreciation, especially in China.

Paperweight

Paperweights are used to weigh down paper. Paperweights come in several types: some are oblong wooden blocks carved with calligraphic or pictorial designs; others are essentially small sculptures of people or animals. Like inkstones, paperweights are collectible works of art on their own right.

Desk pad

The desk pad (画毡 huàzhān) is a pad made of felt. Some are printed with grids on both sides, so that when it is placed under the translucent paper, it can be used as a guide to ensure correct placement and size of characters. These printed pads are used only by students. Both desk pads and the printed grids come in a variety of sizes.

Seal

Works of calligraphy are usually completed by the artist putting his or her seal at the very end, in red ink. The seal serves the function of a signature.

Study

How the brush is held depends on which calligraphic genre is practiced. For Chinese calligraphy, the method of holding the brush is more special; the brush is held vertically straight gripped between the thumb and middle finger. The index finger lightly touches the up-

per part of the shaft of the brush (stabilizing it) while the ring and little fingers tuck under the bottom of the shaft. The palm is hollow, and one should be able to hold an egg within that space. This method, although difficult to hold correctly for the beginner, allows greater freedom of movement, control and execution of strokes. For Japanese calligraphy, the brush is held in the right hand between the thumb and the index finger, very much like a Western pen.

A paperweight is placed at the top of all but the largest pages to prevent slipping; for smaller pieces the artist's left hand is also placed at the bottom of the page for support.

In China, there are many people who practice calligraphy in public places such as parks and sidewalks, using water as their ink and the ground as their paper. Very large brushes are required. Although such calligraphic works are temporary (as the water will eventually dry), they serve the dual purpose of both being an informal public display of one's work, and an opportunity to further practice one's calligraphy.

Calligraphy takes many years of dedicated practice. Correct stroke order, proper balance and rhythm of characters are essential in calligraphy. Skilled handling of the brush produces a pleasing balance of characters on the paper, thick and thin lines, and heavy and light inking. In most cases, a calligrapher will practice writing the Chinese character "Yong" (永) many, many times in order to perfect the eight basic essential strokes contained within the character. Those who can correctly write the yong character beautifully can potentially write all characters with beauty.

Basic calligraphy instruction is part of the regular school curriculum in both China and Japan.

Nearly all traditionally educated men (and sometimes women) in East Asia are proficient in calligraphy.

Chinese scripts are generally divided into five categories: the seal character (Zhuanshu), the official or clerical script (Lishu), the regular script (Kaishu), the running hand (Xingshu) and the cursive hand (Caoshu.)

■ by Richard R. Wertz
Calligraphy work by
Zhang Pingsheng 张平生

Spring Festival Through the Eyes of a Child

I HAVE LIVED IN Shenzhen since I was born, but I have never had Spring Festival in Shenzhen. Every year I go to Zhaoqing City, that is my father's hometown and then Panyu, that is my mother's hometown, to celebrate Spring Festival. It was the same for this year. The first stop was, of course, my father's hometown. It takes 3 hours for my father to drive there. Shenzhen must be very quiet and empty at Spring Festival, since so many people have gone home to be together with their families.

When my father's car stopped beside the roadside, I got out and ran to my grandmother's house. My grandmother already knew of my arrival, she came out from her house to meet me with a big happy smile. I greeted her, then I rushed to the top of the house to visit my grandfather's bonsai garden. My grandfather began to plant bonsai after his retirement. The balcony on the top of the house is his paradise. He took two of his most beautiful bonsai to the living room to decorate the house. Also, we had a big orange tree in the living room, which I knew every family got one, that would bring luck and wealth to the house.

It was Spring Festival Eve. Everyone returned home, including my two uncles, two aunts, my parents and my cousin. We sat around the table chatting with laughter. My cousin and I were the happiest, we ate nuts, candies, cookies and played firecrackers with big noise.

After lunch, my grandmother asked me to have a bath, then I wore my new clothes. No one likes white color on Spring Festival Holidays, so she was not happy when she found the white elastic band on my ponytail. She took off it and then put red thread around it. She likes every thing in red.

At 3pm, we began the ceremony. She had already prepared a lot of food on the tray, including a chicken, red carrots with long roots, three cups of alcohol, a big lotus cakes, and then she burned three incense sticks in the vessel. She kneeled down and whispered: "Please protect my sons for their health and business, my grandchildren, for their good performance in schools". Then she kow-towed three times. She looked up at the ancestor photo on the wall, put her hands together and murmured the same thing: "Ancestors on the heaven, please protect [...]". I followed my grandmother's gesture. After that, my grandmother took the cups and dropped the alcohol on the ground, and said, "Please come back, please eat and drink slowly", then she began to burn paper money as an offering for the dead. It was really fun to burn something, I liked doing that. The ceremony was over with the burning out of the paper money.

I was looking forward to the rich New Year Dinner. Surprisingly, this year's dinner was different from the year before, because we dined out. My uncle had reserved a New Year Dinner in the restaurant. We had a rich dinner with chicken, fish, sea food... a lot, I couldn't count. Then we went home and sat together to watch television. That night we stayed up very late to send the old year going and the new year coming. At 12 o'clock, people called to each other to say "Happy New

Year!". I sent a lot of messages to my classmates and got a lot back. After that, we went out for a walk along the river. My grandparents said that would bring us good luck. After the walk, I went to bed. I was so exited because tomorrow morning was the first day of the new year, I would get red pocket money from my grandparents, my parents, my uncles and aunts.

I got up very early on the second day. I dressed up with my new clothes, and left my bedroom. I knew greetings must be given to everyone in order to get red pocket money. My grandmother gave me two red envelopes, my mother kissed me and gave me two, my aunts also gave me two. Oh, I got a lot of money. I took my red envelopes to my bedroom to count, because my mother told me it was impolite to count money before guests. Haha, I got 800RMB that day! I was so happy. The moments following that morning were a happy time, my father drove us here and there. We went to different restaurants to have lunch and dinner.

People don't like to do housework on new year days, so we don't sweep the floor until it is the third day of new year. But the second day of new year was the day to visit some relatives and friends. I felt bored of these activities, but my father asked me to go with him. Before he started visiting, he always got ready for some gifts and red envelopes. He visited his friends and chatted with them in their homes, but I didn't understand why they laughed. I just sat there idle, although they served me some candies and peanuts.

New Year "Xin Nian" lasts 15 days, but we stayed 4 days in my father's hometown, then we would drive to my mother's hometown, where I could get more lucky money!

■ Lin Yunlu 林允璐
12 years old

Traditional Chinese Holidays Table

Date	English Name	Chinese Name	Remarks
Last day of 12th lunar month	Chinese New Year Eve	**Chúxī** 除夕 大年夜	Cleaning the house, putting up new posters of "door gods" on front doors, fireworks before the family union dinner, which should be at least 10 course meal with a whole fish entrée symbolizing the abundance of the coming year. (The fish entrée should not be consumed completely because the leftover symbolizes the abundance).
1st day of 1st lunar month	Spring Festival (Chinese New Year)	**Xīnnián** 新年 农历新年 春节 大年初一	More fireworks after midnight, visiting in-laws.
15th day of 1st lunar month	Lantern Festival	**Yuánxiāo Jié** 元宵节 小年	Lantern parade and lion dance celebrating the first full moon.
2nd day of 2nd lunar month	Zhonghe Festival (Zhong He Jie) Blue Dragon Festival	**Zhōnghé Jié** 中和节 **Qinglong Jie** 青龙节	Eating Chinese pancakes (Chun Ping, 春饼) and noodles, house cleaning. Also known as Dragon Raising its Head.
3rd day of 3rd lunar month	Shangsi Festival (Shang Si Jie)	**Shàngsì Jié** 上巳节	Traditional Chinese Women's Day, also known as 女儿节 (**nǚérjié**)
At the jie qi known as qing ming, solar longitude 15 degrees, 104 days after winter solstice (around April 5)	Qing Ming Jie (Tomb Sweeping Day)/ Mourning Day / Ching Ming Festival	**Qīngmíng Jié** 清明节	Visiting, cleaning, and make offerings at ancestral gravesites, spring outing.

5th day of 5th lunar month	Dragon Boat Festival (Dragon Festival) / Tuen Ng Festival	Duānwǔ Jié 端午节	Dragon boat racing, eat rice wrap Zongzi, commemorating the ancient poet Qu Yuan; drink yellow rice wine, related to the White Snake Lady legend.
6th day of 6th lunar month	Bathing and Basking Festival (Xi Shai Jie)	Xǐshài Jié 洗晒节	Putting books, sheets, cloth under the sun.
15th day of 8th lunar month	Mid-Autumn Festival (Moon Festival)	Zhōngqiū Jié 中秋节	Eat mooncake, family union meal, related to the legend of Chang E.
7th day of 7th lunar month	The Night of Sevens /Magpie Festival/ Qi Xi	Qīxī 七夕	According to legend, the goddess "Zhi Nü" (the star Vega) fell in love with the farmer boy "Niu Lang" (the star Altair), but was disapproved by the her mother goddess. As punishment, they were separated by the Milky Way and could only meet once a year on this night.
15th day of 7th lunar month	Spirit Festival (Ghost Festival)	Zhōngyuán Jié 中元节	The day to burn paper "money" and make offerings to ancestors and the dead, so the spirits will not trouble the living.
9th day of 9th lunar month	Double Ninth Festival / Dual-Yang Festival/ Chung Yeung Festival	Chóngyáng Jié 重阳节	Autumn outing and mountain climbing, some Chinese also visit the graves of their ancestors to pay their respects.
15th day of the 10th lunar month	Spirit Festival/ Water Lantern Festival	Xayuan Jie 下元节	Setting flower shaped lanterns adrift in a stream or river at sundown, offerings to deceased who's spirits may return at night to visit.

Day of the winter solstice (solar longitude 270 degrees), around December 22	Winter Solstice Festival/ Mid-Winter Festival	**Dōngzhì** 冬至	Have Tangyuan and Jiuniang and perform ancestor worship, Feast day, family gatherings, also named "Chinese Thanksgiving".
8th day of 12th lunar month	Laba Festival/ Congee Festival	**Làbā Jié** 腊八节	It is the day the Buddha attained enlightenment. People usually eat Laba congee, which is usually made of mixed grains and fruits.

Timetable of Chinese Traditional Festivals (2013-2015)

Year	Spring Festival	Lantern Festival	Qingming Festival	Dragon Boat	Double Seventh	Mid-autumn Festival	Chongyang Festival
2013	Feb. 10	Feb. 24	Apr. 4	Jun. 12	Aug. 13	Sept. 19	Oct. 13
2014	Jan. 31	Feb. 14	Apr. 5	Jun. 2	Aug. 2	Sept. 8	Oct. 2
2015	Feb. 19	Mar. 5	Apr. 5	Jun. 20	Aug. 20	Sept. 27	Oct. 21

For more information about the above-mentioned places visit WikiShenzhen.com

Culture & Sightseeing in Shenzhen

From Expats to Expats
Cinemas (major complexes)

1 Broadway Cinema (Coco Park)   百老汇影院

🖃	2/F, Coco Park, Fuhua 3rd Rd., Futian District
地址	福田区福华三路COCOPARK购物公园2楼
ℂ	2531-3556
🏠	www.b-cinema.cn
ⓘ	Broadway Cinema benefits from a hyper-modern design, spacious screens, and a bustling shopping complex directly outside it. Located in the heart of Futian District, it's obviously a prime choice for those living within or close to the district.

2 Poly International Cinema (Coastal City)   保利国际影城

🖃	3/F, Coastal City, 33, Wenxin Rd., Nanshan District
地址	南山区文心五路33号海岸城购物中心3楼
ℂ	8635-9166
🏠	www.szpolycinema.com
ⓘ	The Coastal City Cinema impresses by its glitzy décor, high number of screens, and the diverse array of restaurants and attractions in the surrounding mall. Its location is convenient, with 10-15 mins away from Sea World by taxi, and situated next to the highway leading towards Futian District.

3 Golden Harvest Theater (The MixC)   嘉禾深圳影城

🖃	3/F, Middle Building, MixC Shopping Mall, Huarun Centre, 1881, Baoan South Rd., Luohu District
地址	罗湖区1881宝安南路华润中心万象成中座3楼
ℂ	8266-8182
🏠	www.yingyuan.cn
ⓘ	Golden Harvest Theater features 12 cinema halls, equipped with state of the art digital projectors and surround sound audio systems. Located within the MixC shopping center, Da Ju Yuan metro station.

4 MCL Cinema (Garden City)	洲立影城

📧	5/F, Garden City Centre, Nanhai Boulevard, Nanshan District

地址	南山区南海大道花园城中心5楼

☎	2685-8870

🖱	www.mclcinema.com.cn

ℹ	Although its screens are limited, Garden City's friendly atmosphere and close proximity to Shekou – 5 mins from Sea World by taxi – make it a good alternative to Coastal City.

5 MCL Cinema (Citygate Mall)	洲立影城

📧	2/F, Hi Citygate Mall, Tai Ning Rd., Luohu District

地址	罗湖区太宁路喜荟城购物中心2楼

☎	2685-8870

🖱	www.mclcinema.com.cn

ℹ	Located within walking distance of Hua Qiang Bei, the city's famous IT district, the cinema in Citygate mall is easy to find for newcomers and conveniently placed in one of Shenzhen's most bustling shopping malls. As such, it's the cinema of choice for those seeking a night out in Luohu District.

Historical Sites & Temples

Hong Fa Temple 弘法寺 in Xian Hu 仙湖植物园 (Fairy Lake) Park is Shenzhen's largest Buddhist temple; there are numerous folk temples scattered throughout the city, including a nice one in the center of Xiasha Village in the south of Futian District. For the ultimate "Old Shenzhen" experience, take a walk in an old village area. Try Hubei Village 湖贝旧村 and Luoling 螺岭, just east of Dongmen, or Xin'an Village 新安村 near Zhongshan Park 中山公园 in Nanshan, which includes a museum.

| **1** Ba Guang Village | 坝光村 |

⌨ East of Kuiyong Subdistrict, Longgang District

地址 龙岗区葵涌镇东部

🚌 360, 364 (Kuichong stop, 葵涌站), change to bus 987 (Ba Guang Cun stop, 坝光村站)

| **2** Chiwan Goddess Temple | 赤湾天后庙 |

⌨ Chiwan Rd., 6, Chiwan, Nanshan District

地址 南山区赤湾六路

🚌 226, 355 (Tian Hou Gong stop, 天后宫站)

⌛ Daily: 8am - 5:30pm

| **3** Dapeng Fortress | 大鹏古城博物馆 |

⌨ Pengcheng Community, Dapeng Str., Longgang District

地址 龙岗区大鹏街道鹏城社区

☎ 8431-9269

🚌 364, 360, 833, 818

⌛ Daily: 8:30am - 6pm

$ ¥20

🖱 www.szdpsc.com (Chinese)

| **4** Da Wan Ancient Residence | 大万世居 |

⌨ Hakka Village, Pingshan Subdistrict, Longgang District

地址 龙岗区平山街道坪山墟客家村

🚌 211, 365 (Pingshan stop, 坪山站)

⌛ Daily: 10am - 6pm

| **5** Dongjiang Guerrilla Memorial Hall | 东江纵队纪念馆 |

	Shihuibei Community, Dongzong Rd., Pingshan Subdistrict, Longgang District
地址	龙岗区坪山街道东纵路石灰陂社区
🚌	365 (Sanyang Hu stop, 三羊站), 360, 364 (Dapeng stop, 大鹏站), then change to 818 (Hedian stop, 核电站)
⧗	Daily: 9am - 5pm

6 Feng Huang Temple	凤凰山
	Fenghuang Cun, Fuyong Zhen, Bao'an District
地址	宝安区福永镇凤凰村
$	Free
ⓘ	310-315 Circle Line 环线 from Window of the World station 世界之窗站 to Tongfuyu Gongye Qu 同富裕工业区, then change bus to 754

7 Guan Di Temple	南山关帝庙
	Guan Gong Temple, Nantou, Nanshan District
地址	南山区赤湾路9号天后宫
✆	2685-3133
⧗	Daily: 8am - 5:30pm
$	¥15 (for the temple)
ⓘ	Located at the Western end of Shennan Rd. Many buses, notably #204, stop at the Nantou stop. From there, walk 20m; the gate will be on your right, just before the larger gate of the Xinan old town area.

8 Guanlan Print Base	观澜版画基地
	Niuhu Community, Guanlan Subdistrict, Bao'an District
地址	宝安区观澜街道牛湖社区
🚌	312, 770, 771, 793 (Niuhu Cun stop, 牛湖村站)

9 Hakka Village & Culture Museum	客家民俗博物馆

🖃	1 Luoruihe North Str., Longgang Str., Longgang District
地址	龙岗区龙岗街道罗瑞合北街一号
☎	8429-6108
⌛	Daily: 8 - 11:30am, 2 - 5pm
$	¥10
🚌	365, 351, 329
①	The Museum is an old Hakka house compound

10 Hong Fa Temple	弘法寺
🖃	160, Xianhu Rd., Liantang, Luohu District
地址	罗湖区莲塘仙湖路160号
☎	2573-8430
🖳	www.szbg.org (English)
⌛	7am - 10pm
$	¥20, children 1.1 - 1.4m tall: ¥10
🚌	57, 65, 218, 220, 382
①	218, 220 (Zhiwu Yuan stop, 植物园站)

11 Hubei Village	湖贝旧村
🖃	Hubei Rd., Luohu District
地址	罗湖区湖贝路
🚌	2, 10, 17, 29, 56 (Guangshen Binguan stop, 广深宾馆)

12 Lamasery Replica	锦绣中华
🖃	Folk Cultural Villages (Splendid China), Nanshan District
地址	南山区锦绣中华华侨城里
⌛	Daily: 8am - 5:30pm

💲	¥120 (Spendid China entrance fee)
🚇	Hua Qiao Cheng station 华侨城站
ⓘ	The "Lamasery" is located in the "Tibet" area of the park; there are prayer cairns and pennants, and a Tibetan-style "house" nearby.

13 Longgang Ancient Residence   龙田世居

▤	Duanxin Community, Kengzi Subdistrict, Longgang District
地址	龙岗区坑梓街道段心社区
🚌	380 (Kengzi Zhen Zhengfu stop, 坑梓镇政府站)

14 Luo Ling Village   螺岭

▤	Wenjin Rd. Central, Luohu
地址	罗湖区文锦中路
🚌	2, 27, 40, 111, 242

15 Nanshan Tian Hou Museum   天后博物馆

▤	9 Chiwan Rd., Tian Hou Temple, Nanshan District
地址	南山区赤湾路9号天后宫
✆	2685-3133
⏳	Daily: 8am - 5:30pm
💲	¥15 (for the temple)
🚌	226, 433

16 Nantou Ancient City Museum   南头古城博物馆, 新安古城

▤	2, Nantou Jiaochang, Nanshan District
地址	南山区南头较场2号
🚌	22, 42, 105, 201, 204, 233, 234, 320 (Xin An Gu Cheng stop, 新安古城站)

17 San Sheng Temple   三圣宫

🖃	Meilin, Futian District (part of Meilin Park)
地址	福田区三圣宫
🚌	218, 222, 240, 242, 30, 324, 334, 35, 361, 374, 44, 45, 60, 67, N9

18 Siyue Library		思月书院
🖃	Loajie Cultural Square, Dongmen, Luohu District	
地址	罗湖区东门步行街老街文化广场	
🚌	113, 300, 337 (Laojie stop, 老街站)	
🚇	Lao Jie station, exit A 老街站	

19 Tomb of the Young Song Emperor		宋少帝陵
🖃	Chiwan, Shekou, Nanshan District	
地址	南山区蛇口赤湾	

20 Xi'an Village		新安村 / 中山公园
🖃	Beside Nantou Footbridge, Nanshan District	
地址	南山区南头天桥旁	
🚌	201, 204, 210, 226, 227	

Mountains

1 Nanshan Mountain		大南山
🖃	At the corner of Dongbin Rd. and Nanhai Av., Nanshan District	
地址	南山区东滨路与南海大道交界	
🚌	70 (Lianhe Yiyuan stop, 联合医院); 226 (Sea World stop, 海上世界); 113 (Haiyang Dasha stop, 海洋大厦)	
⧗	6am - 7pm	

$	Free

3 Mount Ma Luan	马峦山郊野公园
📇	Mount Maluan, Pingshan Zhen, Longgang District
地址	龙岗区坪山镇马峦山
🚌	103, 360, 364, 380 (Xiaomeisha stop, 小梅沙)
⏳	24 hours
$	Free

4 Phoenix Mountain	凤凰山
📇	Fenghuang Cun, Fuyong Zhen, Bao'an District
地址	宝安区福永镇凤凰村
🚌	310-315 Circle Line 环线 from Window of the World station 世界之窗站 to Tongfuyu Gongyequ 同富裕工业区, then change bus to 754
$	Free

5 Qiniang Mountain	七娘山
📇	Dapeng Peninsula, Longgang District
地址	龙岗区南澳街道七娘山
$	Free
🚌	360 (Nan'ao stop, 南澳站), then by taxi/motorbike
🖥	www.qiniangshan.cn (Chinese)

2 Wutong Mountain	梧桐山
📇	Dawang Cun, Shawan, Luohu District
地址	罗湖区沙湾大旺村
🚌	103, 202, 205, 220, 218, 113
⏳	8am - 7pm

$	Free
📖	www.szwtm.org (Chinese)

6 Yangtai Mountain	羊台山

🖃	Yangtai Shan, Bao'an District
地址	宝安区石岩镇
🚌	325, 326 (Luozu Cun stop, 罗租村站), then transfer to 769 to the foot of Yangtai Mountain
⏳	Closes at 6pm
$	Free

Museums & Galleries

No matter what you've heard, there's plenty of culture to be had in Shenzhen. If you are looking for art, try the Shenzhen Art Museum 深圳美术馆 at the north end of Donghu (Eastlake) Park 东湖公园; the Guan Shanyue Museum 关山月美术馆 in Lianhuashan Park 莲花山公园; or the He Xiangning Art Gallery 何香凝美术馆 in OCT 华侨城. The He Xiangning Museum also sponsors the OCT Contemporary Art Terminal 当代艺术中心 at OCT, across the street and a long walk to the east. Though it is not a museum, Dafen Village 大芬油画村 in Buji 布吉 is a great place to see and buy art.

Other cultural venues include the Shenzhen Museum 深圳博物馆 across from Citic Plaza 中信城市广场 Ke Xue Guan station (科学馆站), and further out, the Hakka Museum 深圳龙岗客家民俗博物馆 in Longgang Town, Longgang 龙岗区; and the Dapeng Fortress 大鹏古城博物馆 a Ming-period naval fort on the Dapeng Peninsula in south Longgang District.

There is an old tower at the base of Bao'an's Phoenix Mountain 宝安区福永凤凰山 and a temple (with grottoes) on the top. You may have to spend an hour on a bus, or hire a car, to see them.

See chapter "Arts in Shenzhen" for a complete listing of Museums and Galleries.

Sightseeing: OCT East and Beyond

East and Northeast of downtown Shenzhen lie Yantian and Longgang Districts. These little known districts are an intriguing place for a family holiday or romantic weekend away from the pressures of the city. There are great beaches with all kinds of water sports, theme parks, historic sites as well as some great hiking trails.

Beaches

Shenzhen isn't known primarily as a beach destination, but don't let that put you off. The coast is pretty and has something for just about everyone to enjoy. Just 30 minutes from Luohu, Dameisha is the first beach you will encounter. It is a busy free public beach 1.8-km long. There are plenty of water sport activities (paragliding, windsurfing, jet skis etc), restaurants and shops for tourists.

Xiaomeisha is another 20-minute drive further East. This beach charges a small entrance fee (¥20 p/p), which seems a small price to pay for a slightly more exclusive atmosphere. Xiaomeisha has a few beach front hotels and a nice area for barbecuing, as well as plenty of water sports. Shenzhen's Xiaomeisha Sea World Ocean Park is located inside of Xiaomeisha. Sea World has 8 different areas with all kinds of shows and performances like dolphin and seal shows and other things fishy. This is a fun spot for the little ones.

Dongchong and Xichong Beaches in Longgang District are the furthest away from Shenzhen and far less commercial. The location, southeast of Nan'ao Town, has a pristine natural environment. The attractions include speed boat rides out to Lover's Island where you can collect sea urchins and have them prepared at the local restaurants. If that isn't your thing, bring along a picnic as there isn't much in the way of restaurants. If you spend the night in the rustic cabins (clean but very basic), you will have the beach to yourself in the early morning hours. Bring a bucket to collect your seashells and some hiking shoes to scramble over the trails up into the hills. The views are worth all the effort. By car: Luosha Road (through Wutong Shan Tunnel), Yanba Expressway, Kuichong exit (¥10 toll), Pingxi Rd., Nanxi Rd.

"Jia You! (加油!)" These are the words you will hear coming from the crowds wearing identical T-shirts or hats. It means "Step on it!" or "Try harder!" These beaches are a magnet for China's ubiquitous company picnics. It's a cultural phenomena to watch them playing tug of war and other rousing team building activities.

Hiking Trails

If you feel the need for some serious exercise, there are plenty of hiking options in this area. Wutong Mountain and Maluan Mountain offer various trails for all fitness levels. Or you can follow the coast (up the steep hillside in part) between Xichong and Dongchong. Do bring along water, proper hiking shoes, a hat and sunscreen. It's best to have a guide, if this is your first time in the area, as the trails are not always clearly marked.

Maluan Mountain is located in Longgang District of Shenzhen, connecting with Sanzhou Tian Reservoir in Yantian District in the west, reaching Kuiyong Town in the east and abutting to the beaches in the south. This trail is less than 500m above sea level and has a moderate slope. Verdant virgin mountain forests characterize most of the park with lots of waterfalls and streams. Expeditions to Maluan Mountain usually start at Diecui Reservoir, 15 minutes from Xiaomeisha beach, and end at Dameisha beach. The summit is accessible from various routes, but the most attractive one follows along a stream.

Wutong Mountain is one of the loveliest hiking areas in Shenzhen, featuring one paved road and several winding paths leading to a summit. With spectacular views of Dapeng Harbor to the east and Shenzhen city to the west, Wutong's peak at 943.7m is Shenzhen's highest peak and is often misted by clouds. Because of its location between the city and the sea, it is a favorite for nature buffs. You can expect to see many rare plants and animals such as goshawk, pangolin and lesser civet cat etc. Keen photographers often hike up before dawn to get shots of the sunrise from Brave Man Slope over the bay. There are few concessionaires so bring plenty of water and snacks.

Theme Parks

If you prefer your culture a little more refined, head to OCT East just up the road from Damiesha. The brain child of the curious OCT Group, this resort complex has an interesting combination of Swiss and Asian themes, replete with Alpine gingerbread houses, artificial lakes, huge waterfalls, an amazing spa and the five-star OCT Interlaken Hotel.

The theme park has 3 valley sections. Tea Stream (Chaxi) Valley is composed of the Interlaken Village, the Ancient Tea Town, Sanzhou Tea Garden and a Wetland Garden. The highlight of this area is a large award-winning multimedia Tea Show performance. Knight Valley can be reached by bus or by a cable car. It features lovely views and when complete will have 8 different themed districts with rides. Wind Valley (Yunhai) focuses on Olympic military sports. An old fashioned steam train circles the valleys. There is a golf club with a posh residential compound for well-heeled Shenzheners.

Closer to Luohu, in Shatoujiao one can find the very curious tourist attraction, CITIC Minsk World. The Minsk is a decommissioned Soviet Union air craft carrier with Russian military displays, as well as entertaining singing and dancing shows in their self described "merry military harbor!" Every hour on the hour, pretty young girls in military costumes perform a dance routine with martial flair and twirling rifles. Aside from the dancing, the highlight is an exciting recreated naval battle that tourists can witness from the control room. A visit to Minsk World is a must to military buffs and fans of truly odd theme parks.

Historical Sites

In Longgang District, there are several important historical spots. There are 100 buildings built by Shenzhen's aboriginal population, the Hakkas. Hakka Folk Customs Museum and Enclosures are a large number of old Hakka residences, some of which are still filled with tools and furniture left over from the Qing Dynasty. According to Fodor's travel guide: "The site is somewhat feral; once you pass the ticket booth, you're pretty much on your own and free to stroll around the grounds and explore inside the residences themselves, many of which seem to have been left in a mostly natural state. Although some restoration projects pretty things up to the point of making the site look unreal, the opposite is true here. Parts of the enclosures are so real as to seem downright spooky; visitors might get the feeling that the original inhabitants may return at any moment, crossbows cocked."

Dapeng Fortress was built over 600 years ago, and is an excellent example of a Ming Dynasty-military encampment (1368-1644). The fortress was originally built to resist pesky Japanese pirates who had been harassing the southern coastal areas of Guangdong. However, the fortress is best known as the site of the British Naval attack of September 4, 1839, in which British forces attacked China in what is widely considered the beginning of the Opium Wars. As local legend goes, Chinese troops in fishing boats, led by General Lai Enjue, defeated the better-equipped enemy. Today, visitors flock to the fortress to admire the inside of the walled town, which is replete with ornately carved beams and columns, with poetic couplets painted over each door.

The Tomb of Zhenwei General (who Manifests Might) Lai Enjue is located is Wangqitang Village of Dapeng Town. Lai Enjue was originally buried in Dakangshang Village and was relocated to the present place in the Third Year of Guangxu Period of Qing Dynasty.

There is so much to see in this area. Make sure you allow enough time to really explore. One small caveat for the visitor; while there is plenty to offer tourists in this part of Shenzhen, little information is available in English. Bring a friend who can translate or bring your patience.

Sightseeing: OCT East and Beyond, *Getting There*

■ OCT East	东部华侨城
OCT East, Dameisha, Yangtai District	
地址 盐田区大梅沙东部华侨城	
© 8888-9888	
www.octeast.com	
Weekdays: 9:30 - 9pm, weekends: 9am - 9pm	
$ ¥280	
53, 103, 103B, 239, 308, 242, J1 (Dongbu Hua Qiao Cheng stop, 东部华侨城站)	

Parks in Shenzhen

Shenzhen is blessed with dozens of parks, large and small. Our favorite is Lizhi 荔枝公园 (Litchi or Lychee) Park at the intersection of Shennan and Hongling Road (Da Ju Yuan station, exit B 大剧院站). Here on a Sunday afternoon you will find Chinese folk doing Chinese things: playing Chinese chess, practicing musical instruments, doing Taijiquan 太极拳 (aka Taichi), all these and more.

If you rather do than watch, head for Lianhuashan (Lotus Mountain) Park 莲花山公园 and take a walk up to the statue of Deng Xiaoping at the top of the hill, where there's an excellent view of the city center. Or buy a kite near the southeast entrance and fly it in the Kite Square. More ambitious view-seekers might "climb" Nanshan 大南山, the mountain just north of Shekou in Nanshan District. By all accounts it's more of an uphill walk than a climb. For more strenuous climbs check out Mount Wutong 梧桐山 and Maluan Mountain 马峦山郊野公园 in the east, and Yangtai Mountain 羊台山 in Bao'an, just north of Xili in Nanshan.

Parks in Futian District

1 Bi Jia Shan Park	笔架山公园
76, Mei Gang Nan Jie, Hua Fu Rd., Futian District	
地址 福田区华富路梅岗南街76号	
11, 30, 53, 59, 79, 102, 209, 213, 216, 234, 244, 302, 317, 319, 323, 357, 365, 398, K302	

2 Cai Tian Park	彩田公园
Cai Tian Park, Bei Huan Av., Futian District	
地址 福田区北环大道	
35, 102	

3 Ecology Plaza, OCT	华侨城生态广场
OCT, to the north of Shennan Av., Nanshan District	
地址 南山区深南大道北华侨城	

🚇 Hua Qiao Cheng station 华侨城站

3 Haibin Shengtai Park (Hongshulin Park)	海滨生态公园

🚏 Bin He Av., Futian District

地址	红树林 福田区滨河大道

🚌 J1, 76, 80, K105, K113, K204, 229, 231, 236, 305, 337, 339, 353, 362, 369, 382

4 Huang Gang Park	皇岗公园

🚏 2002, Yi Tian Rd., Futian District

地址	福田区益田路2002号

🚌 71, 76, 80, 219, 317, 374, 385

5 Lianhua Shan Park (Lotus Hill Park)	莲花山公园

🚏 Hongli Rd. West, Futian Central

地址	福田区红荔西路

🚌 N9, 14, 15, 25, 38, 41, 54, 60, 65, 71, K105, 107, 108

⏳ 5:00am - 11:30pm

6 Lizhi (Litchi) Park	荔枝公园

🚏 Lizhi Park, Futian District

地址	福田区荔枝公园

🚌 10, 13, 24, 30, 105, 202, 228

⏳ 5:30am -11pm

7 Mangrove Nature Reserve	红树林

🚏 By Binhai Av., Futian District

地址	福田区滨海大道

🚌 K105, K113, K204, 229, 231, 317, 322, 337, 382

8 Martyr Cemetery Park (Shenzhen -) 深圳革命烈士陵园

| | Beihuan Da Dao, Futian District |
| 地址 | 福田区北环大道 |

9 Meilin Park (Meilin Reservoir) 梅林公园 / 梅林水库

	Meilin Yi Cun, Futian District
地址	家乐福后面梅林公园梅林公园山顶
🚌	15, 35, 44, 45, 60, 102, 111, 216, 218, 388

10 Shenzhen Zhongxin Park (Central Park) 深圳中心公园

	Shennan Av., Futian District
地址	中心公园深南大道
🚌	41, 65, 80, 107, 234, 236, 373, 375, 395
🚇	Gou Wu Gong Yuan station, exit B

Parks in Luohu District

11 Cuizhu Park 深圳翠竹公园

	1078, Cuizhu Rd., Luohu District
地址	罗湖区翠竹路1078号
🚌	3, 17, 29, 52, 53, 64, 211, 300, 306, 351

12 Dong Hu Park (East Lake Park) 东湖公园

	11, Rd. 1, Aiguo Donglu, Luohu
地址	罗湖区爱国路一街11号
🚌	3, 17, 23, 29, 52, 53, 64, 211, 300, 306, 308, 320, 351, 372, 386, 528
⏳	8am - 10pm
$	Free

13 Er Tong Park (Children's Park)	深圳儿童公园
12, Tong Le Rd., Luohu District	
地址 罗湖区童乐路12号	
1, 5, N7, 11, 13, N16, 62, 65, 69, 102, 107, 111, 202, 213, 225, 303, 361, 379	

14 Hong Hu Park	深圳洪湖公园
2023 North Wenjin Rd., Luohu District	
地址 罗湖区，东起洪湖东路和文锦北路	
6, N10, 27, 33, 63, 80, 82, 213, 300, 303, K307, B307, 307, 309, 312, 313, 322, 323, 357, 361, 363, 366, 369, 371, 377, 383	

15 Luohu Cultural Park	罗湖文化公园
2012, Leyuan Rd., Luohu District	
地址 罗湖区乐园路2012号	

16 Ren Min Park (People's Park)	人民公园
Renmin North Rd., Luohu District	
地址 罗湖区人民北路人民公园	
61, 321	

17 Wutong Mountain National Park	梧桐山风景区
Da Wang Cun, Sha Wan, Luohu District	
地址 罗湖区沙湾大旺村	
61, 321	

Parks in Nanshan District

18 Li Lin Park	荔林公园
Li Lin Park, Dong Bin Rd., Nanshan District	

地址	南山区东滨路
🚌	70, 113, 328, 329

19 Li Xiang Park	荔香公园
🖃 (1) Shennan Av., (2) Nanguang Rd., Nanshan District	
地址 (1) 南山区深南大道, (2)南山区南光路	
🚌 10, N11, 21, 36, 42, 78, 81, M200, 234, 327, 368, 369, B628	

20 Nanshan Park	大南山公园
🖃 At the foot of Nanshan Mountain, Shekou, Nanshan District	
地址 南山区东滨路与南海大道交界大南山脚下	
🚌 70, 113, 328, 329	

21 Shigu Shan Park	石鼓山公园
🖃 Shi Gu Rd., Nanshan District	
地址 南山区石鼓路	
🚌 122, B604	

22 Sihai Park	四海公园
🖃 6, Gongyuan Rd., Nanshan District	
地址 南山区公园路6号	
🚌 N1, N4, 70, 77, 80, 122, K204, 204, 232, 233, 331, 332, 390	

23 Zhongshan Park	中山公园
🖃 Opposite side of Hui Quan Square, Nanshan District	
地址 南山区汇泉广场对面	
🚌 21, 22, 37, 201, 226, 332, B628	

Scenic Spots

1 Ba Guang Scenic Spot	坝光乡村风景区
📧 Ba Guang Scenic Spot, Kui Chong, Longgang District	
地址 坝光乡村风景区龙岗区葵涌	

2 Diwang Building (Mansion)	地王大厦
📧 Diwang Dasha, Shennan Zhonglu, Luohu	
地址 罗湖区深南中路	
🚌 101, 10, 233	
🚇 Da Ju Yuan station, exit D 大剧院站	
⏳ 8:30am - 11pm	
$ Sightseeing on the top of Diwang: ¥60	

3 San Zhou Tian Scenic Spot	三洲田风景区
📧 Southwest of Bi Ling Cun, Ping Shan Town, Longgang District	
地址 龙岗区坪山镇碧岭村西南方向	

4 Yuan Shan Scenic Spot	园山风景游览区
📧 Gong Yuan Rd., Da Kang Cun, Heng Gang, Longgang District	
地址 龙岗区横岗大康村公园路	

Seaside

1 Dameisha Beach Park	大梅沙海滨公园
📧 94, Dameisha, Yantian District	
地址 盐田区大梅沙94号	
🚌 53, 103, 239, 360, 364 (Dameisha stop, 大梅沙站)	
$ Free	

2 Dongchong Beach	东涌海滩
📧 Dongchong, Nan'ao Subdistrict, Longgang District	

地址	龙岗区南澳街道东涌村
🚌	360, 364 (Nan'ao stop, 南澳站, then by taxi/motorbike)

3 Nan'ao Village	南澳村

🖵	Shuitousha, Nan'an Subdistrict, Longgang District
地址	龙岗区南澳街道水头沙
🚌	360, 364 (Nan'ao stop, 南澳站)

4 Judiaosha Beach	桔钓沙海滩

🖵	Judiaosha, Nan'ao Subdistrict, Longgang District
地址	龙岗区南澳街道桔钓沙
🚌	360, 364 (Nan'ao stop, 南澳站, then by taxi/motorbike)

5 Xiaomeisha Beach Park	小梅沙海滨度假村

🖵	Xiaomeisha, Yantian District
地址	盐田区小梅沙
🚌	130, 360, 364, 380, 387 (Xiaomeisha stop, 小梅沙站)
⏳	9:30am - 8:30pm; peak season: 9:30am - 0:30am
$	¥20
🖱	www.szxms.com.cn (Chinese)

6 Xichong Beach	西涌海滩

🖵	Nan'ao Subdistrict, Longgang District
地址	龙岗区南澳街道
$	¥10
🚌	360, 364 (Nan'ao stop, 南澳站, then by taxi/motorbike)

7 Yangmeikeng Beach	杨梅坑海滩

地址	Near Daya Bay, Dakeng Village, Dapeng Subdistrict, Longgang District
	龙岗区大鹏街道大坑村麻角山大亚湾畔
	360, 364 (Nan'ao stop, 南澳站, then by taxi/motorbike)

Theaters & Halls

See chapter "Arts in Shenzhen" for complete listing of Theaters and Halls in Shenzhen.

Theme Parks

If you have read anything at all about Shenzhen, you probably know about Window of the World 世界之窗 where you can "see all the world's landmarks in one day." This might appeal more to Chinese citizens, who may not have traveled abroad. World visitors, however, will probably find China Folk Cultural Villages 中国民俗文化村 and Splendid China 锦绣中华 more interesting, where you can see full-sized traditional architecture from twenty-some Chinese minorities, as well as miniatures of most of China's major tourist attractions.

Both of these theme parks are easy to reach near the west end of Metro Line 1 (Window of the World is at Shijie Zhichuang 世界之窗, Splendid China 锦绣中华 and China Folk Cultural Villages 中国民俗文化村 at Hua Qiao Cheng 华侨城). Also located at Shijie Zhichuang 世界之窗 is Happy Valley 欢乐谷, more of a thrill-ride place. This is probably not the best bet for short-timers, but could be good for residents. In addition to the "Big Three Theme Parks," there is a zoo 野生动物园 out in Xili Lake Resort 西丽湖度假村; again, this is probably better for long-time stays. But for your money, one of Shenzhen's best-kept secrets is the Shenzhen International Botanical Garden 深圳国际园林花卉博览园 (Yuan Boyuan), near Qiao Cheng Dong station 侨城东 on Line 1. At this writing admission is free; the extensive gardens include pavilions, bridges, statuary, and other elements that replicate some of China's most elegant and relaxing places.

1 China Folk Cultural Villages	中国民俗文化村
Overseas Chinese Town, Nanshan District	
地址 南山区华侨城	
Hua Qiao Cheng station 华侨城站	
101, 204, 209, 223, 301	
9am - 9pm	
¥120	
www.cn5000.com.cn (English)	

2 Dapeng Fortress	大鹏古城博物馆
Pengcheng Community, Dapeng Str., Longgang District	
地址 龙岗区大鹏街道鹏城社区	
360, 364 (Da Peng stop, 大鹏城站)	
Daily: 8:30am - 6 pm	
¥20	
www.szdpsc.com (Chinese)	

3 Evergreen Resort	深圳青青世界
1, Qingqing Str., Moon Bay, Nanshan District	
地址 南山区月亮湾青青街1号	
www.evergreen-cn.com (Chinese & English)	
8:30am - 6:30pm	
¥50; children below 1.1m: ¥30	
42, 210, 350, 369 (Qingqing Shijie stop, 青青世界站)	

10 Fairy Lake Botanical Garden	仙湖植物园
🗺 160, Xianhu Rd., Liantang, Luohu District	
地址 罗湖区莲塘仙湖路160号	
🏠 www.szbg.org/English%20web/main.htm (English)	
⏳ 7am - 10pm	
$ ¥20; children 1.1 - 1.4m tall: ¥10	
🚌 218, 220 (Zhiwu Yuan stop, 植物园站)	

10 Guangming Farm	光明农场
🗺 Guangming Farm, Bao'an District	
地址 保安区光明农场	
$ ¥80	
🚌 301, 325, 626, 788 (Guang Ming stop, 光明站)	

4 Happy Valley	欢乐古
🗺 OCT, Nanshan District	
地址 南山区华侨城	
🏠 www.happyvalley.com.cn (Chinese)	
$ ¥150; ¥80 if entered after 7pm	
⏳ 9:30am - 10pm	
🚌 101, 105, 113, 204, 209, 222, 223, 301	
🚇 Shi Jie Zhi Chuang station, exit A 世界之窗站	

5 International Botanical Garden	深圳国际园林花卉博览园
🗺 Shenzhen Botanical Garden, Zhuzilin Xi, Futian District	
地址 福田区深圳国际园林花卉博览园	
🏠 www.szyby.cn	

$	The admission is free; ¥20 for adults; ¥10 for children for the dinosaur exhibition
⏳	9am - 8pm
🚌	104, 105, 107, 108, 109
🚇	Qiao Cheng Dong station 桥城东站
ⓘ	There are four entrances to the park, but the main one is just north of Shennan Road near Qiao Cheng Dong station on the #1 Metro line - two metro stops east of Window of the World.

6 Minsk World (CITIC)	中信明思克

🖳	Jinrong Rd., Shatoujiao, Yantian District
地址	盐田区沙头角金融路
🖥	www.szminsk.com (Chinese)
$	¥110; ¥55 for children 110-140 cm; free for children under 110 cm
⏳	9:30am - 7:30pm
🚌	103A, 202, 205, 239, 358, 360 (Hangmu Shijie stop, 航母世界站)

7 Ocean World (Shenzhen -)	深圳海洋天地

🖳	Inside Shenzhen Safari Park, East side of Xili Lake, Nanshan District
地址	南山区西丽湖畔深圳野生动物园园内

8 OCT East	东部华侨城

🖳	OCT East, Dameisha, Yangtai District
地址	盐田区大梅沙东部华侨城
🖥	www.octeast.com
⏳	Weekdays: 9:30 - 9pm, weekends: 9am - 9pm
$	¥280
🚌	53, 103, 103B, 239, 308, 242, J1 (Dongbu Hua Qiao Cheng stop, 东部华侨城站)

8 Safari Park Shenzhen	野生动物园

🖳	Next to Xili Lake park, Nanshan District

地址	南山区西丽湖东侧
🖰	www.szzoo.net (Chinese)
⏳	8:30am - 6pm
$	¥100 (for frequent users, one can buy a one-year pass)
🚌	101 from Luhuo train station, 226 from Shekou Ferry Terminal, 66, 101, 104, 237 (A Line)

9 Shenzhen Zoo	野生动物园
🗒	Eastern Part of Xili Lake, Nanshan District
地址	南山区西丽湖东侧
🚌	101 from Luhuo train station, 226 from Shekou Ferry Terminal, 66, 101, 104, 237 (A Line)
⏳	8:30am - 6pm
$	¥120
🖰	www.szzoo.net (Chinese)

10 Splendid China	深圳锦绣中华
🗒	Hua Qiao Cheng, Shennan Av., Nanshan District
地址	南山区华侨城深南大道华侨城
🖰	www.cn5000.com.cn
$	¥120
⏳	9am - 9:30pm; evening performance starts at 7pm
🚌	101, 113, 201, 204, 209, 223, 301
🚇	Hua Qiao Cheng station, exit D 华侨城站

11 Waterlands Resort	海上田园
🗒	Waterland Resort, Bao'an District
地址	宝安区海上田园

	www.szwaterlands.com
$	¥60
⧗	9am - 10:30pm
🚌	337, 338, 779 (Haishang Tianyuan stop, 海上田园站)

11 Window of the World	世界之窗
🖥	Window of the World, OCT, Nanshan District
地址	南山区华侨城世界之窗
	www.szwwco.com
$	¥120
⧗	9:30am - 10pm
🚌	101, 105, 113, 204, 209, 222, 223, 301
🚇	Shi Jie Zhi Chuang station, exit I or J 世界之窗站

5 Xiaomeisha Sea World	小梅沙海洋世界
🖥	Xiaomeisha, Yantian District
地址	盐田区小梅沙
$	¥120
🚌	130, 360, 364, 380, 387 (Xiaomeisha stop, 小梅沙站)
⧗	10am - 5:30pm; peak season: 9:30am - 5:30pm
	www.szxms.com.cn (Chinese)

12 Xili Lake Resort	西丽湖度假村
🖥	Xili Zhen, Nanshan District
地址	南山区西丽镇
🚌	442, 101 from train station 火车站, 434 from Splendid China 锦绣中华, 435 from Nantou Bus Station 南头车站
⧗	8am - 10pm

$	Free

Chinese Corner & Culture & Sightseeing

Afternoon	下午	xià wǔ
Beach	海滩	hǎi tān
Bench	长凳	cháng dèng
Bicycle	自行车	zì xíng chē
Booking	预订	yù dìng
Botanical	植物	zhí wù
Bus	巴士	bā shì
Car	车	chē
Cinema	电影院	diàn yǐng yuàn
Climbing	攀登	pān dēng
Cloud	云	yún
Don't / not ...	不...	bù
Evening	晚上	wǎn shang
Exit	退出	tuì chū
Flower	花	huā
Gallery	画廊	huà láng
Garden	花园	huā yuán
Go home	回家	huí jiā
Going out	出去玩	chū qù wán
Happy	快乐	kuài lè
Hike (to -)	徒步旅游	tú bù lǚ yóu
Hiking trail	步道	bù dào
History	历史	lì shǐ
Hungry	饿	è
Metro	地铁	dì tiě
Monastery	修道院	xiū dào yuàn
Money	钱	qián
Motorbike	摩托车	mó tuō chē
Mountain	山	shān
Movie	电影	diàn yǐng
Museum	博物馆	bó wù guǎn
Ocean	海洋	hǎi yáng
Ocean wave	海浪	hǎi làng

Park	公园	gōng yuán
Plant	植物	zhí wù
Please	请	qǐng
Promenade	散步	sàn bù
Relax	放松	fàng sōng
Rent (to -)	租	zū
Reservation	预订	yù dìng
Sand	沙	shā
Scenic spot	名胜	míng shèng
Sea	海	hǎi
Sit (to -)	坐	zuò
Sky	天空	tiān kōng
Sport	运动	yùn dòng
Station	站	zhàn
Sun	太阳	tài yáng
Sunburn	晒斑	shài bān
Sun cream	防晒霜	fáng shài shuāng
Surfing	冲浪	chōng làng
Swimming	游泳	yóu yǒng
Taxi	出租车	chū zū chē
Temple	寺庙	sì miào
Thank you	谢谢	xiè xie
Theme park	主题公园	zhǔ tí gōng yuán
Thirsty	渴	kě
Ticket	票	piào
Time	时间	shí jiān
Tired	累	léi
Tree	树	shù
Water	水	shuǐ
Weekend	周末	zhōu mò

Health in Shenzhen

THE TECHNICAL LEVEL of public health has improved greatly in China. The management & supervision of medical work have been strengthened. An urban and rural medical insurance system combining state planning and fee paying has been established. Traditional Chinese Medicine and Western medicine have been promoted simultaneously. The incidence of many epidemic diseases has dropped considerably, and some endemic diseases are now under control. Rural health work has been improved, greatly contributing to the overall health of the population. The average life expectancy of Chinese people, the death rate of infants and childbirth death rates have almost reached the levels of developed countries.

However, even thought the technical level of public health has improved greatly lately, it is advisable to follow the following basic health information in China.

From Experts to Expats
Basic Health Information in China

HOSPITALS AND CLINICS in Shenzhen vary in quality, consistency and specialties offered. Quality control is applied inconsistently in China compared to European or North American standards. Practitioners with English language skills are the exception rather than the norm.

Most Hospitals in Shenzhen:

1. Require payment or deposit in cash on admission, either to emergency department or for out-patient care.

2. Don't offer appointments, even for specialists. One will have to show up and find out if a doctor is available. Many specialties commonly practiced in other countries may not exist in China: Physiotherapists, General Practitioners, Doctors of Osteopathy, and

Chiropractic to name a few.

3. Overall appearance, cleanliness and privacy can be poor depending on facility. Nursing support is limited to specified medical care, and patients are often expected to provide their own bedside support, for example bathing and meals.

4. Traditional Chinese Medicine practice (herbal medicines, massage, acupuncture) is still incorporated in many practitioners' training and is a large part of most clinic and hospital practices. Though separate from "Western" practice, it is offered and reflects the interpretation and practices of many "Western-trained" Chinese doctors.

For long-term expatriates and for newcomers to Shenzhen, I recommend the following:

1. Make sure one has medical insurance in place (what is the plan coverage and payment options; process of filing claims and reimbursement;

are evacuations & repatriations covered)

2. Make sure one has had all vaccinations required and up-to-date;

3. Learn as much as possible about the area you live:
   • Climate peculiarities (altitude, seasonal changes, potentially risky animals and insects);
   • Pay a visit to a few local hospitals, know their addresses, emergency entrance, etc;
   • Find out if dental/pediatric services are available in the area;

4. Have a first aid kit handy that is stocked with appropriate medications if not available locally;

5. Ensure one has enough specific/prescribed medication supply from the home country;

6. Carry an information card/note, written in both English and a local language with you with your name/basic medical information (blood type, allergies, etc.) emergency contact

phone numbers;

7. When traveling it is wise to have reliable means of communication;

8. Make sure that all documents/visas are valid and in place;

9. Keep emergency numbers readily available (ambulance, International SOS Alarm Center);

10. Plan your itinerary carefully, have your documents (ID, insurance policy records, medical records) copied and saved, so in an emergency or if documents are lost, someone can get access to them and retrieve necessary information;

11. Ensure that people who work and travel with you (family, driver, office assistant) know how to seek medical assistance as they may be the only people able to help you when in need.

■ by Jonathan Hyman

Recommended Hospitals in Shenzhen

Futian District

1 Beijing University Shenzhen Hospital 深圳市北京大学深圳医院

Hours: 8am - 12pm, 2h30pm - 5h30pm

Add.: No. 1120 Lianhua Road, Futian District

地址: 福田区莲花路1120号

Tel: 8392-3333

Web: www.pkuszh.com (Chinese)

Buses: 470, 446, 415, 2, 104, 209, 11, 14, 6, 2, Stop at Lianhua North Cunxin Rd (莲花北村西站)

①: English-speaking staff, good cardiology.

2 Shenzhen Second People's Hospital 深圳市第二人民医院

Hours: 8am - 12pm, 2pm - 5pm

Add.: No. 3002 Sungang West Road, Futian District
地址: 福田区笋岗西路3002号
Tel: 8336-6388
Web: www.sp120.com
①: English-speaking staff.

Luohu District

3 Shenzhen First People's Hospital 深圳市第一人民医院
Hours: 8am - 12pm, 2pm - 5pm
Add.: No. 1017 Dong Men North Road, Luohu District
地址: 罗湖区东门北路1017号
Tel: 2553-3018
①: English-speaking staff.

4 Shenzhen Sun Hospital 深圳市阳光医院
Hours: 8h30am - 8pm
Add.: No.1048, Bao'an Road South , Luohu District
地址: 罗湖区宝安南路1048号
Tel: 24 hours hotline: 2556-3998
       Free consultation phone: 800-830-5851
Web: sun.91.cn/english/index.htm (English)
①: English-speaking staff.

Nanshan District

5 Nanshan Hospital 深圳市南山医院
Add.: 89, Taoyuan Road, Nanshan
地址: 南山区桃源路89号
Tel: 2655-3111, ext. 23100

6 Shenzhen Longzhu Hospital 深圳市龙珠医院

Hours: 8h30am - 12h30pm, 2h30 - 5h30pm

Add.:   Longyuan Road 3, Xili, Nanshan District

地址: 南山区西丽龙苑路3号

Tel: 8625-8888, 8625-8999

Web: www.longzhuhospital.com (Chinese)

①: English-speaking staff.

7 Shenzhen Wuzhou International Clinic 深圳市五洲医院

Hours: 8h30am - 12h30pm, 2h30 - 5h30pm

Add.:   7 Ke Hua Road in the Technology Park, Nanshan District

地址: 南山区科技园北区科华路7号

Tel: 2649-1185

Web: www.szwz.cn (Chinese)

①: This clinic is proving to be quite popular as they have English speaking personnel and provide a free 24-hour pick and drop off service.

Bao'an District

8 Shenzhen Hengsheng Hospital 深圳市恒生医院

Hours: 8am - 12pm, 2pm - 5h30pm

Add.:   Baoyuan Road, Xixiang, Bao'an District

地址: 宝安区西乡碧海中心区宝源路

Tel: 2779-1848

Web: www.hsyy.com.cn/html/index.html (Chinese)

①: English-speaking staff.

9 Bao'an Traditional Chinese Medicine Hospital 宝安区中医院

Hours: 8am - 12pm, 2h30am - 5h30pm

Add.:   Yu'an Road, Bao'an District

地址: 宝安区裕安路

Tel: 2780-2422, 2780-6830

Web: www.bazyy.com.cn (Chinese)
ⓘ:   English-speaking staff.

Recommended Dentists in Shenzhen

Shenzhen has good dental care and many clinics will have an English speaking dentist. The standards are quite high and relatively cheap compared to Western dental costs.

Futian District

10 Arrail Dental 瑞尔齿科

Hours: 9am - 8h30pm, weekends and holidays 9am-5h30pm

Add.:   Room A, 2F, Noble Center, No. 1006, 3rd Fuzhong Road, Futian

地址: 福田区福中三路1006号诺德金融中心2层A单元

Tel: 8202-8928

Web: www.arrail-dental.com/en/index.aspx (English)

ⓘ:   Western style dentist office with Western trained dentists.

11 U-Dental 友睦齿科

Hours: 9am - 8h30pm, weekends and holidays 9am-5h30pm

Add.:   24F Jingrun Mansion,No.6019 ShennanRoad, Futian.District

地址: 福田区深南路6019号金润大厦24F

Tel: 8280-0366, 8280-0399

Web: www.u-dental.cn (English)

ⓘ:   Western style dentist office with Western trained dentists.

U-Dental has another office in Nanshan, check their website.

12 Viva Dental 维雅齿科

Hours: 9am - 6pm, Mon - Sun

Add.:   International Chamber of Commerce Building A,
         Room 18, 11/F, Fuhua Road 1, Futian District

地址：　福田区福华一路深圳国际商会大厦A座1118室

Tel:　　8205-6515, 8205-6516

Web:　　www.viva-dental.com (Chinese)

①:　　Located near Coco Park in Futian, Viva Dental is a modern and professional clinic offering a full range of dental services.

Luohu District

13 Arrail Dental 瑞尔齿科

Hours: 9am - 8h30pm, weekends and holidays 9am - 5h30pm

Add.:　Unit 2, G3&G4 /F, Office Tower, Shunhing Square Di Wang Commercial Center, 5002 Shennandong Road, Luohu

地址：　罗湖区深南东路5002号信兴广场，地王商业中心G3&G4层2单元

Tel:　　2583-7588

Nanshan District

14 A-Top Dental 同步齿科

Hours: Everyday 9am - 6pm

Add.:　1, Taizi Rd., 2F, Bitao Yuan building, Shekou, Nanshan District

地址：　南山区太子路一号碧涛苑二楼

Tel:　　Emergency line: 2681-2063, enquiry line: 2698-2266

Web:　　www.top917.com (Chinese)

Buses:　70, 113, K113; get off at Haiyang Dasha (海洋大厦)

15 Huamei Dental 华美齿科

Hours: Everyday 9am - 8h30pm

Add.:　6F, Baoli Building, Intersection of Nanhai Avenue and Chuangye Road, Nanshan District

地址：　南山区南海大道创业路口保利大厦6楼606室

Tel:　　2642-9141, 2642-9142

Chinese Health Phrase-Book

Useful phrases

I would like to register in the Department of Internal Medicine.
Wǒ xiǎng guàhào, kàn nèikē.
我想挂号，看内科.

I am not feeling well today.
Wǒ jīntiān bù shūfú.
我今天不舒服.

I catch a cold,cough heavily.
wǒ gǎnmào le, késou hěn lìhài.
我感冒了，咳嗽很厉害.

I have a stomachache/ toothache.
wǒ wèi/yá tòng.
我胃/牙痛.

I feel a bit feverish.
Wǒ yǒudiǎn fāshāo.
我有点发烧.

I am allergic to ...
Wǒ duì …guòmǐn.
我对…过敏.

My blood type is A.
Wǒ shì A xíng xuè.
我是A型血.

Is there a doctor who speaks English here?
zhè lǐ yǒu huì jiǎng yīng yǔ de yī sheng ma ?
这里有会讲英语的医生吗?

I will take sick leave today, because i have a cold.
wǒ jīntiān qǐng bìngjiǎ, wǒ zhòng gǎnmào le.
我今天请病假，我重感冒了.

Where can I get some headache pills?
wǒ qù nǎlǐ kěyǐ mǎi dàotóu
tòng yào?
我去哪里可以买到头痛药?

I have stomachache, could you please buy me some medicine?
wǒ wèi téng , néng máfan nǐ bāng wǒ mǎi xiē zhǐ téng yào ma?
我胃疼，能麻烦你帮我买些止疼药吗?

Health issues

Diarrhea
lā dù zi
拉肚子

Fever
Fā shāo
发烧

Cough
ké sou
咳嗽

Hign blood pressure
gāo xuè yā
高血压

Dentistry
yá kē
牙科

Body parts

Eye / yǎn jing / 眼睛
Nose / bí zi / 鼻子
Teeth / yá chǐ / 牙齿
Mouth / zuǐ / 嘴
Ear / ěr duo / 耳朵
Throat / hóu lóng / 喉咙
Waist / yāo / 腰
Back / bèi / 背
Arm / gē bo / 胳膊
Leg / tuǐ / 腿
Foot / jiǎo / 脚

From Experts to Expats
Traditional Chinese Medicine

TRADITIONAL CHINESE MEDI-CINE, (中医; Zhōngyī) in-cludes a range of traditional medical practices originating in China. Although well accepted in the mainstream of medical care throughout East Asia, it is considered an alternative medical system in much of the Western world. Traditional Chinese medicine practices include such treatments as herbal medicine, acupuncture, dietary therapy, and both Tui na (推拿) and Shiatsu massage. Qigong (气功) and Taijiquan (太极拳) are also closely associated with Traditional Chinese medicine.

Traditional Chinese medicine theory originated thousands of years ago through meticulous observation of nature, the cosmos, and the human body. Major theories include those of Yin-yang (阴阳), the Five Phases, the human body Channel system, Zang Fu (脏腑) organ theory, six confirmations, four layers, etc.

Traditional Chinese medicine is largely based on the philosophical concept that the human body is a small universe with a set of complete and sophisticated interconnected systems, and that those systems usually work in balance to maintain the healthy function of the human body. The balance of yin and yang is considered with respect to qi ("breath", "life force", or "spiritual energy"), blood, jing ("kidney essence", including "semen"), other bodily fluids, the Wu Xing (五行), emotions, and the soul or spirit (shen, 神). Traditional Chinese medicine has a unique model of the body, notably concerned with the meridian system. Unlike the Western anatomical model which divides the physical body into parts, the Chinese model is more concerned with function. Thus, the Traditional Chinese medicine spleen is not a specific piece of flesh, but an aspect of function related to transformation and transportation within the body, and of the mental functions of thinking and studying.

There are significant regional and philosophical differences between practitioners and schools which

in turn can lead to differences in practice and theory.

Theories invoked to describe the human body in Traditional Chinese medicine include:

- Channels, also known as "meridians"
- Wu Xing, "Fine Elements"
- Qi, "Universal Energy"
- Three jiaos also known as the Triple Burner, the Triple Warmer or the Triple Energiser
- Yin and Yang
- Zang and Fu

The Yin/Yang and five element theories may be applied to a variety of systems other than the human body, whereas Zang Fu theory, meridian theory and three-jiao (Triple warmer) theories are more specific. There are also separate models that apply to specific pathological influences, such as the Four Stages Theory of the progression of warm diseases, the Six Levels Theory of the penetration of cold diseases, and the Eight Principles System of disease classification.

Diagnostics

Following a macro philosophy of disease, traditional Chinese diagnostics are based on overall observation of human symptoms rather than "micro" level laboratory tests. There are four types of Traditional Chinese medicine diagnostic methods: observe (望 wàng), hear and smell (闻 wén), ask about background (问 wèn) and touching (切 qiè). The pulse-reading component of the touching examination is so important that Chinese patients may refer to going to the doctor as "Going to have my pulse felt."

Traditional Chinese medicine is considered to require considerable diagnostic skill. A training period of years or decades is said to be necessary for Traditional Chinese medicine practitioners to understand the full complexity of symptoms and dynamic balances. According to one Chinese saying, a good (Traditional Chinese medicine) doctor is also qualified to be a good prime minister in a country. Modern practitioners in China often use a traditional system in combination with Western methods.

Techniques

- Palpation of the patient's radial artery pulse (pulse diagnosis) in six positions;
- Observations of patient's tongue, voice, hair, face, posture, gait, eyes, ears, vein on index finger of small children;
- Palpation of the patient's body (especially the abdomen, chest, back, and lumbar areas) for ten-

derness or comparison of relative warmth or coolness of different parts of the body;

- Observation of the patient's various odors;
- Asking the patient about the effects of their problem;
- Anything else that can be observed without instruments and without harming the patient;
- Asking detailed questions about their family, living environment, personal habits, food diet, emotions, menstrual cycle for women, child bearing history, sleep, exercise, and anything that may give insight into the balance or imbalance of an individual.

Methods of treatment

The following methods are considered to be part of Chinese medicine:

1. Acupuncture(针灸): (from the Latin word acus, "needle", and pungere, meaning "prick") is a technique in which the practitioner inserts fine needles into specific points on the patient's

body. Usually about a dozen acupoints are needled in one session, although the number of needles used may range anywhere from just one or two to 20 or more. The intended effect is to increase circulation and balance energy (Qi) within the body.

2. Auriculotherapy （耳灼疗法）: which comes under the heading of Acupuncture and Moxibustion.

3. Chinese food therapy （食疗）: dietary recommendations are usually made according to the patient's individual condition in relation to Traditional Chinese medicine theory. The "five flavors" (an important aspect of Chinese herbalism as well) indicate what function various types of food play in the body. A balanced diet, which leads to health, is when the five functional flavors are in balance. When one is diseased (and therefore unbalanced), certain foods and herbs are prescribed to restore balance to the body.

4. Chinese herbal medicine （中草药）: in China, herbal medicine is considered as the primary therapeutic modality of internal medicine. Of the approximately 500 Chinese herbs that are in use today, 250 or so are very commonly used. Rather than being prescribed individually, single herbs are combined into formulas that are designed to adapt to the specific needs of individual patients. A herbal formula can contain anywhere from 3 to 25 herbs. As with diet therapy, each herb has one or more of the five flavors/functions and one of five "temperatures" ("Qi") (hot, warm, neutral, cool, cold). After the herbalist determines the energetic temperature and functional state of the patient's body, he or she prescribes a mixture of herbs tailored to balance disharmony.

5. Cupping （拔罐）: a type of Chinese massage, cupping consists of placing several glass "cups" (open spheres) on the body. A match is lit and placed

inside the cup and then removed before placing the cup against the skin. As the air in the cup is heated, it expands, and after placing in the skin, cools down, creating a lower pressure inside the cup that allows the cup to stick to the skin via suction. When combined with massage oil, the cups can be slid around the back, offering what some practitioners think of as a re-verse-pressure massage.

6. Die da or Tieh Ta (跌打): is usu-ally practiced by martial artists who know aspects of Chinese medicine that apply to the treat-ment of trauma and injuries such as bone fractures, sprains, and bruises. Some of these spe-cialists may also use or rec-ommend other disciplines of Chinese medical therapies (or Western medicine in modern times) if serious injury is in-volved. Such practice of bone-setting (整骨) is not common in the West.

7. Moxibustion: "Moxa," often used in conjunction with acupunc-ture, consists in burning of dried Chinese mugwort (Artemisia vulgaris) on acupoints. "Direct Moxa" involves the pinching of clumps of the herb into cones that are placed on acupoints and lit until warm. Typically the burning cone is removed before burning the skin and is thought, after repeated use, to warm the body and increase circulation. Moxa can also be rolled into a cigar-shaped tube, lit, and held over an acupuncture point, or rolled into a ball and stuck onto the back end of an inserted nee-dle for warming effect.

8. Physical Qigong exercises such as Tai chi chuan (Taijiquan 太极拳), Standing Meditation (站椿功), Yoga, Brocade BaDuanJin exercises (八段锦) and other Chinese martial arts.

9. Qigong (气功): and related breathing and meditation ex-ercise.

10.   Tui na massage (推拿): a form of massage akin to acu-pressure (from which shiat-su evolved.) Oriental massage

is typically administered with the patient fully clothed, without the application of grease or oils. Choreography often involves thumb presses, rubbing, percussion, and stretches.

11.   Some Traditional Chinese medicine doctors may also utilize esoteric methods that incorporate or reflect personal beliefs or specializations such as Fengshui (风水) or Bazi (八字).

Modernization

Traditional Chinese medicine has been to some degree modernized by transforming the plants and ingredients to soluble granules and tablets. Modern formulations in pills and sachets used 675 plant and fungi ingredients and about 25 from non-plant sources such as snakes, geckos, toads, frogs, bees, and earthworms.

Investigation of the active ingredients in Traditional Chinese medicine has produced Western style drugs, for example Artemisinin now widely used in the treatment of malaria.

Settling Down in Shenzhen

From Experts to Expats
Buying a property in China

BUYING A PROPERTY in China can be difficult, probably similar to buying anywhere else outside your own country in a different language.

You can buy a property after one year of legal residency. It is sometimes possible to buy earlier than one year. In that case you must pay cash, as you will not be entitled to a bank mortgage.

There are many taxes and charges associated with a purchase as detailed on the next page. We believe these to be correct at the time of publishing but are subject to change and need to be verified prior to considering a purchase.

Typically the deposit or down payment is around 40% of the price. When you add all the taxes and other costs, you need to have 50% of the capital price to do a transaction. This is very different from many Western countries where the deposit is 10%, so it can be a shock for those who are unaware of this. The government has raised this and also interest rates to slow down the upward spiral of housing prices. It worked.

There will also be a lot of talk about new price and old price. There is a tendency to put down the old price on a contract, as it reduces the taxes paid and may lessen the capital gains tax. In some cases this is a highly risky act.

Getting money out of China is very difficult but getting money into China isn't. What can be difficult is converting foreign currency to RMB on a large scale, as many banks have a daily limit on this. You can get caught with lots of USD or Euro in your account and not be able to pay the housing deposit in RMB, as they will only let you convert US$10,000 per day. There can be fine print in the bank contract allowing larger currency conversions if it is for the purchase of a home or establishment of a business. As most banks don't deal with foreigners buying property, quite often they do not know of these provisions, and this can cause some undue frustration.

Lawyers are not often involved in the purchase process, as the real estate agent does it all. Beware of giving the agent lots of cash (i.e. deposit) as many have gone out of business recently, and a lot of people lost their money. One CEO ran off with 40 million RMB and left a lot of unhappy new clients and very angry staff.

■ by Ian Jones

ITEM	RATE	NOTE
Maintenance & Construction tax	1%	For apartment sold within 5 years.
Education tax	3%	
Stamp tax	0.05%	Seller & buyer.
Business tax	5%	
Deed tax	1.5%	
Stamp duty	0.05%	
Registration fee	50RMB	
Property verification fee	50RMB	
Ownership certificate stamp	5RMB	
Estate agent fee	1.5%	Due from both buyer and seller, but normally pushed all to the buyer.
Transfer fee	6RMB/sqm	
Notarization fees		Varies – can be up to 2,000RMB.
Income tax (capital gain)	20% of profit	Seller will try to push to the buyer.

Table 1: Property acquisition/expenses table

From Experts to Expats
Importing Your Personal Effects into Shenzhen

A S SHENZHEN'S ECONOMY has grown over the last 30 years, so has the number of expatriates working and living in the city. Many people that move to Shenzhen bring a couple of suitcases when they arrive and leave with a 20 or 40-foot container. Others bring in a container of furniture, only to find out that apartments come fully furnished. As an expatriate that has lived in Hong Kong, China and Vietnam for 10 years and having moved four times internationally and many times locally, I will share some of my own personal experiences.

Coming to China for the first time can be an exciting experience for you and your family. Seeing a new country, learning a new language and eating new food can sound like an adventure to begin with, however after a couple of months the novelty will wear off. When this happens, it's nice to know you have a support group of people for your family, as the spouse often times doesn't work.

Before you sign a contract with a prospective employer in China, have a familiarization trip to Shenzhen. During this trip you should contact a realtor and have them show you apartments to get a better idea of what to expect in terms of size and fixtures. You should also ask the realtor to provide a city tour and introduce you to prospective schools for your children, church organizations, supermarkets, sports clubs and other social organizations of interest to you. The faster you understand your new home, the sooner you'll be able to acclimate to your new setting once you arrive. Many of your pre-move questions will be answered in your first trip to Shenzhen. Once you've decided that Shenzhen suits you and your family, then it's time to decide if you need to send a shipment.

Following that, you will have to

order a mover from your original location to do a physical survey and prepare a quotation for sending your personal effects to China. At the time of the survey, you will be assigned a move coordinator who will act as your contact point for any origin-related questions.

One of the major things to consider when sending a shipment to China is the cost of moving services and import duties for the items you will be sending. You should budget USD3,000.00 and up for a minimum sea shipment of 4 cubic meters by "Less than Container Load" (LCL) from larger cities in Europe and North America into Shenzhen. Most Asian cities to Shenzhen will cost considerably less than this due to the proximity and lower cost of services in these countries. Moving companies charge by volume so the more things you take the higher the charges.

Import duty/tax on household effects is uniform throughout China. In general, furniture will be taxed at 10% of the customs assessed value, electrical items at 20%, and luxury items (from golf clubs to cosmetic products) at 30% to 50%. The import duty/tax amount is calculated based on the customs assessed value, solely at the discretion of the local customs bureau and quite often differs from city to city. For example, Shenzhen Customs may assess a DVD player at 500RMB while Beijing Customs may assess the same item at 1,500RMB. Prior to deciding what to bring, you might want to send a list of your things to your moving coordinator to get an idea of the estimated import duties. Sending an old computer and paying more in import duties than its actual value doesn't make much sense.

Once you've decided to move personal effects and have confirmed the quotation, your items will be professionally packed and wrapped by the origin partner. Container ships move in six directions: roll, heave, yaw, pitch, surge and sway. To combat any damage due to transportation, corrugated cardboard, bubble wrap, newsprint paper, tissue paper, hanging wardrobes, folding wardrobes, silica gel (to absorb moisture), dish packs, small, medium and large boxes will be used to protect your items. For things easily damaged, wooden crates can be made around the packaging material for added protection. A packing inventory will serve as your receipt for the items entrusted to the mover. This list will be created by the origin supervisor of your move. Your move coordinator at your origin will discuss the details and requirements of your individual move to ensure your personal effects arrive safely. Prior to packing, be aware of the below items that shouldn't be shipped to China:

- Firearms, Ammunition, Weapons & Explosives.
- TV Satellite dish.
- Telecommunication equipment, including cordless phones.
- Copiers and fax machines.
- Unprocessed food, fresh meat, fresh vegetables, dairy products, and even baby powder milk.
- Live plants.
- Poisons or illegal drugs.

- All kinds of equipment/tools associated with gambling.
- Printed/recorded material deemed detrimental to the political, economic, cultural, or moral atmosphere in China (including all pornographic materials).
- Overlarge office items, such as large photocopier machine, which are not considered for personal or family usage.
- Maps (where the Chinese border is not in accordance with PRC law).
- Endangered and rare animals and their products, such as ivory.
- Counterfeit currencies.
- Motorcycles.
- Any other items that are determined by the local Customs Bureau to be of non-personal or non-family usage. These items may be seized if found in the shipment.

Transit times for a sea shipment will take around 8 weeks for Europe and North America and 5 weeks for Asia. You should factor in temporary hotel accommodation or a fully furnished home until your personal effects can arrive in China. Bringing more suitcases on the initial flight over will suffice until your other things arrive, or you can consider an air shipment to get a small amount of essential items to China faster.

As a foreign passport holder, you'll need a work permit, residence permit and also other documents from your company in order to import household goods into Shenzhen. Your company must be registered in China prior to even starting the work and residence permit. The shipment should not arrive in China until these documents are available.

You should also physically be in China when the shipment arrives, as original documents are needed for a couple of days for customs clearance. Import customs clearance in China tends to progress quite slowly. We frequently encounter problems due to changing customs practices and the often-frequent business travel undertaken by clients, which delays application for the various visa & permits. During the clearance process, patience is needed. After your personal effects have been cleared, a packing team will be arranged to deliver to your residence. An English-speaking supervisor will lead a team to help unpack and set up everything in your new home.

Good planning is key to any successful move. All dates should be confirmed prior to packing in order to minimize the amount of time waiting for your things and also hotel expenses. As soon as you know you will be moving, and the sooner you gather more information the better. Meeting the people on the ground in China who'll be handling your move is also a good step in making sure you will be looked after when your shipment arrives.

■ by Zachary Kever

For more information about the above-mentioned places visit WikiShenzhen.com

From Expats to Expats
Helping Hands in China: Ayis (阿姨)

"**I**NEED AN AYI (pronounced eye-ee)" is one of the first phrases that many expats find themselves uttering when they come to Shenzhen. The term Ayi can mean a housekeeper, maid, child minder or a combination. How the person is viewed in your home is how you define the person's duties. If you talk to expat women about their Ayis, you will find that the Ayi is very important to the workings of the family, usually loves their kids and makes life in China great.

Finding an Ayi

Finding an Ayi can be a quick or laborious process. Many people find their Ayis by word of mouth from other expats thru organizations like Shekou Women's International Club, from local agencies or thru their relocation services company. Agencies within Shenzhen will provide Chinese Ayis. There is no agency at this time for non-Chinese Ayis.

When searching for an Ayi and finding one that suits your needs, make sure that you check out that person by personal references, past employers or through an interview. Set up an interview at your house so that you can explain the duties in the environment they will work in. A health exam can be important to check for infectious diseases if your Ayi is working with children. Ask your Ayi to provide a health certificate or schedule an exam thru a local clinic or hospital. Ask to see their ID card or passport and visa and make a copy for your records.

It is important to have a trust relationship with your Ayi. They will have access to your home when you are not there. Some people are there everyday to open the door for the Ayi, and some people provide a key for their Ayi to come and go independently.

Contracts, trial work periods and work duties

The success of your Ayi is really how you define the work expected. Creating a contract with duties outlined may seem prudent, but if language is a barrier, it is more important that the duties are pointed out and explained thoroughly. An understanding of the job requirements can be agreed upon with a handshake or a paper contract. Most agencies provide a contract. A contract between your Ayi and yourself can be as simple as household duties written down on paper, vacations, holidays, schedule and pay.

Take a week to train and show the Ayi what is expected. Show how you like the ironing to be done and clothes folded. What are your expectations of cleanliness? If vacuuming is required, show the equipment to be used and how to use it. Taking care of a pet is very important. Even an experienced Ayi needs to learn your expectations. Don't assume they know. Take the time to make sure and follow up. Once your Ayi learns your daily requirements, they will plan their work day flow to get the jobs completed.

It is very important to plan for your Ayi to work on a trial basis for 2 weeks to one month. If the arrangement does not work out, pay your Ayi for the time worked and end it. This is a very common occurrence and should not be agonized over. A good fit provides for a stressless and seamless working of the household.

Typical duties of Ayis are dependent upon the household but can include: cleaning all areas of the house including floors and windows, cooking some or all meals both Chinese and Western food, child minding and pick-up from school, checking on the house while the employers are on vacation, caring for the pets; both feeding and walking, liaising with sub-contractors or maintenance people for your apartment or house, dropping off and picking up items from the dry cleaners, grocery and household shopping, laundry and ironing. Many people teach their Ayis to cook the family's favorite dishes. Ovens are not common in China, and you may need to teach your Ayi how to bake.

Language requirements of your Ayi are dependent upon your comfort level. Many Chinese Ayis speak limited or no English but are able to handle the responsibilities of communicating with their employer. For many people, having an Ayi that can communicate with and discipline their children is important, so English may be a highly valued skill for your Ayi. For some, an Ayi can be a means to learn Chinese or practice Chinese. A tri-al period will help determine the right combination for your family.

Working schedule and pay

The going rate of a full-time Ayi can range from 1,500-4,500RMB per month. Certain areas of Shenzhen can command a higher rate based on location. English speaking Ayis can command higher pay. Some Ayis prefer to work part-time or on an hourly basis and the rate can range from 20-25RMB per hour. Providing raises to the base pay are at the discretion of the employer. Some people raise the base salary after a period of time and based on goals reached. If your Ayi is non-Chinese and needs a visa to work, make sure that the discussion of who will pay the visa costs on top of the monthly pay is discussed at the start of employment. Costs for a plane ticket home should also be included.

The schedule your Ayi works should dictate the pay. Full-time Ayis normally work from 8am -6pm Mon. - Fri., but hours can be less or more dependent upon your needs. Some work half day on Saturday. Part-time Ayis are usually less than 5 hours a day or less than 5 days a week. Deciding to have a part-time Ayi may mean that you have to work around a previously set schedule. Live-in Ayis physically live in your house in a separate room and are usually provided a day off once a week, and other mutually agreed upon down time. Separate arrangements are usually made for evening babysitting during the week and weekends.

Pay your Ayi once a month on a set date. Discuss when this will take place with your Ayi. Take this responsibility seriously and provide the pay separate from other financial transactions. They are an employee of your family, so avoid personal loans or other intrusively personal requests.

Holidays and bonuses

For Chinese Ayis, the Chinese New Year is an important holiday to honor. Time off at this time with bonus is the normal requirement.

The bonus should be pro-rated based on the time worked for you. The bonus is given at the start of the Chinese New Year. The amount provided can be a month's pay or less dependent upon other bonuses or perks given over the year. Time off for other National Chinese Holidays are given at the discretion of the employer. Holidays that are related to your home country are usually not celebrated with a Chinese Ayi.

As a final note, don't forget your Ayi is a complex human being with all of the baggage of kids, spouses, parents, home town expectations, etc. that you have. Keep a professional relationship that is friendly and respectful from both sides. Make sure that expectations are clear from the start, and you should have an excellent "helping hand" during your stay in China.

■ by Meribeth Nordloef

For more information about the above-mentioned places visit WikiShenzhen.com

From Experts to Expats
Bringing Your Pet into China

Regulations

YOU ARE ALLOWED to bring pets to China as long as you can prove that they are vaccinated and healthy. In theory, you need to have a Z (resident) visa to bring in your pet. There should be only one pet per Z visa holder (so if you have two cats, for example, make sure that one is registered in the husband's name and one in the wife's). From personal experience, we know that it is possible to waive this requirement by using an agent in the case of a family with two pets and only one Z visa holder (the employee) at the time of entry.

Dogs have to be registered with the Chinese authorities after arrival.

Deciding whether to bring your pet

Bringing a cat or dog to China is quite straightforward provided you get the right documentation sorted out before you come. Bringing a cat is simpler than bringing a dog, as there are fewer rules and regulations concerning cats, and they do not need to be registered with the authorities. Anyone considering bringing their dog to China should be aware that, although the paperwork is manageable (albeit expensive), on arrival they will find that dogs are not as welcome in China as they are in some other places. Also remember that to get your dog out of China, you will need the correct papers. It is suggested you do not list your dog's breed as rottweiler, pit bull or other *dangerous* breeds. This may cause problems, as certain breeds are not allowed. Some cities also have a size restriction for dogs. Check with your agent to see if this applies to your area.

Make reservations to fly non-stop whenever possible or, at least, to minimize flight connections. If your pet will be in the cabin with you, request a forward seat on the right side of the aircraft. Avoid weekend or holiday flights as they tend to be more crowded, and your pet may not get the attention it needs.

Remember that most airlines won't fly animals during periods of extreme temperatures when the weather is too hot or too cold. During the summer, try to schedule a very early morning or late evening flight. During the winter, it's best to fly midday.

Confirm with the airline that you will be bringing your pet 24 to 48 hours before departure.

Preparing your pet's carrier

1. Make sure your pet's shipping crate meets airline requirements, is properly ventilated and of adequate size for your pet to stand up, turn around and lie down comfortably.
2. Place an absorbent towel in the crate. You can also place an item of clothing you have worn but not washed, such as a T-shirt, in the crate. Your pet may be com-

forted by your scent.
3. Label your crate appropriately. Tape a <u>Live Animal</u> label with letters at least 1" high on top and on one side of the crate.
4. Indicate the top with <u>Arrows</u> on at least 2 sides.
5. Attach <u>Feeding Instructions</u> on the outside of the crate, with a small plastic zip lock bag of food, if necessary.
6. Attach <u>Contact Information</u> on the outside of the crate, with your pet's name, your name, addresses and phone numbers at origin and destination.
7. Attach two empty dishes to the crate, one for food and one for water.

Preparing your pet

Never put a choke, pinch or training collar, a muzzle or a leash on your pet. Make a temporary paper collar for your dog with its name, your name, address and phone number on it. Safety collars which attach with elastic or Velcro are recommended for your cat. It is strongly suggested you do not tranquilize your pet.

Transportation

Check with your intended airline(s) as to what rates apply and what rules they have for the carriage of pets. It is important to use an airline-approved pet box. Ensure that you make a reservation for your pet, as space in the appropriate section of the hold is usually limited. It's best to use a Western airline (not a Chinese one) to transport your pet to ensure that conditions in the hold are suitable. Some airlines also allow small pets to travel with you in the cabin.

Many airlines charge a fixed rate for transporting a pet in the hold as long as the owner is also on board, i.e. it is the same price no matter how far you travel, but you pay for each flight taken. Every airline has its own policies regarding pets. If you are using more than one airline, check each of their requirements.

You have a choice of whether to handle everything yourself or engage an agent to help. The advantage of an agent is that they will ensure that you have all the correct documents and will meet you and your animal at the airport. They will speak to the officials there for you and generally smooth the way through the quarantine and import procedures. In theory, this greatly reduces the chance that you will encounter a problem with bringing in your pet. The disadvantage, however, is the cost, which is considerably higher than handling the arrangements yourself. Some families have recently brought in pets without the use of an agent and have not encountered problems. See also 'Requirements for owners' and 'Quarantine'.

Your relocation company can normally handle this.

Cost

1. You can find out the costs of transporting your animal directly from your airline.
2. There is a customs fee per animal of RMB1,000 (China).
3. If your pet is quarantined (see

below) you will have to pay the boarding costs.

4. Agents charge around RMB4,000 (US$500) per pet, inclusive of the customs fee and transport for you and your pet from the airport. This is payable in advance. If you have not paid in advance, then you are advised to have the money in US$ ready to hand over to avoid delays at the airport.

5. For dogs, there is a registration fee which can be arranged through the pet shops in Shekou. You will need a letter from your landlord giving permission to have a pet on property, photos of your dog and copies of the rabies certificate. Check for the most recent regulations. This is very important as there have been culls of all dogs due to rabies outbreaks in some parts of China. Registering your dog will protect them.

Plant and quarantine office

If you choose not to use an agent, you will need to get the application form for importing your animal yourself. The address for this is:

Administration of Entry and Exit Inspection and Quarantine of the People's Republic of China, A10 Chao Yang Men Wai Da Jie, Beijing 100020. Tel. 010-6599-4600.

Quarantine

There is an official quarantine period of **45 days**. If the owner signs an agreement to keep the pet indoors for this period, then official quarantine is usually not demanded. We have not heard of any pet being kept for the quarantine, but if it does happen, you will have to pay for the costs of boarding your pet. We are not sure what the conditions are like for pets, and you will obviously want to avoid your animal being taken into quarantine if at all possible. We are told that the use of an agent greatly minimizes the risk that the pet will be quarantined. However, it appears that this rarely occurs whether you use an agent or not.

Documentation

You will need the following documentation for your pet:

1. Vaccination certificate(s) certifying that your pet has been vaccinated against rabies and other common illnesses (e.g. cat flu, feline encephalitis) within one year prior to the date of entry. The rabies certificate should be separate from any vaccination book you may have, and will be retained by the Chinese officials. You may also need to show the pet does not have Monkey Pox or been exposed to it.

2. Health certificate issued by the vet in the country from which you are traveling. If you are coming from the USA, you must take the health certificate issued by your vet and send it to your state's department of Agriculture. They then certify that the vet is qualified by the state to issue the health certificate. The certificate should be issued no sooner than two weeks in advance of your pet's arrival in China. It should include name of pet, type of pet (dog/cat and breed), age, weight (and height for dogs), gender, plus a general declaration that the pet is vaccinated and in good health.

3. Photo clearly showing the animal's size (photograph beside a ruler).

4. A letter from the management of the residence in which you intend to live, stating that the pet may live there.

5. A letter from your company stating that the employee is employed there.

6. A copy of your passport (one passport per pet).

7. On arrival you should take your pet, fee, and certificates to the Plant and Quarantine office at the airport (if you are using an agent, they will meet you and take you to the office). The officials will keep the health and rabies certificates (but not the vaccination book), so make sure you have copies.

Hong Kong

If you arrive first into Hong Kong,

you will have to go to the cargo terminal to complete the paperwork. Hong Kong has its own unique import requirements. If you do not leave for China immediately, you will have to satisfy Hong Kong requirements as well as the Chinese requirements. The ferry service between Hong Kong Airport and Shekou (Shenzhen) does not take pets so you will need to arrange transportation overland through the truck/car border crossing. After you have completed the paperwork at the cargo department, you will be physically escorted to the China border by a Hong Kong customs official. You will then have to present your documents to the authorities at the Chinese border. They will inspect the documents and the pet. Because all of this can be very difficult if you are not fluent in Chinese, it is suggested you use an agent.

Guangzhou

Arriving into Guangzhou is easier because you are only clearing one countries' set of custom regulations. Upon arrival, present your pet's documentation to the customs officials who will inspect them and the pet. The following link explains in detail the requirements for Guangzhou: www.santaferelo.com/ecs/data/sfguide/CAN/Pet.htm.

The official information as listed by Guangdong Foreign Affair's office is below:

1. It is allowed to carry in only one pet (cat or dog only) per person. When entering with a pet into China, the carrier should declare to the Inspection and Quarantine Authority at the port of entry and present the following documents:

2. The Health Certificate issued by the Veterinary Quarantine Authority of the country/region of export.

3. The Certificate of Immunity from Rabies issued by the relevant government department of the country/region of export. In accordance with the Chinese law, the vaccination against rabies is valid for one year since the in-

jection, and the last vaccination must be done within 30 days before the pet is carried into China.

4. The consular or service identity document or the diplomatic or service passport of the carrier of the pet.

5. The completed Quarantine Inspection Form.

The Inspection and Quarantine Authority at the port of entry will conduct quarantine inspection of the carry-in pet at the port and have it quarantined for thirty days in isolation in the quarantine institute designated by the authority. If the pet can pass the quarantine inspection after the isolation, the Inspection and Quarantine Authority at the port of entry will issue the quarantine certificate to permit the entry of the pet.

If the carrier of the pet is unable to present the Health Certificate and the Certificate of Immunity from Rabies issued by the Veterinary Quarantine Authority of the country/region of export, or the number of pets brought in exceeds the permitted limit, or the pet fails to pass the quarantine inspection, the Inspection and Quarantine Authority will temporarily hold the pet in custody before its repatriation or extermination within the specified time limit. In this case, the carrier will be issued a Receipt of Carried on Articles Held for Quarantine Inspection/Disposition. For the pet to be repatriated, the carrier should complete all the formalities within the specified time limit. Otherwise, the pet will be regarded as the unclaimed. If the carrier decides, in writing, to give up the pet, the Inspection and Quarantine Authority will dispose of the pet in accordance with the relevant regulations.

These are the official rules. In practice, pets are rarely (if ever) quarantined.

Registration of dogs

It is a requirement to register your dog with the local police of your place of residence within a month of arrival. In practice, most people are still in temporary accommodation beyond the first month, so registration inevitably gets delayed. See "Police Stations" on page 308.

As long as you keep your dog within the compound, it is unlikely to attract police attention. It appears that not all dogs are registered, but the police are becoming less tolerant of expats claiming ignorance. If you want to take your dog with you when you leave China, then you must get it registered.

You need to take your dog, import certificate, two photos of the dog, and a letter from your employer requesting registration of the dog and stating that the owner is an employee of the company, your official ID card, and the fee to the above address.

Other pet issues

Pets and the Chinese

Although pets are a relatively new phenomenon in China, they are becoming increasingly popular, and it is now not unusual for Chinese families to have pet dogs or cats. Along with this trend, the facilities for pets are also improving.

Kennels

Boarding facilities are limited and most people leave their pets at home and have their maid or a friend take care of them when on holiday. A few vets provide kenneling.

Vets

There are many vets in Shenzhen with several in old Shekou and on Houhai Blvd., Nanshan. Bring your supply of heartworm medicine and other medications from home. China has quality control issues so it is better to be safe than sorry.

See "Vets" on page 263 for a list of recommended vets in Shenzhen.

Food

Pedigree and Whiskas products are widely available in most supermarkets. Specialist foods (e.g. Hills Science Diet, Eukanuba, and IAMS) are also available at vets' clinics but can be pricey so you might want to consider bringing them in your freight. There are also some local brands.

Note that the above information is subject to change without notice. Please consult the authorities for the most up to date information.

Source: crienglish.com

From Experts to Expats
Judy's Pet Services

FOR MANY PEOPLE, life is not complete without a furry friend. For 12 years, Judy Liang has been helping expats find a new pet by rescuing dogs that need a good home. She also provides referral services. Judy's dogs are smaller, healthy, vaccinated and free of charge. She can refer owners to local vets and help with calling in Chinese if your pet is sick (free of charge). She can organize licensing as well as worldwide shipping (fee applicable). If, for some reason you cannot take your animal with you, Judy can find a good home for it.

Contacting Judy	
✉	Laomu Antiques Shop (next to QSI Shekou) Rm4 GF Crystal Garden Building Taizi Rd., Shekou 蛇口太子路碧涛商业中心底层商铺4号
✆	2668-1871, mobile: 138-0225-8455
✉	judyliang11@hotmail.com
🖱	www.laomu-china.com

See "Vets" on page 263 for a list of recommended vets in Shenzhen.

Children in Shenzhen

From Expats to Expats
Children's Education

For new comers with children, living in Shenzhen may feel like being on a different planet. However, parents can turn it into an enjoyable experience if they are open-minded and try to accept and integrate more into Chinese society. Language is always a barrier, but after a few lessons of Mandarin, parents can have a basic conversation with the locals to express their needs. Sometimes one doesn't need to say much, and any effort is certainly much appreciated. Unlike other major international cities, activities for kids in English are limited in Shenzhen, but in Mandarin such activities are abundant. Use this as an opportunity for your child to pick up another language, which is fun. Research more thoroughly, and your attempts will be paid off. There is always something new happening or opening on the horizon.

Major International Schools in Shenzhen

1 Funful Bilingual School	方方乐趣中英文学校
📧	Goldfield Seaview Gardens, South Xinzhou Rd., Futian District
地址	福田区新洲南路金地海景花园内
✆	2381-0830
🖥	www.funful.com.cn
🚌	70 (Minghua Zhongxin stop, 明华中心)

3 International School of Nanshan Shenzhen (ISNS)	南山国际学校
📧	166, Nanguang Rd., Nanshan District
地址	南山区南光路166号:南山国际学校
✆	2666-1000
🖥	www.isnsz.com

2 Green Oasis International School	城市绿洲学校
📧	Millennium Oasis Tianmian, 4030, Shennan Middle Rd., Tianmian Village, Futian District
地址	福田区田面村深南中路4030号 (花园格兰云天酒店旁)
✆	8395-9000 ext. 207
🖥	www.greenoasis.org.cn
🚌	70 (Minghua Zhongxin stop, 明华中心)
🚇	Hua Qiang Lu station 华强路站

4 OEC International School	东方英文书院
📧	10, Xuezi Rd., Bao'an Education Town, Bao'an District
地址	深圳宝安教育城 (深圳国际机场北) 学子路10号
✆	2900-0566
🖥	www.szoec.com.cn

5 QSI, Quality Schools International, Shekou	QSI国际学校
地址 2nd Floor, Bitao Building, 8 Taizi Rd., Shekou 南山区蛇口太子路8号碧涛中心2楼	
✆ 2667-6031	
🖰 www.qsi.org/shk	

6 QSI, Quality Schools International, Futian	QSI国际学校
8063, Hongli West Rd., Honey Lake, Futian District	
地址 南福田区香蜜湖红荔西路8063号，科爱赛国际学校（科苑宾馆旁）	
✆ 8371-3122	
🖰 www.qsi.org/szn	
🚌 107, 204 or 101, Zhaoshang Yinhang Bldg. stop 招商银行大厦	
🚇 Che Gong Miao station 车公庙站	

7 Shenzhen American International School	深美国际学校
Wenxin 2 Rd., Nanshan District	
地址 南山区美墅蓝山家园裙楼	
✆ 6598-8074	
🖰 www.sziaszh.com	

8 SIS, Shekou International School	蛇口国际学校
Jingshan Villas, Nanhai Rd., Shekou, Nanshan District	
地址 南山区蛇口南海大道鲸山别墅	
✆ 2669-3669	
🖰 www.sis.org.cn	
🚌 70 (Minghua Zhongxin stop, 明华中心)	

Kindergarten

1 Boya Shixia No. 1 Kindergarten	博雅石厦第一幼儿园
🖃	4, Shi Xia North Rd., Futian District
地址	福田区石厦北四街四号
ℂ	8380-4488
🖱	www.yjzjcn.com

2 Funful Bilingual School	方方乐趣中英文学校
🖃	Goldfield Seaview Gardens, South Xinzhou Rd., Futian District
地址	福田区新洲南路金地海景花园内
ℂ	2381-0830
🖱	www.funful.com.cn
🚌	4, 15, 26, 103A, 202, 212

3 LEADS International Kindergarten	理思国际幼儿园
🖃	Xuefu Rd., Bao'an Education City, Bao'an District
地址	宝安区机场北学府路宝安教育城内
ℂ	2970-6679
🖱	www.szleads.com

4 Manhattan Kids Club International Kindergarten	
地名	美加儿童国际教学机构
🖃	(1) OCT, Nanshan District (2) Xiyuan, Xiangmi Hu Rd., Futian District (3) Luhai Mingdu, Xuefu Rd., Nanshan District (4) Bihua Tinju, Mei Xiu Rd., Futian District
地址	(1)华侨城 (2)福田区熙园 (3)南山区绿海名都 (4)福田区梅秀路碧华庭居
ℂ	(1)2692-9592, (2)8289-0659, (3)8606-5461, (4)8316-4486
🏛	Che Gong Miao station 车公庙站
🖱	www.manhattankidsclub.com

5 OEC International School

📧	10, Xuezi Rd., Bao'an Education Town, Bao'an District
地址	深圳宝安教育城（深圳国际机场北）学子路10号
✆	2900-0566
🖥	www.oecis.cn

6 Peninsula Kindergarten School　　　　半岛幼儿园

📧	1, Jinshiji Rd., Dong Jiaotou, Nanshan District
地址	南山区蛇口东角头半岛邦
✆	2685-1266
🖥	www.peninsulakindergarten.com
🚌	80

7 SheckHard Kindergarten　　　　石厦中英文幼儿园

📧	247, Shixia East Village Fumin Rd., Futian District
地址	福田区福民路石厦东村247号
✆	8383-0161
🖥	www.szsheckhard.org

Local Chinese Schools

THERE IS A growing number of expats choosing to educate their children in local Chinese schools in order to command a native-speakers' level of Mandarin. There are many good Chinese schools around. However, for a newly arrived expat, it is no easy task to choose a Chinese school. Local Chinese schools can be government-owned or private. These general tips should equip you with some useful suggestions on how to go about this task:

Choose your schools

1. Go and visit.
2. Talk to as many staff of the school as possible;
3. Get an interpreter (if not a fluent Mandarin speaker) and talk in detail about the schools' curriculum;
4. Hygiene is very important. Spend a day, inspect thoroughly. Private schools are more likely to have higher hygiene standards;
5. Enquire about specifics methods of discipline. After having short-listed, spend more than a day in each school to see for yourself.

Activities for Children

- **C**hildren's World
- **C**hildren's Palace
- **E**vergreen Resort
- **S**afari Park Shenzhen
- **T**eletubbies Children Play & Development Centre
- **G**ymboree
- **H**appy Valley Theme Park
- **S**plendid China
- **W**indow of the World
- **M**insk World
- **S**hekou Skate park
- **S**kating Rink at Mix City
- **S**hekou Youth Sports Program
- **N**anshan book city
- **S**henzhen International Botanical Garden
- **H**aiwan Art School

THERE ARE 2 Children's World shopping malls in Shenzhen. One is located in Nanshan and the second one is located in Futian. These relatively large shopping malls cater exclusively to children. There are many small shops within the mall offering clothes and toys from newborn to teenagers. There is also a department selling basic prams and push chairs together with scooters, bikes and small cars for children. Children's World in Nanshan has an indoor soft play center where you can drop off your child for an hour while shopping. It costs 20RMB. If you wish to accompany your child, there is an additional 5RMB charge. For older kids, there is an art corner where one can pick up pre-made shapes to be filled with various paints. It costs 10RMB.

① ② Children's World	儿童世界
Children's World in Nanshan	
✉ The 1st and 2nd floor, Qingchun Jiayuan, Nanyou Avenue, Nanshan District 深圳市南山区南油大道青春家园一二层	
☎ 2667-6031	
🚌 113,70, 245,329, etc., get off at 海雅百货 - Haiya Baihuo	
Children's World in Futian	
✉ No. 102, Shangbu Industry Zone, North Huaqiang Rd., Futian 深圳市福田区华强北路上步工业区102栋	
☎ 8326-9563	
🚌 **Busses**: 9,12,59,21,16 - **Metro**: 华强北 - Huaqiang Bei	
🖱 www.childrenworld.com.cn (Chinese)	
⏳ 9h30am - 10pm	

CHILDREN'S PALACE IS a large complex with a great variety of activities for children. An Young Mythos Culture arts training base has amazing facilities where children from 2.5 years to 10 years of age can voice themselves through art. There are also DIY, dance and music classes, science and martial arts classes for children of all ages. One must buy a package to participate. On average most classes cost 800RMB for 32 times. There is also children's theater on the premises, which regularly holds performances in Chinese.

③ Children's Palace	深圳市少年宫
✉	Fuzhong First Rd., Futian District 深圳市福田区福中一路市少年宫
✆	8246-8362
🖱	www.szcp.com (Chinese)
⏳	Tuesday-Friday 8h30am - 5pm Saturday and Sunday 8am - 8h30pm
🚌	**Busses**: 25, 34, 64, 65, get off at 少年宫站, Shaonian Gong **Metro**: Line 4, 少年宫站, Shaonian Gong - Exit A

EVERGREEN RESORT HAS more of a small park feel to it than a resort. Proximity to Shekou makes it an easy day's escape from the usual city's hassle and buzz. The place has been recognized as the "Shenzhen Environment Education Base" and rightly so.

Attractions are organized into the Rainforest, Butterfly Park, Melon and Fruit Gardens, which help children to experience the basics of nature. Kids can make pottery, go through a rain forest and fish for goldfish in the pond. It is surprisingly quiet and green. If you decide to stay overnight, accommodation varies from 522RMB for two people to 854RMB for three people.

④ Evergreen Resort	深圳青青世界
✉	1 Qingqing St., Moonbay,Nanshan District 深圳市南山区月亮湾青青街1号
ℰ	2664-6988
⌂	www.evergreen-cn.com/english/01_home/index.asp (English)
⌛	8h30am - 6h30pm
$	50RMB, children below 1.1m: 30RMB
🚌	**Busses**: 369, 210, 350, 396, 42

SAFARI PARK SHENZHEN is located near Xili Lake. The park covers an area of 1.2 square kilometers. It has over 150 species, including 3,000 animals and birds. An attempt to resign from the traditional caging model of most zoos is plausible whilst the reality is far from it. The park is rather run-down and not very well-equipped. Amongst animals displayed there are giraffes, elephants, zebras, tigers and lions, bears as well as various species of birds. There are food stalls on the premises, but it's best to pack a picnic. Animal performances are also available with daily shows provided throughout the day. On the way out, there is also a small amusement park on the premises of the safari park.

⑤ Safari Park Shenzhen	野生动物园
✉	Next to Xili Lake park, Nanshan District 深圳市南山区西丽湖东侧
☎	2662-2888
🖱	www.szzoo.net (Chinese)
⏳	8am - 6h30pm
$	100RMB (for frequent users, you can buy a one-year pass)
🚌	**Busses**: 101 from Luhuo train station **Busses**: 226 from Shekou ferry terminal **Busses**: 101,104,240, 226, 361, 66

Teletubbies children's play & Development Center is a large and modern facility based around famous UK TV characters. The space is well organized into several areas, named after the Teletubbies characters. These include a DIY corner, library, infants' play room, toddlers' play area and a separate room for developmental activities. There are normally supervisors in each area, but children must be accompanied by adults. The singing and dancing activity, together with a DIY activity, are available free throughout the day. They are carried out by a qualified instructor. To join you must become a member and buy a package. There are various packages available. On average it costs 3000RMB for 30 times to be used over a 4-month period. Discounts are offered during children's holidays. It can be booked for birthday parties.

⑥ Teletubbies Children's Play & Development Centre 天线宝宝儿童娱教中心
✉ Room 203, Huacai Tiandi, Haide Road, Nanshan District 南山区商业文化中心海德二楼华彩天地成居商场203
✆ 2649-8851, 2649-8852
⧗ 9h30am - 5h30pm, closed on Mondays
🚌 **Busses**: 113,70,245,329, get off at 海雅百货 - Haiya Baihuo

GYMBOREE IS AN early childhood development program providing classes for babies, toddlers and preschoolers. Founded in 1976 in the USA, it is the global leader in early childhood development programs. The main purpose is to guide young parents to study their child's growth through music, art, and play. Programs are age-specific and are available for kids from 0-5 years old. Typically a package of 12 classes costs 2,680RMB, while a package of 24 costs 4,800RMB.

The greater number of entries, the cheaper it gets. A 25-minute demo is available for free. No free preview classes are available.

⑦ ⑧ Gymboree	金宝贝
Gymboree in Nanshan	
✉ 1st Floor, Garden City Center, Nanhai Road, Nanshan District 深圳市南山区蛇口南海大道花园城中心1楼	
☏ 2688-3819	
🚌 **Busses**: 22, 70, 77, 79, 80, 113, get off at 沃尔玛, Walmart	
Gymboree in Futian	
✉ MixCity Center, Shop 465, Luohu District 深圳市罗湖区宝安南路1881号万象城465铺	
☏ 8883-5757	
🚌 **Busses**: 29, 85, 113, 3 - **Metro**: 大剧院 - Da Juyuan	
🖱 www.gymboree.com.cn/app/web_en/index_en.jsp (English)	

GYMBOREE PLAY & MUSIC 金宝贝

A MEMBER OF THE new generation of theme parks set up by OCT, the park offers an endless number of fun activities and adventures.

The park is divided into different themed areas aimed at different age groups, with a rather large section for smaller children. Special train rides are available to get you around all kingdoms. Amongst attractions are the Space Port, Gold Mine Train and Suspended Looping Coaster.

Individual performances with folk dance and acrobatics are typically held in the evenings (enquire at the ticket office on times and locations). These performances are rather amateur, but fun. It gets very crowded during weekends and is suitable for children of all ages.

⑨ Happy Valley Theme Park	欢乐古
✉ OCT, Nanshan District - 深圳市南山区华侨城	
✆ 2690-1309	
🖱 www.happyvalley.com.cn (Chinese)	
$ 160RMB, 80RMB if entered after 7pm	
⏳ 9h30am - 10pm	
🚌 **Busses**: 20, 21, 26, 204, 209, 210, 222, 223, 101, 105, 113, 301, 310, 311, 320, 324, 328, 329, 370 - **Metro**: 世界之窗 - Window of the World	

THE PARK COVERS an area of 300,000 square meters. It is one of the world's largest miniature parks, reflecting China's natural landscape and cultural history. Replicas of China's historical buildings and landmarks are scaled down in the ratio of 1:15, with the exhibits positioned to replicate their geographical locations.

The park is brilliantly designed and gives an excellent introduction to the most famous historical places in China. The scenic spot area has replicas from Terracotta Warriors to Mogao Caves of Dunhuang. The China Folk village which is also part of the park gives a good flare of Chinese peoples' traditions and customs. Small to medium-size performances are featured throughout the day. The three grand performances are the highlights of the day.

⑩ Splendid China	深圳锦绣中华
✉	Huaqiao Cheng Shennan Ave., Nanshan District 深圳市南山区华侨城深南大道华侨城
✆	2660-6526
🖱	www.cn5000.com.cn/english/about/index.asp
$	120RMB
⧖	9am - 6pm. Evening performance starts at 7pm.
🚌	**Busses**: 223, 232, 245, 32 **Metro**: 华侨城 - Huaqiao Cheng

LOCATED ON THE south side of Shennan Thoroughfare, it occupies an area of 480,000 square meters. It collects wonders from around the world; historic sites, natural landscapes, folk architecture, sculptures, paintings, folk singing and dancing. Window of the World is another replica park, but of world's wonders and famous site. The park includes sites from Eiffel Tower to Niagara Falls and the Grand Canyon. The park holds the Cherry festival, the Indian Cultural week, the Beer Festival and Pop music Festival annually. Special programs are also available during holiday times. Numerous adventure trips are also being offered including the Indoor Alpine Ski Run.

⑪ Window of the World	世界之窗

✉	Window of the World, OCT, Nanshan District 深圳市南山区华侨城世界之窗
✆	2660-8000
🖰	www.szwwco.com (not working at the time of this writing)
$	120RMB
⌛	9am - 10h30pm
🚌	**Busses**: 20,21,26,204,209,210,222,223,101,105,113,301,310,311,320,324,328,329,370 **Metro**: 世界之窗 - Shijie Zhi Chuang (Window of the world)

SITUATED ON THE shore of Sha Tau Kok, Minsk World is one of only two theme parks in the world based on a real aircraft carrier (the other being in Tianjin). The park is built around the base of the Minsk, a second-generation Soviet aircraft carrier. It is praised for being both a National Popular Science Education Base and a Guangdong Military Popular Science Education Base.

Minsk World is made up of two parts: the Minsk Aircraft Carrier (at sea) and Minsk Square (on land). Its Aircraft Carrier covers an area of 30,000 square meter. The ship has a well-known Soviet MiG-23 aircraft-fighter and Mi-24 military helicopters on display, while on the second deck, the crew's living area has been rebuilt. There are also exhibitions on space flight, sailing and aviation, and visitors can take part in activities, such as mock warfare, that allow them to experience the excitement of operating hi-tech military weapons. Russian traditional performances and military performances of the honor guard round out the list of attractions available on the ship. The square has extensive shopping and dining. At every turn, there's a souvenir stall, a stall selling obsolete military equipment, or another stall selling radio-controlled toys. It's a wonderful place for boys and their dads.

⑫ Minsk World	中信明思克航母世界
✉	Jinrong Rd, Shatoujiao, Yantian District 深圳市盐田区沙头角大鹏湾
✆	2535-5333, www.szminsk.com (Chinese)
$	110RMB, 55RMB for children 110-140 cm; free for children under 110 cm.
⏳	9am - 7h30pm
🚌	**Busses**: 202, 205, 239, get off at 政府站 - Zhengfu

THERE ARE ONLY two concrete skate parks in all of China. One happens to be right here in Shenzhen. Located in Shekou, behind the new Quality Schools International (Feng Hua campus), Switch Plaza Skate Park has a diverse street course and a drop-in bowl. Expert skateboarders often help the inexperienced skater with tricks and techniques. Switch also has a full-service skateboard shop offering skateboards and inexpensive skate clothing and shoes. They offer service on skateboards. Skateboarding and rollerblading competitions are held regularly. Occasionally, concerts are offered.

⑬ Shekou Skate Park (Switch Plaza Skate Park)	
✉	Shekou Si Hai Park (四海园), Shekou, Nanshan District Off Gong Ye #7 Rd., past the basketball courts and the roller-blading park.
🖱	www.switchcrew.com (news of upcoming events in English)
$	20RMB admission.

FOR A PERFECT escape on a hot Shenzhen day or a rainy day with nothing to do, the skating rink is located in one of Shenzhen's most luxurious shopping malls. The MixC offers plenty of restaurant choices following a few circuits of the rink. Ladies can of course nip off for a bit of shopping therapy.

⑭ Skating Rink at Mix City (MixC)		冰纷万象
✉	Shop No 488, MixCity, No 1881, South Baoan Rd., Luohu District 深圳市罗湖区宝安南路1881号万象城488铺	
☎	8266-8288, 2585-6668	
⏳	10h30am – 10pm	
🖱	www.worldicearena.com/en (English)	
$	Monday-Friday: before 5pm: 40RMB/hour; after 5pm: 50RMB/hour Saturday-Sunday: 60RMB/hour	
🚌	**Busses**: 29, 85, 113, 3 **Metro**: 大剧院 - Da Juyuan, Exit C	

| ⓘ | There are similar skating rinks located at:
• Window of the World;
• Coastal City;
• Holiday Plaza.
Check out the Indoor Alpine Ski Run in Window of the World (80RMB per hour) |

IN 2006 THE QSI International School of Shekou PSG (Parent Support Group) launched SYSP (Shekou Youth Sports Program). This is a three season program operated by parents and other volunteers along with a supervisor supplied by QSI Shekou. This fun, instructional sport program is open to the entire Shekou community of children regardless of nationality or school attendance ages 5 to 11. The program is offered on Saturday mornings from September through May: Soccer in fall and spring, Basketball in winter. Each session begins with an instructional period of basic skill and rule understanding, and later competitions replace practices. Student volunteers from the QSI Secondary School participate by providing registration, coaching and officiating assistance.

⑮ Shekou Youth Sports Program (SYSP)	
✉	Shekou, Nanshan District Contact Howard Wilson for more details
✆	2667-6031 (Howard Wilson)
⌛	Saturday mornings from September through May. Soccer in fall and spring, basketball in winter.
✉	hwilson2235@gmail.com
$	A nominal fee for each season is required for equipment, uniforms and field rental.

MOST OF THE 5th floor is dedicated to books for children pre-school ages and up, with a wide selection of books mainly in Chinese. There is a small section of books in English. There is also a DIY corner for kids. Pre-made shapes must be filled with colored sand, which keeps one's child entertained for at least 30 minutes. Its costs 10RMB for a small shape and 15RMB for a big one.

| ⑯ Nanshan Book City | 南山书城 |

✉	Shenzhen Nanshan Commercial and Culture Center (the crossing between Nanhai Avenue and Haide Second Rd.), Nanshan District 深圳市南山区商业文化中心区 南海大道与海德二道交界处
✆	8612-2001
⧗	9h30 - 10pm
🚌	**Busses**: 113, 328, 226, 332, 331, 19, 71, get off at 海雅百货 - Haiya Baihuo

THE SHENZHEN INTERNATIONAL Botanical Garden is an oasis of tranquility in the heart of Futian. This free city park is a bit different than other botanical parks that heavily emphasize specific plant species. The theme of this vast park is to show the various ways that gardens are used all over China. The unique weaving together of art, history and the use of plants and water features makes for a very interesting experience. Over 100 different gardens, lakes and cultural areas grace the extensive park.

There are things to do for the young and old alike. At this time, the exhibition center has a fossil display of dinosaurs. The children's park sports typical exercise equipment for the kids and also a slide built into a staircase.

Throughout the winding walkways, there are plentiful places to eat a picnic or sit and enjoy the sculptures and scenery. If you are more into physical activity, there are numerous trails that beckon further investigation of the forest. There is also the 2,000+ stair climb up Jufu hill to the large pagoda that can be seen throughout the park. This offers a scenic view of the city, especially on a clear day.

Each garden has a description translated into English that relates information about the region or city that contributed to the design and building of the garden. Bolivia and Pakistan also made contributions. Maps are conveniently located throughout the park and have English names for all the areas. There are four areas to the garden. The main entrance off Shennan Road is in the south area where a large performance building is under construction. The exhibition hall with the current dinosaur exhibition is located within the west area. The pagoda and hill are in the north area, and the east area sports the large lake.

⑱ Shenzhen Int'l Botanical Garden 深圳国际园林花卉博览园

✉	Shenzhen Botanical Garden, Zhuzilin Xi, Futian District, Shenzhen There are four entrances to the park, but the main one is just north of Shennan Road near Qiaocheng Dong Station on the #1 Metro line - two metro stops east of Window of the World. 深圳市福田区深圳国际园林花卉博览园
✆	8282-9075
🖱	www.szyby.cn
$	The admission is free. 20 RMB for adults, 10 RMB for children for the dinosaur exhibition.
⏳	9am - 8pm
🚌	Metro: Qiaocheng Dong Station - 桥城东站 Bus: 104, 105, 107, 108, 109

Learning Chinese

From Expats to Expats
Starting a life-long hobby...

I WOULD NEVER HAVE signed up for the Beginners Class had someone told me beforehand that, right from Week 1, all lessons included Chinese characters (or, as my father and a few other select sinologists insist on calling them, Chinese 'units'). How, I kept asking the teachers could we, as adults, possibly be expected to learn in one semester what a Chinese primary school child learns over the course of several years. Two students (one a 60-year-old American and the other a 35-year-old Frenchman) proved to me that not only was it perfectly possible to learn all the different components which together make up the complicated sounds and compound meanings of Chinese words, but they were able, after a few weeks, to write them up on the blackboard every day (dictation) in front of a class of fellow Korean and Japanese students. Teacher Chen admitted she had no idea why it was possible for foreigners to learn to write characters so fast, she just invited me to her class to come and see for myself.

The American style was to write

out characters fast, in fact as fast as possible, onto acetate and then delete immediately. Larry is now successfully continuing his life-long hobby at Beijing University. The recommendation from France was to write each character within a box, in pencil, on graph paper, each one to be written out 50 to 100 times.

You may have to rise rather early to have time to write out each word 100 times before an 8 am class. For me an early rise was essential, because I knew that Chen Laoshi was going to pick on me to stand up, in front of a whole class of students (all of them were 30 years younger than me), in order to demonstrate how easy it was for foreigners to write about 25 – 50 new words a day. My only companions during this painful process of learning and copying out characters into little squares 100 times were the eight little ducks that swam serenely on the lake and once laid an egg for me.

A pleasant morning stroll through the campus with your iPod takes care of your lesson preparation. Walk out of the dorm, cross over the bridge on the lake, past the heron and fish (a captive audience for Chinese students who stand shouting their lesson at the edge of the water), walk down the tree lined avenues; climb the gently rolling hills covered with lychee trees, and you will end up at my favorite alfresco dining area by the lake, only a short walk from the class room building.

A meeting with your private tutor in the afternoon will help your pronunciation. Every afternoon Lizzy tried patiently to tutor me on my tones and consonants. I think we eventually gave up on the 'c's and 'zi's. Some things are just impossible, at least for some people.

As one blogger put it, the worst thing about the course was the complaints from the other students about how difficult it was to learn Chinese.

■ by Heather Letterman

Universities

1 Jinan University	暨南大学深圳汉语教学中心风貌
✉	Shenzhen Tourism College of Jinan University, OCT, Nanshan District
地址	南山区华侨城暨南大学深圳旅游学院综合楼103室
☎	2693-1911, 137-9835-3255

2 Shenzhen University	深圳大学
✉	Nanhai Av., 3688, Nanshan District
地址	南山区南海大道3688号 邮编：518060
☎	2655-8894
☎	Ms. Li Yaying; Ms. Liao Wensui (English spoken)
🔖	www.szu.edu.cn/en/students.asp szulxs@szu.edu.cn

Cost	
Classes	¥10,000 / semester + ¥1,000 deposit.
Dorm Opt.	¥8,500 single room, ¥4,500/p double room (per semester)
$	Shenzhen University also runs full-time winter (February) and summer (August) classes over a period from 4 (¥3,500) to 7 weeks (¥5,500)
ⓘ	There are 3 stops to the Uni; West Gate (西门), Main Gate (正门), and North Gate (北门). To get to the Int'l Student Dept building, get off at the Main Gate, pass the security, turn left, walk about 200m, the building is on your left hand side, go the 2nd floor. English spoken.

Chinese Schools

3 Chongyan Mandarin CYBS	
✉	Rm 302, Haihong Bldg, Seaview Garden, Xinghua Rd., Shekou, Nanshan District
地址	蛇口工业区海上世界海滨花园海虹阁302室
✆	2685-8139
🖰	www.dcm.hk

4 Dragon Mandarin	崇言双语学校
✉	Rm 302, Haihong Bldg, Seaview Garden, XinghuaRd, Shekou, Nanshan District
地址	南山区蛇口工业区，海上世界，兴华路3号，海滨花园，海虹阁302室
✆	2685-8139
🖰	www.dcm.hk

5 Hanbridge Mandarin	汉桥汉语学校
✉	Room 102, Block E, Meijia Plaza, Qiaocheng West Str., Nanshan District Shekou centre: 16B, Seaview Plaza, Taizi Rd, Nanshan District, Shekou
地址	侨城西街美加广场E栋102室南山区(欢乐谷对面) 太子路16B号南山区蛇口
✆	2424-2990
🖰	www.hanbridgemandarin.com
🚇	Shi Jie Zhi Chuang station 世界之窗站

6 Horizon Language Center	
✉	Dongmen, Luohu; Horizon Language Center will pick you up at the metro and bring you to the office
✆	English: 150-1946-3614, 中文: 137-2421-8916
🚇	Lao Jie station, exit A 老街站

7 iMandarin Language Training School　　　爱马德汉语学校

✉	1 West Floor, Xincheng Bldg., Zhennan Zhong Rd., Futian District
地址	福田区深南中路新城大厦西座1F
☎	2598-7981
🖥	www.imandarin.net
🚇	Kexue Guan station, exit D 科学馆站

8 Jiahua Language School　　　加华语言学校

✉	Modern International, Futian District
地址	福田区金田路现代国际大厦
☎	400-631-9518
🖥	www.jiahuaschool.com

9 Linda Lee Interactive Chinese

✉	12, Bihua, Taizi Rd., Shekou, Nanshan District
地址	南山区蛇口碧桦路12号
☎	2686-2019
🖥	www.lindalee.com.cn

10 New Concept Mandarin　　　新理念汉语学校

✉	3/F, Bitao Centre, 8 Taizi Rd., Shekou, Nanshan District
地址	南山区蛇口太子8路碧涛中心3楼
☎	2686-4975
🖥	www.newconceptmandarin.com

11 SKY Language Learning Center

✉	Rooms 0103-0104, Block B, Mingxiang Yuan, China Tea Place, 82 Jintian Rd., Futian District

地址	福田区景田北路82号中国茶宫左侧茗香苑B栋0103-0104
✆	139-2376-2737

12 Union Mandarin

✉	Room 2A, Biboge, Haibing Garden, Xinghua Rd., Shekou, Nanshan District
地址	南山区兴华路海滨花园碧波阁2A
✆	2688-4090

Business in Shenzhen

From Experts to Expats
An Introduction to Doing Business in Shenzhen

SHENZHEN WAS ESTABLISHED as a special economic zone in 1980. Before this, Shenzhen was a small village in southern Guangdong Province. As the earliest and fastest growing special economic zone in China, it has won the reputation as the window of China's opening-up drive and the testing ground for the country's economic restructuring. Now with a population of over 12 million, the city is regarded as one of China's economic powerhouses.

The rapid growth of the local economy is mostly attributed to the vigorous inflow of overseas investment and expansion of foreign trade. Between 1980 and 2003, Shenzhen's GDP enjoyed an average annual growth of 33.3%, which is unmatched almost anywhere in the world. In 2007, its GDP reached over $90 billion, ranking 4th among all mainland cities, while per capita GDP ranked 1st in the nation at $10,628. Its to-tal import and export amount was $287.5 billion, including an export value of $168.5 billion which has ranked first among all mainland cities for 12 consecutive years, and import value of $119 billion. By the end of 2007, accumulated foreign direct investment (FDI) reached $41.2 billion.

Shenzhen was an ideal location for Deng Xiaoping's reform and opening for two reasons. One was that it was far away from the capital, and would not threaten any existing urban centers. The other is Shenzhen's proximity to Hong Kong, which has been quite useful in terms of existing family and cultural linkages. In fact, more than 60% of Shenzhen's FDI has come from Hong Kong. While that seems high, much of this is classified as Hong Kong-based investment even though it is done through Hong Kong-based holding companies of companies from other countries. Indeed, more than 10% of Shenzhen's FDI comes from other offshore tax havens such as the British Virgin Islands and others.

The Shenzhen Municipal Government has placed its economic development focus on four major industries; high-technology, logistics, financial services, and cultural industry. Because for the past 30 years Shenzhen has focused almost exclusively on export-oriented manufacturing (as is the case with many of China's coastal cities), the economic structure has become too reliant on manufacturing while not placing enough emphasis on services and higher value-added parts of the product value chain. In addition, the heavy reliance on export manufacturing has taken its toll on the environment, both in terms of

air quality and destruction of the land. Thus in recent years, the government has shifted from a strategy of promoting "more" investment to promoting "better" investment. Incentives for foreign investment in traditional sectors such as toys, furniture, and garments have been almost completely eliminated. In fact many such businesses are being pushed out of the city to help improve the environment and make room for more hi-tech, cleaner, service-oriented and higher value enterprises.

Relative to other locations in China, Shenzhen, while far from perfect, features one of the most business-friendly operating environments. One reason for this is the strong local administrative system run by the Shenzhen government. While many decisions are made arbitrarily and behind closed doors, Shenzhen has among the highest compositions of foreign-invested enterprises and private enterprises in its economy. This helps align the interests of the local government with international

norms of economic oversight and administrative transparency and efficiency. With that said, foreign companies and individuals operating in Shenzhen should take all the same precautions that are advised in other parts of the country. Generally this includes paying attention to due diligence, intellectual property, rapid employee turnover, and quick changes in government policies such as tax, labor and land use, all of which can impact bottom lines.

Companies operating in Shenzhen should be aware of the highly competitive environment across almost every industry. The city has an abundance of retail outlets, a large amount of foreign companies competing for high-caliber Chinese managers and employees, and a vast array of local suppliers who can undercut prices. While Shenzhen is a famous home for Wal-Mart, IBM and a number of large companies, it is easy for small and medium-sized companies to think they need a presence in China and look to the city, due to its proximity to Hong Kong, as the ideal starting point. Many companies do this because it is fashionable or because they read about China in the Wall Street Journal and believe they need a presence on the mainland, when in fact there is no reason for them to be in the country, or in a first-tier city like Shenzhen, based on their goals, capabilities and needs.

With that said, Shenzhen offers numerous opportunities to companies looking at sourcing from third party manufacturers and brokers. Shenzhen is a very useful "nearshore" platform for supporting operations in Hong Kong, and is a great location for any industry with a heavy transportation and logistics component. There are also numerous government incentives in place for service industries and service outsourcing operations, including finance and accounting, software development, and research and development. Also, with China's highest GDP per-capita (i.e. most affluent consumer base), Shenzhen can also serve as a very desirable location in which to enter China's vast retail and specialty consumer markets.

As China's testing ground for new government policies, it can be expected that Shenzhen will usually be on the front edge of nationwide policy announcements, both economic and political. Shenzhen and Hong Kong are in the process of planning a scheme which will enable free cross-border travel for high-tech industry employees, and will enable direct train travel in and out of Hong Kong from the mainland. Any company or individual looking to do business in Shenzhen should stay informed about new developments, and should be prepared to invest considerable time and energy into any new venture in Shenzhen.

■ by China Briefing
www.china-briefing.com

 For more information about the above-mentioned places visit WikiShenzhen.com

From Experts to Expats
Setting Up a Legal Entity in Shenzhen

As CHINA'S FIRST special economic zone, Shenzhen began to open up to diversified foreign direct investments in the 1980's and has managed to stay one of the fastest growing cities in Mainland China. The fate of Shenzhen particularly changed after the visit of Deng Xiaoping, the architect of China's reform and opening-up policy, on January 19-22, 1992. Deng Xiaoping called for bold measures to accelerate the reform and opening of the economy of the southern region of China.

From 1980 to 2001, the average growth rate of GDP in Shenzhen exceeded 30%. By 2006, 120 Fortune 500 companies had made their way to Shenzhen. Thanks to the diversity of its transportation network (by sea, land and air) and the specialization of the local market as a production site or research base as well as commodities trade center of high-tech products, Shenzhen has become the most important industrial hub in South China. Shenzhen also has its own Stock Exchange, which is one of the two national scale securities markets in China.

In general, foreign investors choose the place of their first establishment in China on the basis of their business needs; location of their main suppliers, customers or competitors, the quality of the available infrastructure and its competitive prices, the size and specificities of the local market and its synergies, and the offer of local incentives. Notwithstanding the increase of production costs in Shenzhen (including but not limited to the increasing labor costs and rents) and the national tax reform which came into effect on January

1st, 2008, Shenzhen remains an attractive market for foreign direct investment, especially for all business related to high-tech products and services, as State Council still grants tax incentives to high-new technology enterprises that will be established in Special Economic Zones such as Shenzhen even after January 1st, 2008.

Considering the main stream of Shenzhen market, the following guidelines will focus on the setting up of: (A) representative offices (hereafter RRO) and (B) foreign invested enterprises (in particular: wholly foreign-owned enterprises "WFOE") which are the most frequent forms of legal entities set up in Shenzhen.

Setting-up of Representative Offices

Despite having several projects in China, some foreign investors are still reluctant to establish a company in Mainland China unless mandatory regulations require it. However, many foreign investors decided or plan to set up representative offices in Mainland China for market research, promotion and liaison works.

Chinese laws expressly provide that RROs shall not engage in commercial activities. RROs of foreign enterprises are strictly limited to indirect trade activities. Such indirect trade activities includes liaison works in the name of foreign enterprise, such as research of Chinese business partners or networking with foreign invested enterprises, promotion of products, market studies and technical exchanges, as well as any other activities that are not deemed to constitute direct trading activities. According to the State Administration for Industry and Commerce (SAIC), production, direct agency or selling activities are prohibited for RROs.

The SAIC is authorized to impose penalties on representative offices engaging in direct trading activities, and in serious cases, it may order the closing of the RRO. In practice, certain liaison works which might be assimilated into commercial activities are tolerated by the SAIC and some RROs such as representative offices of foreign law firms or accounting firms can carry out commercial activities. Except the specific cases provided by Chinese laws such as the above-mentioned cases, RROs cannot directly bill any services or sell any products. However, the scope of activity of representative offices of foreign enterprises in China is broad and the main interest of its establishment in Mainland China is to guarantee a legal status of its employees and to provide a stable working environment at a limited cost.

Considering the Tax regime of RROs, the most common method is known as the "cost-plus regime". Under this tax regime, the China-sourced gross income of an RRO is computed based on its operating expenses. In general, RROs may not operate for profit and can only conduct ancillary and coordination activities for their head offices. Accordingly, most RROs are cost centers and do not derive incomes.

RRO's do not have legal personal-ity and the foreign company which established its RRO in Mainland China shall therefore bear all liabilities related to the operation of the RRO.

Setting-up of WFOEs

In the frame of its commitments in order to become a member of the World Trade Organization (WTO), China undertook to open progressively its local market to foreign direct investments according to a defined timetable. According to the WTO's commitments, foreign investors can engage in most commercial activities in Mainland China via a Chinese subsidiary. Such a Chinese subsidiary will be considered as a foreign invested enterprise which can be set up under the legal form of a joint venture between a foreign investor and a Chinese partner (JV) or as wholly foreign owned enterprise (WFOE). Should the activity of the subsidiary to be set up by the foreign investor in Mainland China not require any assistance or cooperation of any Chinese partner due to its specific knowledge of the market and its networks, the foreign investor shall choose in most of cases to set up a WFOE in Mainland China. The setting-up of a WFOE to engage in all activities related to high-new technology is especially recommended if foreign investors intend to control the use of its own intellectual properties.

Foreign investors may be foreign enterprises, economic organizations or individuals.

If a foreign investor wants to establish a WFOE in Shenzhen, attention must be paid to the following steps of incorporation:

- **Its intellectual properties shall be protected before commencing any related business activities in Mainland China;**
- **The foreign investor shall apply for the pre-approval of the future registered name of its subsidiary by the SAIC;**
- **The foreign investor shall open a temporary account to receive the initial funds transferred from the head office's bank account in the frame of the WFOE's incorporation in China. Such temporary**

accounts will allow the WFOE to integrate the received funds to its registered capital after obtaining the business license and the tax certificate of the WFOE;

- **The foreign investor shall apply for the registration of the WFOE with the Committee of Foreign Trade and Economic Cooperation Bureau (COFTEC);**
- **The foreign investor shall obtain the registration of the WFOE with the SAIC which will issue the business license;**
- Post registration formalities with all relevant Chinese administrations shall be carried out after the issuance of the business license.

Neither the regulations related to the WFOEs, nor its implementing Rules provide any mandatory management structure for WFOEs. In practice, most foreign investors choose a management structure which is similar to or simpler than the one applicable to the mother company (i.e. a President with a General Manager and, as the case may be, a deputy general manager; or a board of directors, a supervisory board, etc.). The rules related to corporate decisions (i.e. conveyance of annual meeting(s) of shareholders, quorum, etc.) are also more flexible than in most of Western country's legal system.

The minimum registered capital of a WFOE depends on the local market practice and the contemplated activities. Nevertheless, the registered capital must be consistent with the business scope of the WFOE, and the ratio between the registered capital and the total amount of investment must comply with the mandatory provisions of Chinese laws. During its term of business operations, any increase or decrease of the registered capital of the WFOE shall be submitted to and registered with the Chinese authorities.

Foreign investors can contribute to the registered capital of the WFOE by installments within a defined period starting from the date of opening of the temporary bank account of the WFOE or can fully pay the registered capital at the registration of the WFOE.

The maximum duration of a WFOE depends on its business scope. Some Chinese regulations such as the regulations related to distribution companies in Mainland China (Foreign Invested Commercial Enterprises or FICE) limit the duration of a WFOE to 30 years. The procedure of renewal of the WFOE's duration shall be specified in the articles of association of the WFOE.

According to a recent notice issued by the State Council, transition incentives for enterprise income tax purposes are still granted to foreign invested enterprises newly set up in Special Economic Zones (SEZ, such as Shenzhen) and qualified as "State encouraged high-new technology enterprises". These tax incentives (i.e. tax holidays or exemptions) are exceptions to the tax reform entering into effect on January 1st, 2008. This key tax reform, which introduces a single tax rate of 25%, replaces the former distinctive tax regimes of domestic companies and foreign invested enterprises in Mainland China.

In practice, a State encouraged high-new technology enterprise is an enterprise that independently owns core intellectual property and is qualified as a "high-new technology enterprise" according to the criteria set forth in Article 93 of the "EIT Implementation Rules"

and the "Measures for Verification and Administration of High-New Technology Enterprises".

The dynamism and specialization of its local market combined with remaining exceptional tax incentives for high-new technology enterprises make Shenzhen the "Silicon Valley" of South China.

■ by Antoine Schapira
& Rong Le

From Experts to Expats
Starting Operations in Shenzhen

CHINA HAS BECOME an international magnet for buyers coming from every country, and for every kind of consumer or professional goods. Traditionally, Hong Kong has always been the gateway of choice to the Chinese market. Since the 90s and the creation of the first special economic zone, Shenzhen has become the natural mainland extension for all kinds of manufactured goods. The best way to establish a business in China would be to ask for the help

of a specialized agency, a lawyer or accountant.

Why Shenzhen?
Most companies wanting to develop trade between China and Europe or the USA want to offer the most competitive prices with uncompromised quality. Shenzhen thus becomes an obvious choice for the reasons listed above.

Some businesses start to operate from Hong Kong, but soon find out that it is not a suitable location because a close relationship with suppliers in Shenzhen is indispensable. An intermediate step is to open a representative office with local staff whose job is to follow up on production and orders. The final stage, creating a foreign company in Shenzhen, can be quite an adventure. You may decide to hire the services of a specialized company that can lead the way through the mountain of red tape to register such a company, and open a bank account. Most rep offices are advised to open an account with China Merchant Bank. Communication is very difficult because few employees speak English. To the surprise of many Westerners, in China even though you have an account you cannot withdraw more than 10% of the balance in cash. The remaining is used as a local currency account to pay the local expenses or suppliers. So be careful not to leave more than what is necessary for your petty expenses or monthly tax payments in this account.

Although taxes in Shenzhen are higher than in HK, the lower office rent price and the closeness to your suppliers and partners more than compensate for this drawback.

Finding your office

Finding a good location and an office space is not so difficult. There are plenty of real estate agents, and many office buildings are being built. Some companies will choose to set up their rep offices in Shekou, because it is close to the ferry with a sea view and not too far from the new bridge to the New Territories. Others may wish to be closer to the manufacturing centers in Dongguan. However, the conditions you will find your new office may vary a lot depending on what you expect. You may decide to refurbish it from floor to ceiling. Be careful to choose a good architect and to make sure you follow up progress on a daily basis. This is the only way to avoid disappointment.

Hiring people

You cannot hire people in China for a rep office the same way you could in Hong Kong. This is however, the most crucial exercise for the survival of your company. Finding skilled and English speaking professionals can be a difficult exercise. Salaries tend to grow faster than inflation, and the turnover is rather high. For keeping good staff, you should think of a retention plan as early as possible.

For a rep office, you are not allowed to directly employ local people, although you are free to hire who you want. One must go through an official employment agency (i.e. FESCO) that will prepare the work contracts under its name and answer all tax and social security questions. Although helpful from an administrative point of view, you are in a situation where people work for you but are not directly contracted to your company.

Quality Management

For some businesses, it is critical to set up a permanent presence in China. The amount of added value is based on the customized services provided to overseas clients. When buying in China, they expect to receive the same good quality products and services but at Chinese prices. Although it is still rather easy to source at competitive prices, it can be difficult to ensure a continuous quality of production. Quality in China is the result of a full time investment with different suppliers, from taking care of all simple quality details to quality management. Although many foreign visitors come for a short trip and expect their instructions to be respected, they often discover belatedly many problems. One example is packing: The Chinese can produce the finest piece of furniture, but pay no attention to the packaging and transport conditions. The result at arrival is frustration and a waste of time and money. Another example is substitution of goods. Your carefully chosen "forest green" outdoor furniture can turn up in hot pink or purple.

This apparent lack of attention to details and creativity stems from cultural differences and a shortage of multicultural management.

For more information about the above-mentioned places visit WikiShenzhen.com

■ by SOYO Global

From Experts to Expats
China's Taxes

THE FORMULATION OF tax law in China follows four steps; drafting, examination, voting and finally promulgation by the National People's Congress or its Standing Committee. Detailed implementation rules are created, as appropriate, by the Ministry of Finance, the State Administration of Taxation, or the General Administration of Customs (GAC). The People's Congresses of the four municipalities of Beijing, Shanghai, Tianjin and Chongqing, and Hainan province, have powers to make local tax legislation.

Since China began "reform and opening up" in the early 1980s, it has carried out two major reforms of its taxation system. Most recently, in 1993, VAT was introduced for the first time. In 1994, further reforms introduced the division of tax collection and revenue between the central and local governments.

The main laws with which foreign investors are likely to be concerned are as follows (although bear in mind that there are some detailed implementation rules and amendments, so do take advice on the specifics):

• **Individual Income Tax (IIT) Law of the PRC - adopted on September 10, 1980, and revised on October 31, 1993, August 30, 1999, October 27, 2005, and November 2006.**

- **Interim Regulations of the PRC on Value-added Tax – made December 13, 1993.**
- **Interim Regulations of the PRC on Business Tax – made December 13, 1993.**
- **Corporate Income Tax Law of the People's Republic of China – adopted March 16, 2007.**

Below we examine some of the key aspects of China's tax regime.

Business tax

This is a tax payable against turnover by all enterprises and individuals undertaking the following businesses; providing taxable services, including communications, transport, construction, finance and insurance, telecoms, culture, entertainment and service industries; transferring the provision of intangible assets; and selling immovable properties.

The basic formula is:

Tax payable = Turnover x Tax rate

Only a very few items can be excluded from the turnover. Please

also note that business tax rates vary considerably, dependent on industry. When you first register, the tax bureau will issue you a form showing all the taxes applicable. You must be careful if you are selling goods and services simultaneously, as in these cases there are complicated criteria to judge whether business tax or VAT is applicable. Professional advice is recommended.

VAT

VAT applies if your company is selling, manufacturing, processing or repairing tangible goods. It also applies to the importation of raw material and equipment. Rates vary between 0 and 17 percent, and the regulations are complex.

The Chinese government rules that all enterprises and individuals engaged in the sale of goods, provision of processing, repairs and replacement services, and import of goods within the PRC shall pay VAT. There are a few exemptions, such as self-produced agricultural products sold by agricultural producers, contraceptive medicines and devices, and antique books. However, pretty much every business will be liable for this tax.

The VAT rate for general taxpayers is generally 17%, or 13% for some goods. For taxpayers who deal in goods or provide taxable services with different tax rates, the sale amounts for the different tax rates shall be accounted for separately. If this is not done, the higher tax rate shall apply.

However, there are lower rates for "small scale taxpayers", 4 percent for trading enterprises and 6 percent for other production and other enterprises. "Small scale taxpayers" are those whose annual taxable sales value fall below a certain level. These are defined as RMB1 million(approx US$125,000) for enterprises engaged principally in the production of goods or the provision of taxable services, and RMB1.8 million (approx US$225,000) for enterprises engaged in the wholesaling or retailing of the goods.

Proposals to restructure the na-

tional application of VAT have been put forward to the State Council and are expected to be implemented shortly.

Two measures immediately stand out:

- 1. VAT, which has not yet been levied on services, is to be attached to service contracts and invoices, meaning all service businesses in China can now both levy and offset VAT.

- 2. VAT has not yet been fully able to have been offset against certain purchases, such as equipment purchases; the proposals call for VAT to be offset against all transactions.

The draft proposals broadly follow the VAT pilot scheme that has been adopted for testing by several northeast provinces over the past three years.

The measures are expected to save businesses up to RMB150 billion annually and encourage more investment in industry. Businesses in China will now be able to offset VAT against fixed asset investments (such as equipment purchases), a mechanism previously denied them. The adjustments therefore have a huge impact on manufacturers in China. Although the proposals would see China lose taxable income in the short term, longer term revenues would increase as manufacturing capacity is expanded due to better investment on fixed assets, plants, and machinery encouraged by the new proposal.

Consumption tax

The current consumption tax system was introduced in 1994 along with the nationwide indirect taxes reform including VAT and business tax. According to the "PRC Provisional Regulation of Consumption Tax", consumption tax was initially levied on production or importation of 11 categories of products including automobiles, cigarettes, and alcohol, which were considered to be luxurious.

This tax applies whenever certain luxury or other goods are manufactured, processed or imported. Consumption tax is levied only once. Tax rates vary considerably with the product, and the tax paid is computed directly as a cost and cannot be refunded. In addition, consumption tax is part of the base upon which VAT is levied. Be careful if you are processing taxable goods for others, since you are liable to withhold and pay consumption tax based on the value of the raw material and your processing fee. Consumption tax should be filed and paid monthly.

However, given China's rapid economic development, some of the taxable items and tax rates under the current rules are no longer considered appropriate, and the authorities are also seeking to expand the scope of the consumption tax to influence domestic consumption. A major revision to consumption tax came into effect from April 1, 2006. This is intended to influence the consumption of energy and natural resources, and to narrow the gap between the rich and the poor by collecting consumption tax on luxury items in China.

Please note that the new policy does not change the scope of the consumption tax levy. It continues to apply to most taxable items at the production level.

Withholding tax

Withholding tax is a PRC tax levied on overseas companies providing services to China based businesses.

If you are based outside the PRC but are supplying services to clients in China, your invoices are in effect "China derived income", and the Chinese tax authorities levy taxes on these amounts. These are withheld by your client in China, being deducted from your gross invoice amount. This is why many overseas companies without a legal presence in China cannot receive the total gross amount due on their invoices to the China entity.

Your client has the responsibility of passing this tax onto the tax bureau. If they do not, or do not subtract the relevant amount of tax from your invoice, then the Chinese tax bureau will pursue the local business, and not the overseas operation, for settlement.

There are two types of withholding taxes:

- **Withholding tax – this applies when a non-China based company signs an agreement with a China based company and assigns an employee to provide the contracted service in China. It is a combination of business tax (5% of gross contract value) and foreign enterprise income tax, of which the rate varies depending upon whether any double tax treaties are in force between China and the invoicing entity's country of origin;**

- **Withholding income tax – this**

is applicable to non-China based companies if they are obtaining income in such forms as rental, royalties, dividend, interest, or

crete proof of your earnings elsewhere. If you can't provide this, they may refuse to register you, effectively and immediately mak-

Salary minus 4,800 X tax rate, less quick deduction figure = IIT tax bill		
Monthly taxable salary	Tax rate	Quick calculation deduction
From RMB5,000 to RMB20,000	20%	RMB375
RMB20,001 to RMB40,000	25%	RMB1,375
RMB40,001 to RMB60,000	30%	RMB3,075
RMB60,001 to RMB80,000	35%	RMB6,375
RMB80,001 to RMB100,000	40%	RMB10,375
In excess of RMB100,000	45%	RMB15,375

other profits, but not provision of services.

Withholding income tax is calculated at 10 percent on the gross invoice value, but may be reduced if double tax treaties or China preferential rates apply, such as in free trade zones.

Individual income tax

The first RMB4,800 of your earnings in China are tax free. That does not mean you can rush out and declare salaries of RMB5,000 however, the tax bureaus are wise to this and will demand to see con-

ing your presence in China illegal.

China's individual income tax rates are high compared to neighboring countries. The following table demonstrates salary brackets and tax rates, plus the quick tax deduction system. Your total liability can be calculated as shown in the table below.

China is also pretty reasonable as regards to non-taxable elements as part of an expat package, however some attention may need to be paid to the structuring of the inclusive package with certain items needing to be properly defined in the employment contract. As a rule of thumb, if you pay for the expenses yourself (against local official invoices), and the company provides you with cash allowances, then these are considered taxable. However, if the company pays for certain expenses on your behalf (e.g. your apartment rental), then this kind of allowance is not taxable and can be deducted from your company CIT computation basis.

Enterprises are obligated to withhold employees' IIT when paying salaries to them; failing to do so will cause penalties. Meanwhile, the enterprises can get 2% of the IIT withheld from the tax bureau as commission or handling charge. Pay attention to the calculation of the IIT if the companies are paying IIT for the employees, in this case the income has to be grossed up for the purpose of calculating IIT.

Individual Income Tax calculations for standard salaries are fairly easy to assess, but get more intricate according to the complexity of the expatriate's salary package.

It makes sense to take professional advice when structuring expatriate salary packages to ensure liabilities can be planned in the most tax-efficient manner.

No government likes tax evasion, and China is no exception to the rule. The penalties for late payments, nonpayment and other transgressions (naivety is no excuse) can be severe, often up to five times the amount due, plus the original liability. In cases of blatant evasion, businesses can have their licenses withdrawn and assets seized. If you have any doubts, please seek professional advice immediately. This is the one area it is best not to mess about with, fees spent on decent advice are less than the amounts levied in fines and penalties.

■ by Dezan Shira & Associates
www.dezshira.com

For more information about the above-mentioned places visit WikiShenzhen.com

From Experts to Expats
Doing Business with the Chinese

I T IS NOT surprising at all that many foreign investors complain when doing business in China. Many wonder why their years of experience in the business world can not be applied in China immediately. Doing business is about building mutual trust and benefit amidst establishing relationships with people. If you do not understand your counterpart well, it will be quite difficult to establish good cooperation with them. An old Chinese saying goes: know yourself and your enemy well, and you can fight a hundred battles without any fear of defeat. This greatly emphasizes the importance of knowing and understanding your counterpart.

Modern economic models differ greatly from the traditional one, whereby people in the past 'fight' till the last man standing. Today, people seek to achieve a "win-win" situation, and pursue long-term trade cooperation under a fair and healthy, competitive environment. Understanding factors such as China's history, humanity and culture will be the key to investors' success in China. As Western thinking and China's traditional values do differ, encountering the cultural differences is therefore inevitable. Thus a better understanding of the cultural differences is necessary when doing business in China:

1. **Learn how to handle Guangxi (relationship). In China, Guangxi (relationship) is a complicated field. Establishing relationships with others does not mainly deal with achieving one's own self-in-**

terests or personal goals. A special feature of doing business in China will be that Guangxi (relationship) in China will have to include relationships with the government body, investors, partners and even relationships with your own staff. China's government plays a large role in administrating the investment in China. This is because China is a socialist state; the economy is still largely controlled and managed by the government. So when doing business in China, it is important for foreign investors to learn to coordinate with the Chinese government. At the same time, seeking a suitable local partner may be a shortcut and helping hand in developing your business in China's market.

2. How to prevail over competition. China, at the moment, can be said to be a big, open market, and the ability to prevail over competition is a very important issue today. Investors should fully realize and maximize one's advantages. Some investors are afraid that China's im-

itation products will hurt the sale of their products. Even though this symptom is a concern, in a free and competitive market, it will always be the one that has the superior quality who will not be afraid of competition and will prevail eventually. China's market is constantly undergoing standardization, and China's government has vowed to protect the quality of the market. The Vice-Minister of the Ministry of Foreign Trade and Economic Cooperation had previously stated in his speech that being a member of the World Trade Organization, China's government will continuously rectify and standardize the economic structure of the market, and will persistently crack down on illegal acts of producing counterfeit products. The level of technology in China is still relatively lagging behind, thus foreign investors should fully make use of their advantages in technology and expertise to produce high-quality products and services. One should not be too concerned with the negative impact brought about by new counterfeited products. Continuous development of one's technology and emphasizing on innovation will be the key to success.

3. **Route for Investment. There are three options to take when make investments in China, mainly: wholly foreign-owned enterprise, Chinese-foreign cooperative enterprise and Sino-foreign joint venture. Which option to take will have to depend on factors such as the investors' investment direction, investment environment, and the amount of investment to be undertaken. Generally speaking, wholly foreign-owned enterprises require examination and approval from many government bodies, and this process can be quite a hassle and time-consuming. Government procedures for establishing Chinese-foreign joint venture and contractual joint ventures will be even more complicated and will require more interactions with government bodies. Thus Sino-foreign joint venture appears to be the ideal investment option as less governmental proce-**

dures and authorization time will be required. The possibility of encountering hiccups will be smaller.

Why do some foreign-funded enterprise became successful when entering the China market while others fail, and why do some grow relatively faster than the rest? Reasons to explain all these are complex and varied. The following factors can determine how well or bad foreign-funded enterprises fare in China:

1. **Establishment and implementation of enterprise's development strategy. In China, successful MNCs and foreign-funded enterprises will definitely implement long-term development strategy, adopting a long-term outlook for their business, unlike other unsuccessful companies which do not look far and only concentrate on short-term gains. Besides adopting a development strategy that is long-term, the strategy will need to be a flexible one as market conditions are constantly changing due to the presence of globalization. The enterprise needs to be flexible to react immediately to**

any changes without affecting its business operations.

2. Leadership of the top management. Leadership of the top management plays a decisive role in the success of the company. In the face of greater competition brought about by globalization, management today will need to possess stronger judgment, decision ability, adaptability and greater foresight. The ability to look ahead is crucial as one needs to be able to anticipate unforeseen circumstances in order to be ready at all times to react to any changes.

3. Growth. Form key competitiveness for the enterprise, and grow together with the economy. Treat your staff with an open heart, cultivate the enterprise's values and vision constantly into them to foster togetherness within the organization and strengthen the organization's strengths.

4. Network. Build and strengthen the institutional framework and economic system of the enterprise. MNCs usually will establish main or Asian headquarters in key cities in China. Beside that, research and development center, training center and logistic base will also be built. Therefore it is vital for the organization to have a strong organizational structure dealing with its cash flow, flow of information and manpower movement, in order to ensure its success in China.

5. Chinese Culture. It is essential for the foreign-funded enterprises to understand the Chinese culture, especially regarding the culture of Guangxi (relationship), so as to be able to gain the popularity and trust of China's population. With a good relationship, business can become smoother and probability of failure will be greatly reduced. Stronger bonds can also be built with the customers, suppliers and partners.

Five tips to invest and do business in China

1. Have clear understanding of China. It is essential to understand the culture of the country before investing in it. Understanding China is vital, as China is a land of vast diversity. As such, it is important for the company to understand the culture and

the society's values before establishing operations in China. Only
through understanding the culture
and values can strong foundations
be built, and higher chance of success can thus be achieved.

2. Understand local business practices. Given China's distinct cultural differences from the rest of the
world, understanding China's business culture is extremely crucial.
What works in one's country will
not be applicable at all in China.
Understanding how the local people think and their business practices can allow one to engage better
and faster with them. Original organizational culture and practices
may have to change in order to ac-
commodate to China's practices.
Thus flexibility and adaptability is
the key for any organization to be
successful in China.

3. Acquire local knowledge and establish local presence. Establishing
a representative office in conjunction with a strong domestic, pri-
vate-sector partner that has access
to all necessary information and
contacts in their field is the formu-

la practiced by foreign firms who
already enjoy success in China.
Another way will be through setting up a joint venture. Most important is the selection of the correct
partner. Finding the right partner
may require more time, patience
and experience. It is never a waste
of time to spend more efforts in
choosing the right partner, because
a wrong partner will definitely
guarantee failure. Chinese expertise and local talent must also be
incorporated into management or
consulted during decision-making
since local knowledge is essential as
a source of information, access to
networks and social and cultural
learning, especially in China.

4. Need for establishing business relationships. Guanxi is an important
element in achieving successful
business in China. Top management must learn to nurture close
relationships with their local coun-
terparts. This not only helps them
to understand the Chinese domestic market, but also creates avenues
for help in times of trouble or in
need of assistance. Building strong

relationships with business partners can aid in mitigating strategic and operational risks.

5. Establish close relations with government officials China's government plays an important role in influencing market movement and administering foreign investments, a strong government relationship remains an important factor to do business successfully in China. Fewer hiccups may be met during paperwork applications or achieving local authorization if a strong relationship with government officials is in place.

■ by Joseph Lee
www.starmass.com

From Experts to Expats
Setting Up a Legal Entity in Hong Kong

THE FIRST STEP to set up a Hong Kong limited company would be the selection of an appropriate name. According to the Companies Ordinance, a new limited company cannot have the same name which has already been incorporated and registered in the Companies Registry.

When the name of the new company is confirmed, the authorized capital and the first shareholders (at least one person) of the company have to be determined. Then, several copies of the memoran-

dum and articles of association to be signed by shareholders for application of the Certificate of Incorporation must be prepared.

According to the Companies Ordinance, the memorandum and articles of association should specify the nature of business, the power of the shareholders, directors and company secretary, and the procedures and regulations of the meetings and resolutions of the company. There are some standard samples of memorandums and articles which contain the basic requirements in accordance with the laws and practices in Hong Kong. The memorandum and articles of association can be amended at any time after the company is incorporated. It takes about one to two days to prepare the memorandum and articles of association. Once this has been done, the Certificate of Incorporation can be applied for. It takes about 10 days for the Companies Registry to issue a Certificate of Incorporation.

After the issuance of the Certificate of Incorporation, the new company has been legally established, but cannot yet operate. The company now has to appoint its first director, a company secretary, issue shares to the shareholders and prepare the necessary memorandum and articles of association, register of shareholder/s, register of director/s, share certificate, company chop and common seal. It will take about one week to prepare all of these documents. The newly appointed director or secretary then has to apply for the Business Registration Certificate (BRC) at the Business Registration Department, which may issue the BRC on the same day. After the issuance of the BRC, the new company can be operated in Hong Kong.

It will take about three weeks to incorporate a new limited company. However, it is also possible to use an off-the-shelf" company that has previously been registered for those who need to shorten the incorporation time. One can transfer all the shares of the shelf company to the appointed shareholder/s and appoint the first director and prepare the other setting up procedures.

When establishing a legal entity Hong Kong, investors should consider the following:

Authorized capital

The authorized share capital is the

maximum amount of capital that a company can issue. Ordinarily, the face value of a share is HK$1.00. The company has to pay a capital fee of 0.1 percent for its authorized share capital. For example, if the authorized share capital of the company is HK$10,000, then the capital fee shall be HK$10.00. A company may increase the authorized share capital when and if it is required.

Quorum of meetings

The minimum requirement under the Companies Ordinance for a quorum is two if the number of shareholders or directors is more than one. If the company only has one shareholder and one director, no meetings should be held, but resolutions should be prepared to record the company resolutions.

Shareholders

The shareholders are the investors and beneficial owners of the company. They may be individuals or companies and have the right to share profits. There is no current restriction on the occupation/nature of business, nationality/registered address and age of a shareholder. The shareholders are not actually the persons who manage the operations of the company. According to the Companies Ordinance, a company shall have at least 1 shareholder.

Directors

Directors are the people who run the business of the company. They have full power to determine the policies in respect to administration, management, financing and general business operations of the company. They can represent the company to negotiate and conclude all kinds of contracts. The directors are appointed by the shareholders.

Their term of service is specified in the memorandum and articles of association. The minimum number of directors in a company is one. A director can be an individual or a company (when the director is an individual, their age shall be over 18).

Reserve director (not compulsory)

If a private company has only one member and that member is the sole director of the company, the company may in a general meeting nominate a natural person to act as a reserve director in the place of the sole director in the event of their death.

Company secretary

The company secretary is responsible for handling all documents and procedures required by the Companies Ordinance, such as; the preparation of minutes, keeping of the statutory records, submitting the annual returns, assisting the directors to prepare the directors' report and preparing all documents and procedures for all changes in the company structure. The company secretary can be an individual or a company ordinarily residing in Hong Kong or a company registered in Hong Kong. If the company only has one individual shareholder, and that shareholder is the sole director of the company, then that sole director cannot act as the company secretary.

Registered office

The registered office is the statutory correspondence address of a company in Hong Kong. Any location in the territory can be chosen as the registered office of the company.

Issued capital

A company may according to its requirement, issue any share capital within the limit of its authorized capital.

Bank account

Business transactions in Hong Kong are normally carried out through bank accounts. A company may open bank accounts in one or more banks. Please note however, that different banks may have different requirements in terms of opening of accounts procedures, one should be familiar with these in order to avoid delays and misunderstandings.

Nature of business

When applying for the BRC, the company has to specify its nature of business. The nature of business will be printed out in the BRC. However, a company's business operation is not restricted by this nature of business.

Normally, a company can do any legal business whenever they are specified in the memorandum and articles of association, without having to notify separately any of the government bureaus (unless restricted by other laws in Hong Kong, such as banking and insurance).

■ by China Briefing
www.china-briefing.com

From Experts to Expats
Empowering Your Business With a Chamber of Commerce

So, YOU'VE SET up your company and are working hard to make it a success. Entering into the China market is a big step, but a chamber of commerce can really give you a helping hand. What are some of the ways that a chamber can help people do business?

A chamber of commerce is an association, primarily of people in business, to promote the commercial interests of an area. It is a non-political, non-profit making organization, owned and directed by its members, democratically accountable to individual businesses of all sizes and sectors. As a network, it achieves a multi-sectoral, multi-size membership across a wide geographic spread. Every chamber sits at the heart of its local business community, reaching the entire business community and providing service, information and guidance to its members.

A chamber of commerce truly is the voice of business, the first choice partner for information and guidance, and the natural choice for business support.

To promote business in Shenzhen and the Guangdong region, chamber members get information about and invitations to regular events such as specially organized seminars and forums. These events address the issues relating to business, whether they be global issues affecting all businesses such as the global credit crisis, or local issues such as the labor market in Shenzhen. As a regional organiza-

tion, a chamber has an extensive network of member companies that provide a wealth of resources, many of which directly benefit members and their businesses by providing information about trading and investing in and between China and other countries.

It's no surprise that the business environment in China has changed rapidly in the last few years, and is still developing. In order to keep up with these changes, seminars feature guest speakers who are recognized as market leaders in their field. If you need to know something, like how the recent changes to the labor law affect you, the chances are that you're not the only one. That's why a seminar with a local legal expert to explain what the law actually means for companies operating here is an unmissable opportunity to get the answers you need.

Getting a foothold in the market can be difficult for a new company, and exposure through chamber activities can give a real advantage. The message gets through to managers and executives at top companies throughout the region. We are able to put together the companies that need each other; buyers with suppliers, consultants with clients, and service providers with end users. Local in-house publications give companies a place to voice their ideas on various themes, and give advertisers an opportunity to put themselves in the spotlight.

The chambers of commerce are not alone in their efforts to promote business, but are proud to work closely with other organizations and other chambers of commerce to maximize the potential benefits for members. Strong ties to local consulates and regional agencies give information about and invitations to government sponsored and supported events, participation in trade missions and lobbying powers.

But it's not all work, work, work. Everyone looks forward to social networking events which give local business people a chance to unwind and enjoy themselves. Regular events such as networking drinks evenings, give people an opportunity to meet outside of the office and share stories about life in China's most vibrant city. One-off special events such as the ball or quiz night are the highlight of the calendar.

A chamber is run by its full-time staff, working directly to look after their members' interests. The only way to really get to know your local chamber is to get involved. Go to the events, meet the people, give your support, input, and feedback about what the chamber could be doing to help businesses be more successful.

■ by Jonathan Gander

 For more information about the above-mentioned places visit WikiShenzhen.com

Major Business Associations in Shenzhen

Australia		Australian Chamber of Commerce (AustCham)	131
		Zernike Australia Pty Ltd	132
Brussels		Brussels Enterprise Agency (BEA)	132
Canada		Atlantic Canada Business Network (ACBN)	132
		Canadian Advanced Technology Alliance (CATA)	133
		The Canada China BUSINESS Council (CCBC)	133
Dubai		Dubai Technology and Media Free Zone	133
Egypt		The Egyptian Chinese Businessmen Council	134
England		South West England Regional Development Agency (SWERDA)	134
		The British Chamber of Commerce (BCC)	134
Europe		European Union Chamber of Commerce	135
Finland		FinChi Innovation Center Co.	136
		Nordic Trade House	136
France		China for the Vienne Council France	136
		French Chamber of Commerce (CCIFR)	137
Germany		The German Chamber of Commerce in China (GCC)	138
		The German Chinese Center for Economical & Technological Cooperation (GCC-ETC)	138
Hong Kong		Applied Science and Technology Research Institute Company Limited (ASTRI)	138
		Productivity (Shenzhen) Consulting Company Limited	138
Hungary		The Hungarian Technology Center (HTEC) China	139

India		Associated Chambers of Commerce & Industry of India (ASSOCHAM)	139
		India China Economic and Cultural Council (ICECC)	139
Israel		SHIRAT Enterprises	140
		The Israel Export & International Cooperation Institute (IEICI)	140
Italy		China-Italy Chamber of Commerce	140
Korea		Korea Electronics Technology Institute, Shenzhen Office (KETI)	140
		Sino-Korea Technology Center (SKTC)	141
		The China-Korea Society of Hi-Tech Industry Exchange	141
		The Korean Chamber of Commerce & Industry (SZKCCIC)	141
Poland		Polish Business Center (PBC)	141
Russia		The Chamber of Commerce and Industry of Samara Region	142
Rwanda		Rwanda Investment, Trade & Technology Office (RITTO)	142
Singapore		Singapore tech-EntreClub Pte Ltd	142
Spain		Spain Aragón Exterior	142
Taiwan		Hi-Tech. & Trading Association of Taiwan	143
USA		American Appraisal	143
		CEO Clubs China	143
		The American Chamber of Commerce in South China	143
		The City of Ontario	144

Australian Chamber of Commerce (AustCham)

AUSTCHAM SHENZHEN WAS founded in 2007 in response to the need to represent the growing number of Australians doing business in Shenzhen, and to help form ties with Chinese businesses investing in Australia or promoting Australian goods and services in China.

⊠   c/o Level 12 Xinghua Insurance Building, Mintian Road, Futian

地址   深圳市福田区民田路新华保险大厦12楼东侧

℡   134-3077-1883 (David Jacobs)

🖷   8251-4340

@   david.jacobs@austcham-shenzhen.org

🖱   www.austcham-shenzhen.org

Zernike Australia Pty Ltd.

ZERNIKE AUSTRALIA PTY Ltd., a joint venture with the Zernike Group of the Netherlands, is specialized in the design, construction, and management of science parks, venture capital and international sales and marketing.

⊠   Chinese Overseas Scholars Venture Building,
            Shenzhen Hi-tech Industry Park, Nanshan District

地址   深圳市南山区高新区南区留学生创业大厦

℡/🖷   Unknown

🖱   www.zernikegroup.com (www.zernikechina.com)

ⓘ   It appears that Zernike Australia Ltd. has ceased operations in Shenzhen, check their website for more information.

Brussels Enterprise Agency (BEA)

THE BRUSSELS ENTERPRISE Agency (BEA) is a non-profit organiza-tion managed by the Brussels Regional Government. It provides free-of-charge advice and consultation services to companies that want to invest in Brussels. Brussels is an ideal springboard for Chinese enterprises to develop their presence in Western Europe. In 2007, BEA opened an office in the Shenzhen International Science and Technology Business Platform, which has attracted 31 overseas organizations from 22 countries and areas within the Shenzhen High-tech Park. BEA has assisted several companies to set up a branch or headquarters in Brussels including large and small companies from electronic, automotive, service sectors, etc. BEA has received several Brussels delegations to Shenzhen and also Shenzhen delegations to Brussels, including 2 delegations led by Executive Vice Mayor Mr. Xuqin to Brussels in 2008.

✉   Rm 222, 2/F, Chinese Overseas Scholars Venture Building, Shenzhen Hi-tech Industry Park, Nanshan District

地址   深圳市南山区高新区南区留学生创业大厦2楼222室

✆/📠   8632-9700, 8632-9705

🖱   www.investinbrussels.com

Atlantic Canada Business Network (ACBN)

ATLANTIC CANADA BUSINESS Network (ACBN) builds trade and investment between Canada and China. ACBN focuses on Canada-China trade in diverse sectors, such as ICT (Information Communications Technology), Aviation, Education and Training, and advanced manufacturing.

✉   Rm 205, 2/F, Chinese Overseas Scholars Venture Building, Shenzhen Hi-tech Industry Park, Nanshan District

地址   深圳市南山区高新区南区留学生创业大厦2楼205室

✆/📠   2658-8371, 2658-8372

🖱   www.atlantic-canada.org

Canadian Advanced Technology Alliance (CATA)

ESTABLISHED IN 1979, CATA is committed to improve a mutual understanding and friendly communication between China and

Canada on economy, science & technology, education, and especially in the hi-tech field through electronics business platform and international business activities.

✉   Rm 317, 3/F, Chinese Overseas Scholars Venture Building, Shenzhen Hi-tech Industry Park, Nanshan District

地址   深圳市南山区高新区南区留学生创业大厦3楼317室

✆/昌   2654-8505, 2654-8531

🖰   www.cata-china.org

The Canada China Business Council (CCBC)

THE CANADA CHINA Business Council (CCBC) provides services in six key areas: event management, facilitation & marketing, consulting, policy advocacy & mediation, business operation and administration support, as well as access to analyzed information.

✉   Chinese Overseas Scholars Venture Building, Shenzhen Hi-tech Industry Park, Nanshan District

地址   深圳市南山区高新区南区留学生创业大厦

✆/昌   Unknown

🖰   www.ccbc.com

Dubai Technology and Media Free Zone

THE DUBAI TECHNOLOGY and Media Free Zone is a tax-free commercial zone set up by the Dubai Government to support the development of knowledge-based industries. The Free Zone was established in 2000 to support and develop ICT, media, and knowledge-focused companies, including education and training institutions.

✉   Rm 316, 3/F, Chinese Overseas Scholars Venture Building, Shenzhen Hi-tech Industry Park, Nanshan District

地址   深圳市南山区高新区南区留学生创业大厦3楼316室

✆/昌   2601-7782, 2601-7782

✆ www.dubaiinternetcity.com

The Egypt-China Business Council

THE EGYPT-CHINA BUSINESS Council is private non-governmental business established in 2002. Its mission is to strengthen the economic and commercial ties between China and Egypt and increase the mutual flows of trade and investment.

✉ Rm 201, 2/F, Chinese Overseas Scholars Venture Building, Shenzhen Hi-tech Industry Park, Nanshan District

地址 深圳市南山区高新区南区留学生创业大厦2楼201室

✆/🖷 8635-0900, 8635-0901

✆ Unknown

South West England Regional Development Agency (SWERDA)

SOUTH WEST ENGLAND Regional Development Agency (SWERDA) is funded by the British Government's Department of Trade and Industry. SWERDA provides a single point of contact for companies and has access to a wealth of resources from local, regional, national and international sources.

✉ Rm 216, 2/F, Chinese Overseas Scholars Venture Building, Shenzhen Hi-tech Industry Park, Nanshan District

地址 深圳市南山区高新区南区留学生创业大厦2楼216室

✆/🖷 2658-8282, 2658-8282

✆ www.southwestrda.org.uk

The British Chamber of Commerce (BCC)

THE BRITISH CHAMBER organizes informative seminars by guest speakers and social networking events. BCC provides a forum where members of the international business community can get together on a regular basis to share experiences, gain useful insights, and develop new contacts.

⊠   Rm 314, 3/F, Chinese Overseas Scholars Venture Building,
       Shenzhen Hi-tech Industry Park, Nanshan District

地址   深圳市南山区高新区南区留学生创业大厦3楼314室

☎/🖨   2658-8350, 8331-5016

🖰   www.britchamgd.com

ⓘ   It appears that the British Chamber of Commerce has ceased
       operations in Shenzhen, check their website for more informa-
tion.

European Union Chamber of Commerce

THE EUROPEAN UNION Chamber of Commerce in China, founded in 2000 in Beijing, is a non-profit business organization to give European businesses a common voice across different business sectors, nationalities and regions of China.

⊠   Rm 308, 3/F, Chinese Overseas Scholars Venture Building,
       Shenzhen Hi-tech Industry Park, Nanshan District

地址   深圳市南山区高新区南区留学生创业大厦2楼308室

☎/🖨   8635-0920, 8632-9785

@/🖰 prd@euccc.com.cn, www.europeanchamber.com.cn

FinChi Innovation Center Co.

FINCHI INNOVATION CENTER Co., Ltd is an extension of Finnish innovation environment to China. FinChi focuses on cooperation and networking between Finnish and Chinese companies and research centers.

⊠   Rm 213, 2/F, Chinese Overseas Scholars Venture Building,
       Shenzhen Hi-tech Industry Park, Nanshan District

地址   深圳市南山区高新区南区留学生创业大厦2楼213室

☎   8632-9408

🖳   8635-0456

🖱   www.finchi.cn

Nordic Trade House

NORDIC TRADE HOUSE jointly works with organizations of VIEXPO, Seinajoki Business Center and Enterprises Association in Ostrobothnia Finland. The NTH focuses in trade, technology and professional exchange.

✉   Rm 305, 3/F, Chinese Overseas Scholars Venture Building, Shenzhen Hi-tech Industry Park, Nanshan District

地址   深圳市南山区高新区南区留学生创业大厦3楼305室

☏   2699-3112

🖳   2697-2993

🖱   Unknown

China for the Vienne Council France

THE CHINA FOR the Vienne Council France helps boost investments and cooperation between France-Vienne and Shenzhen in the fields of economics & trade, science & technologies, cultures, arts & education, environmental protection, law, information and companies with French visa applications.

✉   Rm 223, 2/F, Chinese Overseas Scholars Venture Building, Shenzhen Hi-tech Industry Park, Nanshan District

地址   深圳市南山区高新区南区留学生创业大厦2楼223室

☏   2601-7735

🖱   Unknown

@   Unknown

French Chamber of Commerce (CCIFC)

THE FRENCH CHAMBER of Commerce's main mission is to offer operational assistance services to French firms established in China and the ones willing to do so. Some services offered by the CCIFC are as follows:

✉ Rm 318, 3/F, Chinese Overseas Scholars Venture Building, Shenzhen Hi-tech Industry Park, Nanshan District

地址 深圳市南山区高新区南区留学生创业大厦3楼318室

☏/🖷 8632-9602, 8632-9720, 8632-9736

@/🖰 information@ccifc.org, www.ccifc.org

The German Chamber of Commerce in China (GCC)

THE GERMAN CHAMBER of Commerce in China facilitates communication and the exchange of information among their business communities for the benefit of the economic relations between Germany and China. GCC also offers a variety of publications, both in German and English languages.

✉ Chinese Overseas Scholars Venture Building, Shenzhen Hi-tech Industry Park, Nanshan District

地址 深圳市南山区高新区南区留学生创业大厦

☏/🖷 Not available at the time of this writing

🖰 www.china.ahk.de

The German Chinese Center for Economical & Technological Cooperation (GCC-ETC)

THE GCC-ETC OFFERS services such as; information-services, mediation of contacts, arrangements for cooperation, marketing actions, company presentations, market analysis and business plans, support on projects and business operations, setup of branch offices and agencies.

✉ Rm 307, 3/F, Chinese Overseas Scholars Venture Building,

　　　Shenzhen Hi-tech Industry Park, Nanshan District

地址　　深圳市南山区高新区南区留学生创业大厦3楼307室

©/🖨　　2601-7724, 8635-0901

🖱　　www.shenzhen-bridge.de

Applied Science and Technology Research Institute Company Limited (ASTRI)

ASTRI WAS DESIGNATED as the Hong Kong R&D Center for Information and Communications Technologies. ASTRI performs market leading-edge R&D for technology transfer to industry, and acts as a focal point that brings together industry and university R&D assets.

✉　　Rm 220, 2/F, Chinese Overseas Scholars Venture Building, Shenzhen Hi-tech Industry Park, Nanshan District

地址　　深圳市南山区高新区南区留学生创业大2楼220室

©/🖨　　+ 852 3406-2801

🖱　　www.astri.org

Productivity (Shenzhen) Consulting Company Limited

HKPC PROVIDES SUPPORT for Hong Kong companies in advanced manufacturing, management systems as well as integrated support across the value chain. It is supported by over 30 Centers, 10 laboratories with training facilities and over 600 professional consultants in HKPC.

✉　　Block D, 1/F.,Productivity Building, Gaoxin #2 Avenue (Middle), Shenzhen Science Technology Park, Nanshan

地址　　深圳市南山区科技园高新中二道生产力大楼D座一层

©/🖨　　8616-8488, 020-8616-8822

@/🖱　　www.sz.hkpcprd.com

The Hungarian Technology Center (HTEC) China

ESTABLISHED BY THE Hungarian government, HTEC China links innovative Hungarian ICT companies directly with the Chinese market, and helps Chinese companies do business in the European Union by leveraging Hungary's IT infrastructure and local knowledge.

✉   Rm 319, 3/F, Chinese Overseas Scholars Venture Building,
        Shenzhen Hi-tech Industry Park, Nanshan District

地址   深圳市南山区高新区南区留学生创业大厦3楼319室

✆   2601-7762

Associated Chambers of Commerce & Industry of India (ASSOCHAM)

ESTABLISHED IN 1920, ASSOCHAM is the oldest apex chamber of commerce in India. ASSOCHAM's mission is to facilitate trade, joint-ventures, exchange of information and knowledge between India and business houses and trade & industry associations in China, especially the Pearl River Delta region.

✉   Chinese Overseas Scholars Venture Building,
        Shenzhen Hi-tech Industry Park, Nanshan District

地址   深圳市南山区高新区南区留学生创业大厦

✆   2655-1500

@/⌂   www.assocham.org

India China Economic and Cultural Council (ICECC)

INDIA CHINA ECONOMIC and Cultural Council is an organization of Indian business leaders, professionals and intellectuals engaged in evolving closer relations between India and China.

✉   Rm 304, 3/F, Chinese Overseas Scholars Venture Building,
        Shenzhen Hi-tech Industry Park, Nanshan District

地址   深圳市南山区高新区南区留学生创业大厦3楼304室

✆/📠   8632-9780, 8632-9778

@/⌐ www.icec-council.org

SHIRAT Enterprises

SHIRAT ENTERPRISES HAS been involved in the Israeli Hi-tech and Venture Capital industries for many years. The SHIRAT Enterprises Shenzhen office constitutes a permanent center and exhibition facility for presenting and demonstrating novel technologies and new products developed by Israeli Companies.

✉   Chinese Overseas Scholars Venture Building,
         Shenzhen Hi-tech Industry Park, Nanshan District

地址   深圳市南山区高新区南区留学生创业大厦

✆   2654-8530

The Israel Export & International Cooperation Institute (IEICI)

THE ISRAEL EXPORT & International Cooperation Institute facilitates trade opportunities, joint ventures, and strategic alliances between international businesses and Israeli companies.

✉   Rm 306, 3/F, Chinese Overseas Scholars Venture Building,
         Shenzhen Hi-tech Industry Park, Nanshan District

地址   深圳市南山区高新区南区留学生创业大厦

✆/🖨   2655-1709, 2655-1500

@/⌐   www.export.gov.il/Eng

China-Italy Chamber of Commerce (CICC)

THE CHINA ITALY Chamber of Commerce (CICC) was registered in 1991 and is based in Beijing. The CCIC is present in Guangdong and Shanghai. Its members include major Italian industrial groups, banks, law firms, insurance and transport companies, as well as small and medium sized enterprises.

✉   Rm 217, 2/F, Chinese Overseas Scholars Venture Building,

Shenzhen Hi-tech Industry Park, Nanshan District

地址   深圳市南山区高新区南区留学生创业大厦2楼217室

℡   8632-9518

@/⌂   www.cameraitacina.com

Korean Electronics Technology Institute, Shenzhen Office (KETI)

KETI IS A specialized research institute in Electronics and Information. KETI contributes to the reinforcement of international competitiveness in the electronics, information, and other related components industries by fostering R&D for technological innovation and support of small and medium enterprises.

✉   Rm 226, 2/F, Chinese Overseas Scholars Venture Building, Shenzhen Hi-tech Industry Park, Nanshan District

地址   深圳市南山区高新区南区留学生创业大厦2楼226室

℡/📠   2671-2285, 2671-2284

⌂   www.keti.re.kr

Sino-Korea Technology Center (SKTC)

SKTC IS A specialized research institute in the electronics and information field. SKTC contributes to the reinforcement of international competitiveness of the electronics, information, and other related components industries, by fostering the R&D necessary for technological innovation.

✉   Chinese Overseas Scholars Venture Building, Shenzhen Hi-tech Industry Park, Nanshan District

地址   深圳市南山区高新区南区留学生创业大厦

⌂   www.szistb.org/en

The China-Korea Economy Promotion Association

THE CHINA-KOREA ECONOMY Promotion Association promotes culture exchange, government relationships between China and Korea, as well as mutual communication and technical exchange.

✉ Rm 207, 2/F, Chinese Overseas Scholars Venture Building, Shenzhen Hi-tech Industry Park, Nanshan District

地址 深圳市南山区高新区南区留学生创业大厦2楼207室

✆ 2658-8363

The Korean Chamber of Commerce & Industry (SZKCCIC)

SZKCCIC IS THE sole representative organization of more than 1,500 Korean enterprises and 30,000 Korean emigrants based in Shenzhen. SZKCCIC's mission is to strengthen cultural, physical training and educational exchange between the two countries.

✉ Rm 312, 3/F, Chinese Overseas Scholars Venture Building, Shenzhen Hi-tech Industry Park, Nanshan District

地址 深圳市南山区高新区南区留学生创业大厦3楼312室

✆/🖶 2692-1539, 2690-8654

Polish Business Center (PBC)

POLISH BUSINESS CENTER [PBC] is a management consulting and services organization which has been founded by the Polish Government, the Polish Chamber of Commerce, commercial banks, and investment companies.

✉ Rm 309, 3/F, Chinese Overseas Scholars Venture Building, Shenzhen Hi-tech Industry Park, Nanshan District

地址 深圳市南山区高新区南区留学生创业大厦3楼309室

✆/🖶 8635-0181, 8635-0191

The Chamber of Commerce and Industry of Samara Region (CCI SR)

CCI SR REPRESENTS the members and corporations in Russia, republics of CIS, and other foreign countries. CCI SR organizes business meetings, negotiations, presentations, exhibitions, seminars for both Russian and foreign firms, and encourages export-import transactions.

✉   Rm 311, 3/F, Chinese Overseas Scholars Venture Building, Shenzhen Hi-techanshan District

地址   深圳市南山区高新区南区留学生创业大厦3楼311室

🖱   www.cci.samara.ru

Rwanda Investment, Trade & Technology Office (RITTO)

RITTO SHENZHEN IS a representative office of the Rwanda Investment and Export Promotion Agency RIEPA in Shenzhen. RIEPA is a government agency with offices worldwide, which is charged with the responsibility to promote and facilitate trade and investment in Rwanda.

✉   Chinese Overseas Scholars Venture Building, Shenzhen Hi-tech Industry Park, Nanshan District

地址   深圳市南山区高新区南区留学生创业大厦

🖱   www.rwandainvest.com

Singapore tech-EntreClub Pte Ltd.

SINGAPORE TECH-ENTRECLUB PTE Ltd., incorporated in Singapore, is a club for Singapore Techno-preneurs and enterprises in the technology sectors. Its aims is to promote the exchange of technology transfer and expertise resource, and to provide consultancy services in capital market, finance and investment.

✉   Rm 202, 2/F, Chinese Overseas Scholars Venture Building, Shenzhen Hi-tech Industry Park, Nanshan District

地址   深圳市南山区高新区南区留学生创业大厦2楼202室

Spain Aragon Exterior (Arex)

AREX IS THE official organization of the Aragonese Government, in Spain. The company is responsible for external promotion and attracting foreign investment.

✉   Rm 210, 2/F, Chinese Overseas Scholars Venture Building, Shenzhen Hi-tech Industry Park, Nanshan District

地址   深圳市南山区高新区南区留学生创业大厦2楼210室

🖱   www.aragonexterior.es

Hi-Tech. & Trading Association of Taiwan

HI-TECH & TRADING Association of Taiwan is a non-profit organization which   provides technology, trading and services between Taiwan and mainland China.

✉   Rm 206, 2/F, Chinese Overseas Scholars Venture Building, Shenzhen Hi-tech Industry Park, Nanshan District

地址   深圳市南山区高新区南区留学生创业大厦2楼206室

✆/🖨 8635-0998, 8635-0997

🖱   www.chtf.com/en

American Appraisal

AMERICAN APPRAISAL, PROVIDES valuation or valuation-related advisory services for business, financial, legal or tax purposes. The consultants, located in major financial centers throughout Asia, Europe and North America, have experience with all classifications of tangible and intangible assets

✉   Rm 314, 3/F, Chinese Overseas Scholars Venture Building, Shenzhen Hi-tech Industry Park, Nanshan District

地址   深圳市南山区高新区南区留学生创业大厦3楼314室

🖱   www.american-appraisal.com

CEO Clubs China

THE CEO CLUBS helps Chinese businesses to explore the U.S. market, and at the same time, helps U.S. companies to learn the investment environment in China more directly and comprehensively.

✉   Rm 215, 2/F, Chinese Overseas Scholars Venture Building, Shenzhen Hi-tech Industry Park, Nanshan District

地址   深圳市南山区高新区南区留学生创业大厦2楼215室

🖰   www.ceochina.net.cn (Chinese)

The American Chamber of Commerce in South China

AMCHAM WAS CERTIFIED in 1995 by the U.S. Chamber of Commerce in Washington D.C. AmCham Guangdong has more than 550 corporate and individual members, and represents over 480 American and international companies doing business in south China.

✉   Rm 208, 2/F, Chinese Overseas Scholars Venture Building, Shenzhen Hi-tech Industry Park, Nanshan District

地址   深圳市南山区高新区南区留学生创业大厦2楼208室

@/🖰   amcham@amcham-southchina.org, www.amcham-southchina.org

The City of Ontario, California

THE CITY OF Ontario China Office is the official representative office in China, the purpose of the office is to facilitate international business opportunities for both businesses from the City of Ontario and China business.

✉   Rm 221, 2/F, Chinese Overseas Scholars Venture Building, Shenzhen Hi-tech Industry Park, Nanshan District

地址   深圳市南山区高新区南区留学生创业大厦2楼221室

✆/🖨   8632-9754, 8632-9748

@/🖰   www.ontariocalifornia.cn

Sports in Shenzhen

From Experts to Expats
Sports Associations

SHENZHEN IS A young city without the legacy of expats that more developed places such as Shanghai has, so surprisingly there are wide variety of sports associations run by expats. There is something for everybody. The clubs all seem to harbor a sense of fun and camaraderie, all embrace the various nationalities, and none were bound by age, race or gender. It seems sports is expanding in Shenzhen so don't be surprised if new clubs pop up. The ones that are already around seem fairly well established and here to stay.

Inter Shenzhen Football Club

FOUNDED IN 2001 with a mixture of locals and expats and expanded through word-of-mouth, the team became a magnet for foreigners who wanted to play football regularly. The club name 'Inter Shenzhen' was created in 2004, reflecting the various 'Internationality' of the players. All nationalities and locals are welcome, as are regular and irregular players.

✉	All maps available via the website 1) Shenzhen Stadium Pitch 2) Meilin Reservoir Pitch 3) Qiao Cheng Dong Pitch 4) Xili Pitch 5) Buji Stadium 6) Cui Hai Garden Square 7) Futian Pitch
✆	None
✎	Via website only
⧗	Posted to members via website
🖱	www.intershenzhen.com
$	Full member: 1,500RMB, no pitch fee, entry into league Assoc Member: 500RMB , pitch fee, no entry into league Non-member: 100RMB, pitch fee, no entry into league
🚌	Level: All

Algerian Football Club

THE CLUB WAS set up 2 or 3 years ago by predominantly Algerian members. However, it is open to everyone.

✉	Longfa School, Luohu District
☏	Radouane: 138-2311-6400 Tommy (Founder) 137-5100-6612
✎	ttscoffee@hotmail.com, tommy8689@gmail.com
⏳	Thursday 8pm -10pm , matches on Sunday·
🖰	Unknown
$	Split pitch fee
🚌	Level: All

Shekou Soccer 8's

THE ANNUAL TOURNAMENT is played prior to the start of the new league. The 8 a side one day tournament has been running since 1999 and is a combination of Western and Chinese players (call Kim for latest updates).

✉	China Merchants Pitch, Shekou
☏	Kim: 159-9969-2721
✎	info@shekousoccer.com, holykimhk@hotmail.com
⏳	Once a year, the first weekend in September
🖰	www.shekousoccer.com
$	Application via internet. 2 packages available: 880RMB per person, or 2,800RMB per team (see website for full package details)
🚌	Level: Non professional

Shekou Hash House Harriers

MEETS SATURDAY'S RAIN or shine at The Snake Pit at 2pm. Known as a "drinking club with a running problem" it's a social get-together going on a run or walk, followed by a bit of drinking and an optional dinner.

✉	At the 'Snakepit', above Pizza Hut and behind Watsons, Taizi Square, next to Sea World, Shekou
☎	Ed Hoffman: 138-2377-4701
✎	Via website only
⧗	Every Saturday 2pm
⚲	www.hhhweb.com/shekouhash
$	60RMB
🚌	Level: All

Shekou Touch Rugby

TOUCH RUGBY WAS established in 1996, while the Union side was resurrected 4 years ago. Touch is minimal contact played by men, women and children of all ages and skills. The game emphasizes running agility, ball handling, passing and catching, no tackling, scrumming, kicking etc.

✉	China Merchants Field, Shekou (map on website)
☎	None
✎	touchrugby@shekou-rugby.com
⧗	Wednesday 8-9 pm
⚲	www.shekou-rugby.com
$	Cost of pitch hire divided between no. of players typically 30 or 40RMB
🚌	Level: All welcome

The Shekou Sports & Social Club (The Snake Pit)

THE SNAKE PIT, perhaps the oldest expat club in South China, is a social focal point for the local community. It is also home to Shekou Hash Harriers, Shekou Rugby, Shekou Flag Football and Shekou Softball.

✉	At the 'Snakepit', behind Watsons, above Pizza Hut, Taizi Square, next to Sea World, Shekou
☎	None
✎	exec_committee@the-snakepit.com
⧗	M-F: 5pm-12am, F: 5pm-2am, S: 12pm-2am, D: 12pm-12am

🖱	www.the-snakepit.com
$	A member only bar which sponsors social events and various sports clubs. 400RMB for lifetime membership. Temporary membership book (5 drinks) 100RMB.

Gui Lao Basketball Team

THIS TEAM IS open to anyone who has a passion for the game of basketball and wants to play with other like-minded foreigners.

✉	Mont Orchid Sports Center, Yanshan Rd., Shekou
☎	Eddie Pittman Tel: 137-2372-1755
📧	Ezypzy30@hotmail.com
⏳	Thursday from 8-10pm & matches at the weekend
🖱	Unknown
$	Cost of hall hire, split between number of players (unless playing outside then no fee)
🚌	Level: Intermediate to advanced

Shenzhen Celts Gaelic Football Team

THE CELTS WERE formed in 2004 by expats who experienced similar clubs in Taiwan. Started with friends and sponsored by the players' company, the team was born. The game is Irish in origination, but the players are international. The game is a mixture of soccer and Aussie rules with minimal contact.

✉	Hongli Lu & Xinzhou Lu (map & directions on website)
☎	Ladies Captain: Niamh 136-3266-5027 Men's Captain: Darragh 138-2520-1901 Club President 139-2687-9002 Founder: Peter 135-1039-6321
📧	info@shenzhencelts.com
⏳	Always posted and updated on website
🖱	www.shenzhencelts.com (currently being updated)
$	cost of pitch split between the players typically 50 rmb, free first trial.
🚌	Level: All welcome

Shenzhen Commonwealth Cricket Club

SHENZHEN COMMONWEALTH IS sponsored by McCawleys Irish Pub & restaurant. They welcome all players beginner to expert, and have Canadian, American, Indian, Chinese, Australian, English, South African and Namibian members. They try to practice once a week in Nanshan and have already participated in 2 international sixes tournaments.

✉	Nanshan High School, everyone meets at Futian and goes together via taxi
✆	Jonathan: 138-2873-5650
@	jonathan.hyman@internationalsos.com
⧖	Schedule on Facebook
🖰	www.facebook.com/group.php?gid=5532696353 Facebook "SCCC" group name
$	Free
ⓘ	Form more information, call Jonathan.

Shekou Youth Sport Program (SYSP)

IN 2006 THE QSI International School of Shekou PSG (Parent Support Group) launched SYSP. This is a three season program operated by parents and other volunteers along with a supervisor supplied by QSI Shekou. This fun, instructional sport program is open to the entire Shekou community of children, regardless of nationality or school attendance, ages 5 to 11.

✉	QSI International Shool of Shekou
✆	2667-6031
@	Howard Wilson : hwilson2235@gmail.com
⧖	The program is offered on Saturday mornings from September through May: Soccer in fall and spring, Basketball in winter. Each session begins with an instructional period of basic skill and rule understanding and later competitions replace practices. Student volunteers from the QSI Secondary School participate by providing registration, coaching and officiating assistance.
$	A nominal fee for each season is required for equipment, uniforms and field rental

Go-Kart

1 Xiangmi Hu Go-Kart	香蜜湖小型赛车
🖃 North Xiang Mi Hu, Hongli Rd., Futian District	
地址 福田区红荔路香蜜湖北（香蜜湖娱乐城大门旁）	
ℰ 8394-7962	
$ Standard carts: ¥60 / 10 mins; Fast carts: ¥150 / 10 mins	
⌂ www.kdcchina.com	

2 Shajing Go-Kart	沙井小型赛车
🖃 Shajing Subdistrict, Nandong Rd., Bao'an District	
地址 宝安区沙井街道 黄埔上南东路	
ℰ 2989-7388	
⧗ Weekdays 9:30am - 6:30pm; weekends 9am - 7pm	
⌂ www.szkarting.com	

Golf Clubs

1 Century Seaview Golf Club	世纪海景高尔夫俱乐部
🖃 Yangchou Bay, Nan'ao Town, Longgang District	
地址 龙岗区南澳镇洋畴湾	
ℰ 8440-8888	
⌂ www.centuryseaviewgolf.com	

2 Firestone Golf Club	光明高尔夫球会
🖃 Ti Yu Garden Rd., Guangming, Bao'an District	

地址	宝安区光明新区体育公园路
☎	2788-8999

---

3 Green Bay Golf Club · 碧海湾高尔夫俱乐部

▣	Xinwan Rd., Xixiang Town, Bao'an Distrist
地址	宝安区西乡镇西乡大道新湾路
☎	2769-1888
🖥	www.greenbaygc.com

---

4 Jiulong Hills Golf Club · 九龙山绿色基地高尔夫球会

▣	Jiulong Hills Green Base, Fumin Guanlan Town
地址	宝安区观澜镇福民九龙山绿色基地
☎	2798-6999
🖥	www.jlsgolf.net

---

5 Longgang Public Golf Club · 龙岗公众高尔夫球场

▣	Henggang He Ao Village, Longgang District
地址	龙岗区横岗荷坳村
☎	2893-7188
🖥	www.gzgolf.net

---

6 Mission Hills Golf Club · 深圳观澜球会

▣	1, Guanlan Golf Av., Bao'an District
地址	宝安区观澜高尔夫大道1号
☎	2802-0888

🚌 312, 770, 771, 793 (Gaoerfu Qiuchang stop, 高尔夫球场)

⏳ 8am - 10pm; to play golf you should either be a member or stay in the hotel

🖥 www.missionhillsgroup.com (English)

---

7 Noble Merchant Golf Club   名商高尔夫球会

📧 Dawei, Shahe, Nanshan District

地址 南山区沙河大围

☎ 2690-9999

🖥 www.nmgolf.com.cn

---

8 Tycoon Golf Club   港中旅聚豪高尔夫球会

📧 Jiu Wei, Xi Xiang Town, Boan District

地址 宝安区西乡镇九围

☎ 2748-3999

🖥 www.tycoongolf.com

---

9 Shahe River Golf Club   沙河高尔夫球会

📧 1, Baishi Rd., Nanshan District

地址 南山区白石路1号

☎ 2690-0111

🖥 www.srgc.cn

---

10 Shenzhen Airport Golf Club   航港高尔夫球会

📧 Near Shenzhen Int'l Airport, Bao'an District

地址 宝安区机场侧

☎ 2777-7773

11 Shenzhen Genzon Golf Club 正中高尔夫球会

Inside the Botanical Garden, Longgang District

地址 龙岗区植物园路植物园内

8484-5555

www.china-golf.com

12 Shenzhen Golf Club 高尔夫俱乐部

Shennan Rd., Futian District

地址 福田区深南大道香蜜湖南

8330-8888

13 Shenzhen OCT Golf Club 华侨城高尔夫俱乐部

Xiangshan Str. West, OCT, Nanshan District

地址 南山区香山西街

2691-0333

www.golftx.cn

14 Shenzhen Shekou Grassland Golf Club 蛇口绿草地高尔夫

Sea World (behind the boat), Shekou, Nanshan District

地址 南山区蛇口海上世界

2685-5666

15 Shuanglong Resort Golf Club 双龙生态庄园高尔夫练习场

Qinglin Jing Forest Park, Zhu Gushi Park, Longgang District

地址 龙岗区庆林径森林公园内

✆	8482-9082

16 Xili Golf Club	西丽高尔夫乡村俱乐部
⊡ Tang Lang Village, Xili, Nanshan District	
地址	南山区西丽镇塘朗村
✆	2655-2888
🖰	www.xiligolf.com

17 Yunhai Gu Golf Club	云海谷高尔夫球会
⊡ Yunhai Gutiyu Park, OCT, Dameisha, Yantian District	
地址	盐田区大梅沙东部华侨城云海谷体育公园
✆	2888-1111
🖰	www.octeast.com

Water Sports

Xichong Beach

Xichong beach is about two hours drive east of Shenzhen and Guangzhou. From Shenzhen, to get there by bus from Shenzhen Stadium, take bus 360 or bus E11 to Nan'ao. From there, take a minibus or taxi, or motorbike over the winding mountainous road to Xichong. The best surf is usually in the middle left of the beach. The beach is a lot longer than Dongchong, but Xichong's facilities (the "surf shop", hotels & shops) are scattered out along its length.

Facilities, like bars, hotels and restaurants, are generally fairly basic, but acceptable. Tents, for sleeping on the beach, can be hired too for ¥50 per night. The "surf shop" (consisting of some rental boards locked away in a shed, you may need to improvise leashes) is on the right of the beach, as you face the sea. The shop is hard to differentiate from the other facilities, but it has a corrugated iron blue roof. Boards are about ¥50 and ¥150 to rent for three hours.

Dongchong Beach

Dongchong beach is very close to Xichong; to get here, turn left near the crest of the hill about 3 km before reaching Xichong. There is a risk from the speedboats, so watch out for them and make them aware that you are in the water. The beach and village are conveniently compact, and it is cleaner than Xichong. Facilities, like bars, hotels and restaurants, are also more advanced in Dongchong and there are some decent wooden villas for rent. There are two shops that rent boards just off the beach front by the car park. Boards are about ¥50 to ¥100 for three hours. There is a new surf club in Dongchong village - Blue Surf Club, tel: 138-2526-5825.

Pinghai Beach

Pinghai beach is another option, about three and a half hours drive along the coast from Shenzhen. There is a bus from Luohu bus station to (close to) Pinghai. The beach is very long (and almost empty) beside an interesting fishing village. To find where the waves are breaking best, drive very slowly along the very rough coastal road. The best spot is near the far end of the beach, away from the fishing village, about 4 miles along the very rough coastal road near two nice hotels, but this may vary. There are quite a few nice local hotels, bars and restaurants in the village, but facilities along the huge beach are very limited, though there are a couple of good hotels towards the far end of the beach.

Information & Surfware

Weather Forecast: www.windguru.cz/int/index.php?sc=186632

In Dapeng, about 15km from Xichong/Dongchong, there is a surf shop called Aloha Surf; Kuinan Rd., Dapeng (tel: 135-3426-5025).

Living in Shekou
and Nanshan

From Expats to Expats
An Overview of Shekou

THE PAINT ISN'T dry on most of what we know as Shenzhen, but that is far from the whole story. The town of Shekou (snake mouth in Chinese, 蛇口) has its humble origins hundreds of years ago as a fishing village. Its most famous ancient landmark is the Chiwan Temple, (c 1410) located South of the ferry terminal. Chinese history says that the famous admiral-eunuch Zheng He was commissioned by emperor Zhu Di to "sail west." Reaching the Pearl River Delta near Chiwan, the fleet encountered a violent storm and through the intervention of the sea goddess, Tian Hou, was able to continue its voyage. The emperor,

in thanks to Tian Hou, built the original temple. Because the lovely temple is now surrounded by the industrial port, few visitors or residents discover it. Be one of the few, it is worth the effort.

The Shekou Industrial Zone was Deng Xiaoping's showcase of economic reforms. As China's leader in the 1980s he decided to open a small corner of China to the outside world. With the efforts of a company called China Merchants, Shekou was developed as we now know it. As the base for the petroleum industry in the South China Sea, Shekou attracted many multi-national oil companies. Consequently, foreigners poured in with their families. Suitable housing and schools needed to be developed quickly, and soon Shekou became the expat ghetto of Shenzhen with China Merchants being just about everyone's landlord.

So what's the deal with the landlocked cruise ship in the middle of Seaworld Plaza? Back in 1962, France launched a ship named Ancerville, which was purchased by the People's Republic of China in 1973 and renamed Minghua. After several years cruising to and from Australia, she was permanently berthed in Shekou as a hotel and entertainment complex. The water which originally surrounded her

has been reclaimed to allow construction of the driving range and other tourist attractions. Today the

coastline has been moved several hundred meters, leaving her completely landlocked. She currently houses a hotel named the Cruise Inn. If you are visiting Shekou, this is a fun place to stay in the heart of the action.

The reason so many foreigners choose to live in Shekou is it has a real sense of community. It is a friendly place with excellent schools and a safe, family-oriented environment. Shekou Women's International Club welcomes expat ladies to join in their many social and sporting activities (see "The Shekou Women's International Club (SWIC)" on page 117). The Snake Pit, a local watering hole and social club welcomes all, providing you are willing to drink a shot of real snake wine. I can attest that nothing tastes nastier! Around the lively area of Seaworld, there are dozens of international restaurants that cater to both visitors and locals.

There are many nice residential neighborhoods in Shekou that cater to the needs of the expats. The

original, Jingshan Villa, is a gated community on a hillside. Regular church services are held there as well. Other upscale options include Mont Orchid Riverlet, Coastal Rose Garden, Seaview Terraces, and Peninsula to name of few of the bigger ones. All have a wide variety of apartments and villas that serve the international community.

Shopping in Shekou is easy. Park'n Shop, a large grocery store, carries a wide variety of international foods. In addition there are many other smaller shops that sell imported items. Wal-Mart has a great selection of fruit and vegetables as well all the daily necessities. **Want to live like a local?** Check out the Shekou Wet Market in Old Shekou for a fascinating glimpse of everyday life in China.

This is one place where English is not spoken but a smile and a calculator is really all you need (see "The Shekou Wet Market" on page 249 for details and names of Chinese vegetables and common fruits). For the carnivore, the Butcher Shop next to McCawley's has good quality fresh imported meats.

Old Shekou is the only place that feels like you are in China. It is lots of fun to wander around where the locals shop. You can find tailors, hardware stores, electronics, DVD vendors, shoes and trendy inexpensive fashions (see "Shopping in Old Shekou" on page 244).

Need to get physical? Stop by the

Snake Pit on a Saturday afternoon and join the Shekou Hash House Harriers for their weekly fun run. Aside from the Hash, there are plenty of options for sports in Shekou. There is a Bowling Alley in the Ming Wah Hotel (see "Shekou's Hotels" on page 252). Regular Golf outings for ladies and men are scheduled, plus there is a driving range just behind Seaworld. Badminton is very popular. Cricket matches usually happen on Sunday. Touch Rugby is played every Wednesday. Yoga and Tai Chi round out the options. If you prefer your sports on the big screen, several local pubs in the Seaworld area have a lively crowd for major events. Try McCawley's Irish Pub and the X-Ta-Sea Sports Bar

& Restaurant, inside the Minghua Ship.

Culture is more your thing? The SWIC and the SACS run various activities throughout the year. If you want to spread a little love, a group of ladies regularly visit local orphanages. The French, German, Brazilian, Japanese and Korean communities are also well organized with their own activities.

■ Mary Ann MacCartney

For more information about the above-mentioned places visit WikiShenzhen.com

From Expats to Expats
Shekou from A to Z

ATM

There are many ATMs where you can get cash, and most are bilingual. In Seaworld they are located at China Bank and China Construction Bank. In Coastal Rose Garden Phase II, they are located at China Merchant Bank and inside the 7/11.

ACCOMMODATIONS

There are a lot of high quality apartments for rent in Shekou. Housing complexes such as Jingshan Villa, Coastal Rose Garden, Mont Orchid Riverlet, Sea Taste Garden and Peninsula provide secure, modern accommodations with many of the amenities one would expect in a Western complex. Most are fully furnished.

It is a good idea to ask around to find the real market price. Be careful of inclusions and contract conditions when negotiating.

Most agencies have window displays advertising prices. Be aware that the picture on the advert could be an example. The furnishings in the apartments vary in style and quality, so make sure you keep looking until you find the right fit for you and your family. Most contracts are solely in Chinese, so it is a good idea to get it translated for you.

The normal rental period is a minimum of one year. However, you can sometimes get a six month contract. If this is a must for you, it will limit the number of apartments available as landlords would prefer not to lease for six months.

The standard process is to pay two months deposit, one month rent, and a half month's rent for the agent's commission. The agent also receives half a month rent from the landlord as commission. It helps to pay this money as soon as possible, preferably in cash. International bank transfers can be difficult and time consuming.

Any extra inclusions or work required should be noted in the contract and signed off by both parties. After the deal is done, it is too late. Upon moving in, we advise that you get the management office to change the lock on any entry door. The landlord may have given keys to any number of agents to show the property so dozens of people could have access to your apartment.

In addition to monthly rent, you will be required to pay management fees. These cover items such as garbage removal, security, shared area utilities and gardening. Typically this charge is about 2.5 – 3.0RMB per square meter of your apartment. Other costs are for electricity, water, gas, internet and cable TV. The landlord will provide you with a bank account (probably a bank book too) for you to deposit the rent (in cash) and maybe a second bank book for the utilities.

You must put money in the utilities bank account by a specific day (varies for each complex) of each month as they are auto-deducted shortly thereafter. You will receive an invoice/statement in your letter box each month of all of these so you know how much to deposit. Gas, internet and cable TV are each invoiced separately but management fee, electricity and water are on a single itemized invoice.

The average cost to a family for all the extras is around 1,500RMB per month, for a single it is 600-800RMB.

ADSL INTERNET SERVICE

ADSL is slower than cable. It gets quite slow at peak times of the day (down to 2.5Kb/sec. at times) Cost is 1440RMB per year.

ANTIQUES

▶ Lao Mu - (老木)

Judy Liang of Laomu in Shekou has been collecting and selling Chinese antique furniture, stone carvings and statues since 1995. These items, popular with expats especially, come from every province in China. Also, she specializes in designing and making Western and Chinese furniture from reclaimed antique wood, according to customer specifications. All items are handmade in small workshops. Additionally, she provides interior and exterior design services including the use of exterior antique building materials. Repair and renovation services are also available. When the time comes to move, she can help with customs clearance and worldwide shipping.

✉ Rm4 GF Crystal Garden Building TaiZi Rd., Shekou
蛇口太子路碧涛商业中心底层商铺4号

℡ 2668 1871

🖱 www.laomu-china.com, judyliang11@hotmail.com

⧗ 10am - 7pm

ARTS

See chapter "Arts in Shenzhen" for details.

ASSOCIATIONS

▶ German Association: see "German association" on page 222

▶ L'AFESS (Association Francophone pour l'Enseignement a Shekou, Shenzhen); see "French association" on page 221.

▶ SACS (Shenzhen Asian Culture Society): "SACS" on page 107.

▶ SWIC (Shekou Women's International Club); see "SWIC" on page 117.

▶ See "The Shekou Sports & Social Club (The Snake Pit)" for details.

▶ Sports Associations: see "Sports Associations in Shenzhen" on page 210 for details.

Baby clothes

▶ See "Western Foreign Wholesale Fashion City" on page 247 for details.

▶ Decathlon offers clothes and shoes at good quality and affordable prices.

▶ Wal-Mart (limited selection).

Baby food

▶ Carrefour in Coastal City.

▶ Hong Kong.

Bagels

▶ Jonathan's N.Y. Bagels

Bagels are one of the most popular breakfast & sandwich breads in the USA & Canada. They are boiled before baking for a moist chewy inside & crisp outside, and can be delivered anywhere in Shenzhen.

✉ Sam's Bakery, 101B Yongjing Xuan, Gongye 7 Rd, Shekou
蛇口工业七号101B商铺

☏ 2681-0123 (Chinese, 中文)
139-2341-2188 (English)

$ 8RMB/bagel, 4 per bag, 120g each
Delivered daily, baked fresh every day

Banking (general information)

Banks operate seven days a week, and it is easy to open a bank account. Take your passport and an initial deposit (100RMB will do), and they will issue you a card and often a bank book very quickly. Internet banking is in its infancy here and is mostly in Chinese.

It is relatively easy to get money into China via bank transfer, although things can get held up if the account name doesn't quite match up with the name on the overseas transfer, i.e. Smith John C could cause a problem if the account is John Charles Smith. If a transfer takes too long to hit your account, you need to go to the bank with all the transfer details plus your passport and a Chinese speaker.

It is difficult to get money out of China. China Post has a Western Union facility but the charges can be quite high. Many people change their RMB to another currency (USD, Euro, GBP) and take it to a Hong Kong bank account. HSBC has a good internet banking system, but be aware there may be extra fees.

Banks in Shekou

▶ China Construction Bank, across from McCawley's.

▶ ICBC, next to the new Starbucks.

▶ China Merchant Bank, Time Square building, 1st floor.

Bars

See the companion book "Shopping in Shenzhen for details.

Bay Bridge

See "Shenzhen Bay Bridge" on page 233.

Big sizes

▶ For big size shoes, see "Shoes (big size)" on page 234.

▶ For big size clothes, see "Fashion (big size)" on page 217.

BOOKS

▶ Nanshan Book City

Nanshan Book City has a small English book section for adults, and a English book section for children located on the 5th floor.

▶ English Bookstore

Large selection of original English children's books for readers 2 to 18, and even some French, German and Spanish books. They stock mainly DK, Scholastic Houghton Mifflin, Puffin and Walker books. Many prices are half of or less than the printed prices. They can organize book fairs for international schools.

✉ Located at Linda Lee Interactive Chinese school. Crystal Garden, Bihua #12, Taizi Road, Shekou. 蛇口太子路碧涛苑别墅碧桦路12号

✆ 2686 2031

Chinese@lindalee.com.cn

⧖ Monday to Sunday 9am to 5pm

BOWLING

▶ Located in the Ming Hua Hotel, at the basement.

BREAD

▶ Croissant de France, at Seaworld Square.

BUSSES

Busses are very cheap, and if you have the time, they are a safe way to travel. Shekou to Luohu takes about 75 mins and costs 5-8RMB. Busses are regular and reasonably clean. Mostly there is a ticket collector that will ask where you are going. The fare is based on your destination. It really helps if you can pronounce the area you are going to. Most busses are air conditioned, although the double decker busses are not and are consequently cheaper, but a lot more crowded. Be very careful of pickpockets and thieves on the busses. When exiting the bus, try to be ready prior to its stopping, as new passengers enter the doors without waiting for others to exit. This behavior applies for trains and elevators too.

Cashmere

▶ SCM Merry Carrier Fashion - (华丝企业)

Major products include: Silk & Cashmere Sweaters, Scarf, Hat, Quilt, Pillow Cover, etc. The raw material cashmere is from Inner Mongolia and the silk from Zhejiang Province.

✉ A small shop is located in Coastal Rose Garden Phase II.
　A bigger shop is located in 37, Yanshan Rd., Old Shekou, 蛇口演山路37号
✆ 2682-6840
🖰 www.szcsm.com
⧗ Mon-Sat: 8h30am - 5h30pm

Cheese

Butcher shop, Silver Palate, USA store, Mix Up, and Carrefour.

Childcare

See WikiShenzhen.com for details.

Chinese language

See "Chinese Schools in Shekou and Nanshan" on page 151 for details.

Churches

▶ Catholic Club (in English)

Foreigners only.

✉ SIS International School gym, Jingshan, Shekou, Nanshan District
⧗ Twice a month, 1st 3rd 5th Sunday, 3h30pm

▶ Catholic Church in Nanshan (in Mandarin)

✉ St. Paul Church, 210 Chaoyang Street, Nantou, Nanshan District

✆ 8661-1334
⌛ Every Sunday at 9am and 8pm

▶ Catholic Church in Futian (in Mandarin)

✉ St. Anthony, Jialin Road next to Sam's Club, Futian District
✆ 8371-9372
⌛ Every Saturday at 8pm and Sunday at 9am

▶ Korean Church

There are 15 Korean language churches in Shenzhen below are the principle ones.

✉ Shenzhen Korean Church, Futian District
✆ 8314-5676

✉ Shenzhen Joongang Church, Futian District
✆ 2675-4585, Danica 137-2885 4492

✉ Shenzhen Love Korean Church
✆ 2645-6625, Judy 150-1261 4610

▶ Protestant Church

✉ SIS International School gym, Jingshan, Shekou, Nanshan District
⌛ Every Sunday 10 am they have Sunday school and nursery services

▶ Hispanic Group

✉ Futian St. Anthony, Jialin Road next to Sam's Club
✆ Sra. Marisol Tabazques de Zapata, tabazques@yahoo.com, 139 0244-1524
    Sra. Ivonne Rueda Jong, iprueda@hotmail.com, 138-2872-7425
🖱 www.elperiodista.net (This website listed is not specific of the group but lists the
    monthly activities and other relevant articles for the Hispanic community).
    Activities: day trips, dancing, sport, eating out, etc.

▶ Jewish Synagogue

✉ Holiday Bay Overseas Chinese Town Building 1, 2D, Nanshan District
✆ Rabbi Sholem & Henny Chazan, 135-5689-2441
🖱 www.chabadshenzhen.org

Clinics

See "Recommended Hospitals in Shenzhen" on page 80 for details.

Coffee

▶ Two Starbucks, one is located at Seaworld Square, the one is located on the way to Mama's.

Copies

Two in Seaworld, one is next to 7/11 (Kodak), the other is next to Honlux hotel.

Dentists

See "Recommended Dentists in Shenzhen" on page 83 details.

Electricity

Costs are higher in China than many Western countries. For urban residents the price is 0.78RMB per KWH. For information on voltage, see "Voltage" on page 242.

Electronics

▶ Nanshan Computer Market

These markets are where local people shop for computer equipment. Things purchased here appear to be genuine, considering the packaging, pricing, and quality. There are many stores under one roof, so it is easy to shop around for the best deal. Little English is spoken there but enough to get what you want. Locals say that "Saige" offers better quality products than "Xibu Dianzi", but prices tend to be lower at "Xibu Dianzi" than at "Saige".

▪ Saige - (南山塞格)

✉ Saige, Nanshan Dianzi Guangchang, Nanshan District
南山区南山电子广场

✆ 8612-9172

▪ Xibu Dianzi - (西部电子)

✉ Xibu Dianzi Time Square, Xuefu Rd., Nanshan District
南山区学府路西部电子时代广场

✆ 8113-7746

ENGLISH LANGUAGE FOR CHILDREN

QSI International Schools offer English tutoring for kids, see "Children's Education" on page 120 for details.

EYE GLASSES

▶ Shenzhen Doctor Glasses - (博士眼镜)

They sell many name brand spectacles (Silhouette, Gucci, Tag Heuer, etc.) and offer excellent service and quality product. Glasses are much cheaper than similar quality that is available overseas. It is possible to place special or custom orders. Judy, the optometrist, is Singaporean, and her English is very good.

✉ 310 Shuibu Xing Street, New Shekou Walking Street, Shekou
蛇口水步行街310号

✆ 2669-5572

🖱 www.doctorglasses.com.cn

⧗ Mon-Sun 10am - 9pm

FASHION (BIG SIZE)

The Fallow Ground boutique is located in the Old Shekou, and is specialized in extra large sizes.

✉ 247 Shuibu Xing Street, New Shekou Walking Street, Shekou
蛇口水步行街247号

✆ 138-2430-1292

⧗ 10am - 10pm

FASHION FOR WOMEN

▶ Women's Clothing and Shoes Mall

This popular mall has lots of small shops with a great selection of fashionable Western style clothes and shoes. Located close to Wal-mart in

Shekou, this is a very entertaining place to shop. They carry sizes up to US12-UK16 for clothing, and size 39(US8) for shoes. There are no dressing rooms. If you wear a tank top and a big skirt, you can try on most things without getting undressed. Some shops will hold up a sheet.

✉ NanYou 1st Industrial Zone, NeiHuan Rd, Shekou (next to Wal-mart)
南山区蛇口内环路南油第一工业区
Coming from Shekou on Nanhai Blvd., turn left at Wal-mart, staying to the right of the construction. Once you have made the turn, Little Sheep Hot Pot restaurant will be on you right. Go a little further, until you see UBC Coffee, then Mrs & Mr Heden. The next doorway is the one to enter the mall. There is no English sign over this door, only phone numbers. Enter and go up the stairs. There are also some shops downstairs. Don't forget to bargain. There are lots of shops, so you will need time to see it all.

▶ SHCER - (茜施尔)

SHCER sells underwear small & large sizes.

✉ 189 ShuiBu Xing Street, Shekou
蛇口水步行街189号
☎ 2667 5147
🖱 www.shcer.com
⏳ 10am - 10h30pm

▶ Wan Ji Da Fashion - (万吉达服装精品)

They sell Laura Ashley, Ann Taylor, and Esprit in big and small sizes at very attractive prices. Popular among Westerners.

✉ Building 14, 5th Floor, Nanyou Zhongxing Industrial City (next to Wal-mart)
南山区蛇口南油中兴工业城 14栋5楼
☎ 2606 4573
⏳ Mon-Fri: 8am-6pm, Sat: 8h30am-5pm

▶ Ming Wei Fashion - (明媚国际品时装批发)

Ming Wei offers a good range of Western dresses.

✉ Youji Center Mall, 2nd floor, stall 216A (next to Wal-mart)
南山区南油世纪广场二楼216A铺
☎ 8189 9080, 137 1399 8986
🖱 www.mmgj668.com/engdigi/ (English)

⧗ 10am - 6h30pm

▶ Old & New Walking Streets
See "Shopping in Old Shekou" on page 244 for details.

▶ Western Foreign Wholesale Fashion City
See "Western Foreign Wholesale Fashion City" on page 247 for details.

Ferry

The ferry is a great way to get to Hong Kong or Kowloon (55 mins) or the HK airport (30 mins). You can also go to Zhuhai and Macau in about 80 mins. Kowloon ferry frequencies have dropped dramatically since the Shenzhen Bay Bridge has opened and is now down to only one or two per day. See www.xunlongferry.com for their timetable, or www.WikiShenzhen.com for a clickable map.

The cost to HK is 110RMB, and the fare varies from HK to Shekou as it increases to 125RMB in the evening. A round trip ticket costs 180RMB, but you must know the exact time you will return. The last ferry from HK (Central) is at 8h30pm. If you miss this, then you need to take the MTR then KCR to get to either Luohu (before midnight) or Huanguang (24h) border, then take a taxi or bus from there. It can be a long and exhausting journey.

Ferry to Hong Kong International Airport

The ferry service to the airport is one of the best things around. If you fly with Cathay Pacific (and some others now), you can check your luggage in at the ferry terminal and collect it at your final destination point. For other airlines you will need to check it in when you get to the ferry terminal at HK airport. This is where you check into the flight and get your boarding pass. Many passengers are also entitled to claim a refund of their departure tax, and you will be given a small three part voucher to do so. There is a tax claim desk on the left hand side at the rear of the departure lounge. The refund is about 110HKD.

We suggest that you buy your ferry ticket at least one day prior to your flight. This gives you advance warning of any issues that may occur. This is especially useful around holidays. It does get booked out occasionally, but also some airlines have restrictions on which ferry you can catch for their flights. Most airlines require you to catch a ferry at least three hours prior to their departure time.

If you get to the ferry terminal and get confronted with this situation, you need to get a taxi to the Shenzhen Bay bridge border crossing and then get a bus to the airport.

Ferry from International Airport to Hong Kong

To catch the ferry from HKIA to Shekou, you need to buy a SkyPier ticket at the ferry counter and provide them with your luggage tag one hour before the ferry departs. See www.hongkongairport.com/eng/tbu/skypier_to.htm. The staff will then go and retrieve your luggage from the carousel, and it will be taken to the ferry for you. It is always reassuring to be at the bus departure area (Gate 10) a bit early and actually see they have your luggage (though we have not heard of and missing baggage on this service).

<u>Do not go through Immigration Control</u>, or else you will not be able to get to the ferry as the ticket counter is behind security in the transfer zone. The staff will tell you how to get down to Gate 10. You are subject to another baggage check here, and the 100ml fluid restriction applies to all hand carry items, even duty free.

Ferry to Macau & Zhuhai

Traveling between the Shekou Ferry Terminal and Zhuhai (60mins) or Macau (80mins) is very convenient. See www.xunlongferry.com for their timetable, or www.WikiShenzhen.com for a clickable map.

Film festival

SACS runs 2 film festivals a year; see "SACS" on page 108.

Flowers

▶ Flower street in Old Shekou

This shop does a lovely job at reasonable prices and has a lot of business with the expat community in Shenzhen. Very little English is spoken, so have your housemaid or Mandarin speaking friend call to order. If not, stop there yourself and make the order. Look through books for ideas or point out what you want. Delivery is free in Shekou and Nanshan. Here are some sample prices: bouquets (generous proportions): small 6-80RMB, medium 100RMB, and large 200RMB. Single flowers (can be had alone or put into a bouquet): roses 2-4RMB, orchids 3-5RMB, Lily 13-15RMB, carnation 1RMB, more available seasonably.

- ✉ Gonye No 7 Rd., shop #105
  蛇口工业七路105号
- ✆ 2686-8102
- ⧗ 7h30am - 10h30pm

French association

The "*Association Francophone pour l'Enseignement a Shekou, Shenzhen*" (L'AFESS) was organized by parents for children. The association organizes activities to give them a chance to mix with other French children.

- ✆ Contact Charlotte Rouquet
- ⌂ afess.canalblog.com
- @ crouquet@hotmail.com

Gas

Gas is mostly used for cooking and hot water heating. It is relatively cheap, and most complexes are supplied via gas lines.

Gas delivery

Mr. Su delivers canisters of gas to your home for kitchen or gas grill. Mr. Su can also provide a converter kit to enable use of a gas grill. No English is spoken.

- ✆ 2682-3817, 132-4664-1189, Mr. Su
- ⧗ 8am - 10pm

German association

The German association gathers twice a month. German rounds "Stammtisch" for German speaking people are held in the two German Microbreweries.

- ✉ Loewenburg Restaurant, Shekou, Taizi Road, Cruise Inn, 6th floor, Shekou or Galleon Bar and Restaurant, Intercontinental Shenzhen Hotel, Futian
- ✆ Christian Liepke, 134-1093-5385
- ⌂ www.etreff.cn
- @ clbeermaster@yahoo.de
- ⧗ 8pm first (Shekou) and third Tuesday of the month (Nanshan)

Golf

There is one golf course in Shekou, the Grassland Club, next to the boat (see "Golf equipment" below for details). Also, there are several good courses within 30 – 45 mins drive of Shekou. The largest golf course in the world is the Mission Hills Club in Shenzhen about one hour away. The cost of golf is quite high in China. An average round costs US$80-120 plus caddy fees.

▶ Golf @ Grassland Club - (绿草地值乐部)

Golf pros are available to give lessons. Driving range costs: mat charge: 10RMB, 1 bucket of 45 balls, 25RMB. Little English is spoken at reception, but there are bilingual brochures in the reception area to help you communicate. Rental golf clubs are available.

- ✉ Seaworld Square, next to the boat, Shekou
  蛇口太子广场
- ✆ 2685-5666
- ⧗ 8am - 11pm

Golf equipment

This shop offers everything you need for golf.

✉ Taizi Rd., next to Yinghui building, between the QSI school (yellow building) and Post Office, Shekou
蛇口太子广场
☎ 2685-0169, 138-2877-0919
@ shekou_golf@hotmail.com

Grocery

There are a lot of good quality inexpensive fruit and vegetables available at markets and local supermarkets. If you go to the market, be prepared to bargain. Western foods are considerably more expensive than at home (as you would expect) and are available at Park'n Shop, Silver Palate, and the USA Shop (all near QSI school) and also at Mix Up, two City Shops, and a new Silver Palate in Coastal Rose Garden Phase II. Most of these stores have a range of foreign foods, frozen meat, cheese, wines and tinned/packaged groceries available.

▶ Silver Palate

Silver Palate sells meats, poultry and seafood. They carry mostly Western products. The staff is English speaking, and they offer free delivery in Shekou. There are 2 locations.

✉ Shop1: Taizi Rd. Bitao Center, I:太子路133号海滨商业中心3号
Shop2: Coastal Rose Garden Phase II, II:玫瑰园一期
☎ 2668-2657
⏳ 10am - 11pm

▶ USA Charlies & Co

Import grocery store. Large choice of Western products i n c l u d i n g wines at good price, some cheeses, Western flour etc.

✉ Taizi Rd. Bitao Center, Shekou
蛇口太子路碧涛中心一楼

ℂ 2667 2701
⏳ 9am - 9pm
🖱 www.usacoshop.com (Chinese)

▶ Park'n Shop

Park'n Shop sells both Chinese and Western products including fresh milk, yogurts, some fresh vegetables and fruits. They also have a good selection of wines.

✉ Taizi Rd. BiTao Center, Shekou
蛇口太子路碧涛中心一楼
ℂ 2669-1940
⏳ 9am - 9pm

Hair removal

Peng'Ai hospital is specialized in cosmetic surgeries and other related services. The office in located on the second floor. Take a Mandarin speaker with you for a consultation.

✉ Peng'Ai Hospital, 1122, Nanshan Bld., Nanshan District
鹏爱医疗美容医院，南山区南山大道1122号
ℂ 2665-0533, 2665-0522, Dr. Lu
⏳ 9am - 9pm
🖱 www.payy.cn (Chinese)

Health

See "Health in Shenzhen" on page 77 for details.

Hiking

There are 3 possibilities, one is to join the Hash House Harriers (see "Shekou Hash House Harriers" on page 151 for details), the second is to hike with SWIC members (expat women only, see "SWIC" on page 117), and the third one is to hike Nanshan mountain. There are 5 ways to access the mountain, the most popular is the trailhead located past the driveway to Fraser and the Ming Hua Hotel.

Hong Kong (transportation)

See "Shenzhen Bay Bridge" on page 233.

Hospitals

See "Recommended Hospitals in Shenzhen" on page 80 for details.

Hotels

Shekou has a range of hotels suitable for foreigners. The Nan Hai Hotel is a long serving five-star property close by the ferry terminal. Honlux Group has two properties in the SeaWorld area, one is the Cruise Inn on the Ming Hua ship (landlocked now), the other is the Honlux Hotel on Taizi Road opposite McDonalds. Fraser Place provides serviced apartments on a short or long term basis. Prices are on the high side. The Fuzon Hotel, behind Luna Bar, is budget priced with nice rooms and a viable alternative. See "Shekou's Hotels" on page 252 for details. See also the companion book "Shopping in Shenzhen", available at www. WikiShenzhen.com.

Ice delivery

All ice is made from purified water. Prices: 15RMB for a 10 kg of ice, 30RMB for a large block of ice (2' x 3'), 20RMB for 1lb. of dry ice. The ice provider, Mr. Sun, does not speak English. Mr. Sun will deliver the same or next day.

- ℂ   137-1413-9626, 137-1389-2078
- ⌛   10am - 9h30pm

Internet cable

Cable provides reasonable speed and reliable uptime but don't expect broadband speed as you may have in your home country. Cost is 1,440RMB per year. See www.sktv.com.cn, with this you also get a basic cable TV package. For Internet via ADSL, see "ADSL internet service" on page 210.

MAID

See "Helping Hands in China: Ayis (阿姨)" on page 101.

MARKET

See "The Shekou Wet Market" on page 249.

MASSAGE

▶ MeDo Catenation - (美都 足浴城)

MeDo Catenation is recommended by many expatriates for its very reasonable prices. It offers various types of body massage, foot massage, acupuncture, facials, etc. Traditional Chinese Medicine and acupuncture are also available. Little English is spoken by the helpful staff. Request for a VIP room for an extra 5RMB.

✉ 175 ShangLe Street, Old Shekou Walking Street, Shekou
蛇口商乐街175号
✆ 2683-3377
⌂ www.sz-md.com
⧖ 11am - 2am

▶ Eastern Athens Business Hotel (东方雅典商务酒店)

Located on the first floor of the Eastern Athens Business Hotel are 2 vast areas for massage, facials, Chinese traditional treatment, foot massage, and more. The massage rooms are very clean and peaceful. The staff is well trained. Prices are reasonable.

✉ Chuangye East Rd., Nanshan District
南山区创业东路
✆ 8619-5933

www.dfyd-hotel.com

24h, if you come after 10pm and you spend more than 200RMB, you can spend the night there.

▶ Sakura foot massage - (樱花苑)

Sakura is a favorite among expats for foot massage. It is located opposite Seagull restaurant, near China Construction Bank, Seaworld.

✉ 18, Taizi Rd., 2F, building D, Haijing Square, Seaworld, Shekou
蛇口海上世界海景广场二楼D座

✆ 2682-0010

MEAT

▶ Premium Meats

Meats are high quality. Staff are English speaking and helpful. English is spoken. Delivery is available.

✉ Coastal Rose Garden Phase II, Shekou
南山区蛇口南海玫瑰园二期31号街铺

✆ 2667-9795

⏳ 10am - 8pm

▶ The Butcher Shop

The Butcher Shop serves homemade English sausages, bacon, steaks, a huge range of different meats as well as deli items such as fine cheeses. All meats are chilled and not frozen, to ensure the products are as fresh as possible. The Butcher Shop imports meats from Australia, New Zealand and further afield from the USA and Brazil. Free home delivery service.

✉ Honlux Hotel, First floor, Shekou (Next to McCawleys' Irish Bar & Restaurant)
南山区蛇口鸿图公寓一楼侧

✆ 2685-8295 - email service: shekou.butcher@hotmail.com

⏳ 9am - 8pm

ⓘ Quality meats are also available at Carrefour, Metro, and Jusco with slightly lower prices. Metro carries the least expensive meat.

MEDICAL INSURANCE

Many countries' healthcare coverage does not extend to overseas postings. It is necessary to purchase insurance to get appropriate protection for any medical services required, especially hospitalization in Hong Kong which can become expensive. The policy should provide for outpatient, in-patient care and medical evacuation. Dental and optical services are normally an optional extra. You may be able to get treated in your own country under some policies. HSBC Hong Kong offers a "China Medical Card", with a MultiTrip policy. See www.WikiShenzhen.com for details.

MEDICATION

See "Pharmacy" on page 231.

METRO

See Transportation.

MOBILE PHONE

There are over 300 million mobile phone users in China. Many of them are using prepaid top up cards sold at small convenience stores and phone shops. You will not get all the added features you may be used to i.e. voicemail, call forwarding, incoming call alert, etc. There is a China Telecom store about 200m east of McDonalds, and they normally have one English speaking person there. If you want to get a service that includes roaming you will need to take your passport, but be advised the roaming charges will be expensive. It can be cheaper to purchase a SIM card at your destination.

MONEY

Cash is king in China. Credit cards are still in their infancy in many businesses as local debit cards rule. Do not automatically expect your credit card to work even if your home bank assures you it will. Also see "ATM" on page 208.

MONEY CHANGERS

There are several money changers in Shekou, ask a fellow foreigner to guide you. Their rates are nearly always better than the banks.

MOVIE THEATER

There is a movie theater at Garden City Center, next to Wall-Mart.

MUSICAL INSTRUMENTS

This shop is located in Nanshan, close to the University of Shenzhen. Many instruments are available for rental; pianos can be rented for 5RMB/day, electric pianos for 3RMB/day. Delivery charge for piano is 750RMB, which includes tuning. Little English is spoken there.

✉ Meiyin Qinxing, 46, Yukang Building, Xuefu Rd., Nanshan District
美音琴行—南山区学府路愉康大厦一楼46号
☎ 2656-5274
⏳ 9am - 10pm

There is also a musical instrument shop located on Gongyuan Road (公园路), opposite QSI High Scool, close to Wal-Mart.

ORGANIC FOOD

There is an organic section in Wal-mart and Ole.

ORPHANAGE

There is a group of volunteers that visit local orphanages Tuesday and Wednesday afternoons and Friday mornings. The children are all ages, sizes and capabilities. There is a government registration requirement that takes a few weeks. The children really appreciate the cuddles. For more information, contact shentoddler@hotmail.com.

Paintball

▶ Paintball at Nan Hai Hotel - (野战乐园)

Paintball is a war game played with several guns which shoot paint pellets instead of bullets. You can play at the Nanhai Hotel any day from 9am to 9pm. The cost is 140RMB per person, which includes 100 paint pellets, the gun, special protective clothing and a helmet. You can buy an additional 100 paint pellets for 60RMB. To get to the paintball area, enter the hotel and go outside, near the pool. If you ask at the concierge desk, they will also be happy to direct you. Ask for the War Games (野战乐园, Yezhan Leyuan.)

✉ Located at the Nanhai Hotel, 1, Gong Ye 1st Rd. Nanhai Blvd, Shekou
   南海大道工业一路南海酒店
℗ Contact the swimming pool attendant at 2669 2888 ext. 378 or 516
⧗ 9am - 9pm (max 3 hours), Mon - Sun

Photos for passport/visa

There are 2 small boutiques in Seaworld. Kodak is next to 7/11, the other is next to the Honlux hotel.

Pets

Pets are welcome in China but you need to ensure that you have your pet immunized and bring all the immunization certificates with you upon entry to the country. It is best if the immunization is done between one and six months prior to arrival.

Judy Liang helps expats find a new pet by rescuing dogs that need a good home. She also provides referral services. Judy's dogs are healthy, vaccinated and free of charge. See "Judy's Pet Services" on page 115 for details.

For information on vets, see "Vets" on page 241.

Pharmacy

There are many pharmacies/drug stores in China providing Western style medications. Often these do not require prescriptions, but you do need to know what you want as not much English is spoken. Many of the pharmacy chains have a drug "dictionary" so if you have the name of the drug they can look up the Chinese equivalent. It is wise to get assistance from a Chinese friend as it can be confusing.

Recommended pharmacy: "Medicine Shoppe" in 47, Coastal Rose Garden Phase II, between 7/11 and the SIS International school. Ask for Salley, 2683-0657. Free delivery.

Phone (land line)

Land lines are relatively cheap to enable and use. The monthly rental is about 35RMB and calls at 0.11RMB per minute are also quite cheap. If you want to use it for international calls, buy a calling card. It is possible to purchase a 100RMB card for 35RMB. International rates are high. For mobile phone, see "Mobile phone" on page 228.

Police

The police station is located in Shui Wantou and they are helpful and respectful of foreigners. You will definitely need a Chinese interpreter with you.

Post Office

There are 2 conveniently located post offices; one between the Old and New Shekou Walking Street, behind the green market, the other one is next to the QSI International school (the yellow building on Taizi Road).

Postcards

You can find postcards at the post office located next to the QSI

International school (the yellow building on Taizi Road).

Real estate

See "Accommodations" on page 208.

Restaurants

Shekou has a good range of Western restaurants including Thai, Italian, French, Indian, Mexican and Australian cuisines. Most of these are within the main square at Shekou SeaWorld. All take credit cards and have some English speaking staff. Tipping is not expected (or mandatory as in some countries) but is gratefully received. Many restaurants have a 10-15% service charge, which does not necessarily go to the serving staff.

SACS

The Shenzhen Asian Culture Society (SACS) is a non-profit organization working to strengthen relationships, promote understanding and provide cultural enrichment for the Shenzhen community. SACS welcomes both local and expatriate members. See www.shenzhenacs.com.

Schools

See "Children's Education" on page 120 for details.

Security

Most of the popular housing complexes have 24/7 security guards, and the more modern have keycard access to the main gates, car park and individual blocks. Some have a concierge per block for additional security. There are not that many personal security issues around Shekou, but like any major urban area it is not wise to walk alone in deserted areas late at night. Always keep handbags, purses and mobile phones in your grasp.

Serviced apartments

Three options are available in Shekou, all located at the base of the Nanshan Mountain, next to Seaworld.

▶ The Ming Hua Hotel offers serviced apartment for reasonable prices.

▶ The Maillen Club offers 8 clean and reasonably priced serviced apartments

▶ The Fraser Place offers clean and comfortable serviced apartments with prices on the high side.

Shenzhen Bay Bridge

The bridge opened July 1, 2007 and provides an inexpensive and effective means to get to and from Hong Kong.

Shenzhen Bay Bridge to Hong Kong

From Shekou, take a taxi to the bridge "Shenzhen wan" is what you tell the driver. The cost is roughly 30RMB. There are 3 alternatives for Hong Kong transport; one is to use public transport, another is to buy a bus ticket, or take a taxi.

Bus tickets can be purchased at the blue ticket booths located in front of the immigration building. For 40HKD you can take a bus directly to Kowloon, Kowloon Tong and Prince Edward Metro Stations. They will give you a sticker and a ticket and tell you which bay the bus leaves from. The busses are located on the Hong Kong side of immigration and to the right.

Public transport is very convenient. Once through immigration walk straight by the moving sidewalks. The B2 bus at the end of the walkway goes to Tin Shui Wai Metro Station and costs 8.5HKD. From there the Metro is a cheap and easy way to get around Hong Kong. You can use the Octopus card for the bus and the Metro.

Shenzhen Bay Bridge from Hong Kong

To return you can catch a bus in Jordan at Chinalink Travel at 11 Pak Hoi St. The street runs off Nathan Road and has a Starbucks on that corner. Chinalink is opposite the Eaton Hotel, look for the pink ladies, or you can take the Metro back to Tin Shui Wai and catch a B2 bus to the bridge.

Shenzhen Bay Bridge to HKIA

The shared van service from Shenzhen Bay to the Hong Kong Airport is very convenient. Tickets can be purchased at the blue ticket booth in front of the immigration building. There is a sign that says Hong Kong International Airport on the right end of the bank of booths. The cost is 140-150RMB per person each way. It is also helpful that they drive through immigration.

Shenzhen Bay Bridge from HKIA

From the Hong Kong Airport to Shenzhen Bay, the ticket counters can be found in Terminal 2. Follow the signs that say "Coach to Mainland." It is very well marked.

Shoes (big size)

There is a shop under the boat with a good selection of shoes. Other shoe shops can also be found next to the boat, by the statue.

Shopping (general information)

There are small shopping areas around Sea World and a larger area known as "Walking Street" in the Shui Wan Tou area. Bargain hard and be prepared to walk away; if they don't chase you then you have got their best price. Never buy at the first shop you go to.

Wal-Mart at Garden City, Carrefour, and Jusco at Coastal City, are about 10mins by bus or taxi from Shekou (Carrefour has a free shuttle bus.) The formats are the same but the products are different as they primarily cater to Chinese customers. In the same area as Garden City and Coastal City, there are other specialty stores plus Starbucks and Papa Johns.

One of the best sources of information is our companion book Shopping in Shenzhen, which is available from many hotels and restaurants for 98RMB. See www.WikiShenzhen.com.

Silk

▶ China Silk - (上海名扬服饰)

China Silk factories make clothing for higher-end brands for Europe and the USA. Samples up to size US16 are for sale at very reasonable prices. You must have a Chinese person with you in order to enter. You must sign in at the entrance, and you will be given a tag. There are 4 selling areas in this building. Two on floor 3 and two on floor 4. Take the elevator to the third floor; Turn left into the sewing room. Go into the first office on your left and say you want to look at the clothes. You will be shown to the next door down. Ask the office for the directions to the other three selling areas. Show receipt and return tag at the exit doorway.

✉ Huaijing Industrial Building Block 4 Xinghua Rd, Shekou industrial Zone
To find China Silk, start from McDonald's and walk toward Old Shekou for two blocks. The entrance has a large glass window labeled "China Silk". It's on the same side of the street as the new Starbucks.
蛇口兴华路华建工业大厦第四栋
🖱 www.chinasilk-ltd.com

Sports

▶ The Shekou Touch Rugby
▶ The Shekou Sports and Social Club
▶ Shekou Hash House Harriers

▶ Shekou Soccer 8's
▶ Shenzhen Commonwealth Cricket Club
▶ Shekou Youth Sport Program (SYSP)
See "Sports Associations in Shenzhen" on page 210 for details.

Sport - Golf
See "Golf" on page 215.

Sport - Yoga
See "Yoga" on page 258.

Sports for children
See "Activities for Children" on page 135 for details.

Sport equipment
▶ Decathlon - (迪卡儂)
A huge range of equipment for the beginner and the professional in over 60 sports, both indoor & outdoor: skiing & snowboarding; running & fitness; team sports and water sports. All managers speak English. They have a bike repair shop on site. Delivery is available in Shenzhen. There is another Decathlon Center in Nanshan, next to IKEA, along Bei Huan Rd. (北环路).

✉ Intersection of Nanhai Av. and No. 8 Gongye Rd., Nanshan (near Walmart)
　 南海大道与工业八路交汇处
☏ 2689 7878
🖰 www.decathlon.com.cn
⏳ 10am-10pm, Mon-Sun
🚌 113, 22, 204, 105

▶ Giant
Giant is a well-know mountain bike retailer. The quality of the bicycles tends to be better than at what you would find at Decathlon for very

reasonable prices. Located opposite Decathlon, in Nanshan.

✉ Intersection of Nanhai Av. and No. 8 Gongye Rd., Nanshan (near Walmart)
南山区蛇口南海大道与工业八路交汇处

🚌 113, 22, 204, 105

▶ See also Carrefour, Coastal City, and Holiday Plaza.

Sport equipment for children

▶ Decathlon
▶ See "Sport equipment" on page 236.

Stationery

This stationery store offers a wide range of office and school supplies.

✉ 81, Haichang Street, Shekou, Nanshan District
南山区蛇口海昌街81商铺

☎ 2668-2901

ⓘ It is located on the road between McDonald's and Mama's.

SWIC

The Shekou Women's International Club (SWIC) is a social club open to membership for all expatriate women living in Shekou, Shenzhen and the surrounding areas. See "The Shekou Women's International Club (SWIC)" on page 117 for a full introduction, or SWIConline.com.

Swimming pools

There are 3 swimming pools in Shekou; one in Jingshan Villa, one in Coastal Rose Garden Phase III, and one in the Maillen Club.

TAILOR

▶ Christina Tailor

CALL CHRISTINA FOR all your tailoring and home design needs. With Christina's experience in designing and tailoring, enjoy affordable quality with reliability you can count on. For your convenience, <u>in-home or in-office appointments</u> are available in Shenzhen and Hong Kong with free delivery on finished goods. Items can also be shipped anywhere in the world. Whether you want to have a copy made from an existing piece of clothing or a photo, or you have your own unique idea, Christina's experience working with customers from all over the world makes the process easy. Her fluency in English also ensures accuracy.

Clothing:	Home Fashion:
• Men's shirts and suits	• Curtains
• Ladies' shirts and skirts	• Bed covers
• Linen suits	• Chinese and Western-style cushions
• Chinese traditional clothing	• Seat covers
• Wedding dresses - Western and Chinese styles	
• Maternity clothing	Special occasion items:
• Chinese silk clothing	• Fabric envelopes
• Wool suits and coats	• Bags of all kinds
	• Party favors

Convenience:
In-home or office appointments for measuring and adjustments
Free delivery in Shenzhen and Hong Kong, shipping services available

✉	5055A 5/F Luohu Commercial City, Railway Station, Luohu District 罗湖区罗湖商业城，5楼，5055A铺
☎	8427-2778, 136-3298-8513
@	yangchristina007@yahoo.com.cn

▶ Shanghai Xinli Western-Style - (上海鑫利洋服)

This tailor offers quality work at reasonable prices.

✉ 161 ShangLe Street, Old Shekou Walking Street, Shekou
　 蛇口商乐街161号
℡ 2667 8156, 138 2525 2081
⧖ 9am – 11pm

▶ Shanghai Mingyang Fashion - (上海名扬服饰)

This tailor offers quality work at reasonable prices.

✉ 81 ShangLe Street, Old Shekou Walking Street, Shekou
　 蛇口商乐街81号
℡ 2682-9009, 135-3776-9299
⧖ 10am – 11h30pm

▶ Classical Charm Clothing - (古韵坊)

Traditional Chinese dress, Tang costume, suit, uniform, and various styles are offered.

✉ 55 ShangLe Street, Old Shekou Walking Street, Shekou
　 蛇口商乐街55号
℡ 2682-6468, 132-6555-8445
⧖ 10am – 11pm

▶ Crystal Tailor - (碧涛洋服)

English speaking staff tailors suits men/women, kids, beds/pillows, costumes design. This store is popular among the Western community because of the good quality, design, and prices, and friendly service.

✉ 1 Taizi Rd. Yinghui Building, Shekou
　 蛇口太子路迎晖大厦J号
℡ 2668-7983, 136-2231-5901

▶ Young's Tailor - (杨仕)

Young's Tailor has 15 years experience in Shekou. He trained and worked in Hong Kong for many years. They do very good quality work for both men's and women's clothing. English is spoken well. The have many fabric samples in the shop from which to choose, or bring a garment to copy or a picture of what you want. There are many books at the shop to look at if you need inspiration. Located in the Nan Hai Hotel, go in the lobby and turn right into the shopping corridor. The shop is on the right. The prices are on the high side.

✉ Nan Hai Hotel, Shekou
蛇口南海酒店
✆ 2669 2888 ask for Young's Tailor (ext. 379)
⧗ 8am - 9pm

TAXI

Relatively cheap, the flagfall is 12.50RMB which will get you 2.5km, then the rate is 0.60RMB per 250m or 0.60RMB per 45secs when not moving; an additional 30% is charged after 11pm. The driver will not understand English. You must have a business card or address details to show him. It helps if you have someone Chinese to explain your destination; it is handy to call someone and get them to talk to the driver.

If you arrive at Shenzhen airport and get into a metered taxi, they will offer to take you to Shekou for 200RMB. The actual meter price is closer to 90RMB, so just refuse and point to the meter, do not waiver.

Private taxis are another form of transport often used. These are the guys that solicit "taxi, taxi" inside the airport and ferry terminals. They are not legal but serve a purpose if there are no metered taxis available; they often congregate near the exit points at Coastal Rose Garden as metered taxis are hard to find there. They are quite safe (in our experience). Be careful at the ferry and airport as they might increase the fare; you must know the approximate correct fare beforehand. If you get one to take you to the ferry, pay him well before you get there. If a policeman sees you pay him then you may be detained and questioned, and he may lose his car.

TELEVISION

Shekou has many local free to air TV stations and also gets TV from Hong Kong albeit a little basic. CCTV9 is the China English language station. Shekou Telecom provides loads of Chinese channels plus Star Movies, Star TV and ESPN in the basic package that comes when you buy the Cable Internet service. You can add other channels like HBO, CNN, Discovery, etc for 20-50RMB per channel. Satellite is available only in areas where expats live. There are satellite systems on the local market and typically provide about 60-70 channels including US, UK, German, Korean & Philippine channels.

Toys

In Nanshan, there are several locations where you can purchase toys from:
▶ Jusco in Coastal City.
▶ Children's World (see "Activities for Children" on page 135 for details).
▶ Wal-Mart (many branches in Shenzhen).
▶ Suibao Department Store (南山岁宝百货, Binhai Blvd., 2649-5686).
▶ Haiya Department Store (南山海雅百货, intersection between Nanhai Blvd. and Haide 2 Rd., 2641-2111).

Vets

▶ Angel Pets - (天使宠物医院)
  ✉ No. 25, Coastal Rose Garden Phase II, <u>Shekou, Nanshan District</u>
    南山区蛇口望海玫瑰苑二期25商铺
  ☎ 2669-9995
    Emergency phone: 133-0299-6469
  ⧗ 24h/7. Clinic hours: 9h30am - 9h30pm

▶ Blue Spirit - (蓝精灵宠物医院)
  ✉ 101, Haichang Street Wanghai Huijing Yuan, <u>Shekou, Nanshan District</u>
    南山区蛇口海昌街望海汇景苑101商铺
  ☎ 2686-0505
    Emergency phone: 132-6720-1616 / 131-4883-1549
  ⧗ 24h/7
    Clinic hours: 9am - 9pm

ⓘ This new clinic is fast becoming a favorite of local expats. The friendly staff speaks some English. Boarding and grooming are available.
It is located on the road between McDonald's and Mama's.

▶ Humanity Hospital - (和平仁爱动物医院)

✉ 2047, Heping Rd., Taiping Building, 1&2F, <u>Luohu District</u>
罗湖区和平路2047号和平大厦一、二楼

✆ 2558-6415

⧖ Clinic hours: 9am - 10pm

ⓘ This large hospital is located in <u>Luohu District</u> and offers comprehensive animal healthcare. The staff speaks a little English.

▶ Viking Animal Hopital - (建威宠物医院)

✉ Minyuanju, 108, , Houhai Bld., <u>Nanshan District</u>
南山区后海名苑居108号

✆ 2657-7111

⧖ Clinic hours: 9h30am - 9pm

ⓘ The 2 vets, Ling and Ginger, speak good English and perform all vet services including vaccination, operations, dental, x-ray, ultrasound, lab work, electrocardiogram, and endoscopy. Boarding is also available. The clinic also sells Hills Science Diet and Prescription Diet dog and cat food.

VOLTAGE

Electricity in China is 220V/50Hz with plug types as illustrated below. Most supermarkets sell "power strips" (power boards) that take the majority of international plugs. Be careful to use a transformer when using a 110V appliance.

Modern buildings   Older buildings

VOICE OVER IP

Services such as Skype are quite popular with expats, as the rates are very cheap. Note: it is illegal to use some of the VOIP providers in China (as only a handful of telco companies are licensed to provide it.) The only drawback with VOIP is the lack of internet speed at peak times.

Another innovative VOIP supplier is Jajah see www.jajah.com. From the Jajah site you set up your home, office, and mobile numbers, select which you want to use then enter the other party's number. Your phone will ring, and once you pick up it will call the other party. It beats headsets and microphones and is generally good quality and saves bandwidth on your internet line. You can also do conference calls.

Volunteering

See "Orphanage" on page 229.

Water

Water in Shekou is not drinkable, you must get a water dispenser installed. The deposit on the machine is 50RMB then you pay about 18RMB per bottle (20ℓ). Delivery is normally within 30 mins to most of Shekou. These units can supply chilled or hot (not boiled) water. Alternatively, you can get a water filtration device fitted to your tap. This will be at your expense as the landlord will not pay for it. When looking at apartments you also need to check if there is hot water installed in the kitchen, many older apartments do not have it. If you are looking at the lower end of the rental market definitely do not expect this to be present.

Zen

This entry is partly because this section wouldn't be called <u>Shekou A to Z</u> if there wasn't a letter Z... like in Zen. Talking about Zen, it might be hard to find a such a place in Shenzhen. Our recommendation is a little authentic Japanese restaurant on the outside of the Nan Hai Hotel. It serves traditional Soba and a wide range of Sake. Truly Zen!

From Expats to Expats
Shopping in Old Shekou

OLD WALKING STREET and New Walking Street (aka Old Shekou), just across from A.Best supermarket are Shekou's most appreciated shopping streets.

OLD WALKING STREET

As you make your way down *Old Walking Street*, you will find everything from fruit stalls to jewelry, ornaments, tattoo shop, electronics, traditional Chinese attire, shoes, and a wide range of clothing. Although most shops do not sell large sizes, a few do. Obviously, bargaining is highly expected.

One entrance to the "Old Walking Street"

For a small range of electronics, try *Panama Bar*, *Lucky Shop*, *Yumi*, and *Friendship Shop*. You will find remote controlled car toys there too. As you get further down the street, you will come across a number of shoe stores selling mostly sports clothing and accessories. Try *Joy Shop* for larger sizes.

You will also find many stores for men's business shirts and some attire, though few with English

One entrance to "*Old Walking Street*", opposite A.Best Shopping Market

names. All carry varying sizes and styles.

For DVDs or CDs, try *Ronald and You*. For sunglasses and watches, check out *Tick Tock A Class Glasses* and *Peters Shop*. For handbags, go to *Fashion Shop* located on a corner at the start of *Old Walking Street*. You will find a reasonable range with reasonable prices.

At the end of *Old Walking Street* you will find a few tailors. They do not boast a great range of fabrics but are excellent for alterations, copies, cushion covers and some drapery. If it is relaxation you are after, try *Mei Do Massage* for great foot treatments and body massage. Don't forget to take along a DVD to watch in your private room while you get your treatments.

NEW WALKING STREET

At the end of *Old Walking Street*, take a right turn up and pass Huayang Hotel (in the shape of a horseshoe) to get to *New Walking Street*. Both sides of *New Walking Street* are lined with a good variety of restaurants and stores, mainly selling clothing, shoes, sunglasses and watches. The street is much cleaner than *Old Walking Street* and has some 'chain' retail outlets such as *Daphnes* for shoes, and *Aico* for children's clothing.

For women's wear try *Foreign Reignment*, *B9 JoJo*, *Tomboa*, *Oumena*, and *Sugar by Beans*. There are also many more small women's boutiques for those individual items. Most boutique shops carry some shoes, handbags and interesting accessories.

For men's clothing, try *Fallow Ground*, *Professional Shirt Makers*, *Crocodile*, *YIFA Fashion*, and *Wooden Roy*. If you are looking for an actual retail outlet, there is a great *Dunlop* outlet on the corner opposite *Joy Shop* in *Old Walking Street*. They have good sizes and good selection for foreigners. If it is casual gear you need, check out *Sunday* for men and women.

For some Indian inspired fashion for the ladies, *Songday* is an excellent store, though there is no bargaining there. *Bolun Glasses* is also located on the corner at the start of *New Walking Street* and has a good range of sunglasses and prescription glasses.

For incense, trinkets, gifts, accessories, sarongs, intricate jewelry and Chinese minority style dress, there is one shop you must not miss. Located on the left side half way down and without an English name, with bells hanging over the door, keep an eye out for this very colorful shop.

There are many children's stores that provide good quality and wide range of styles. *Try Hip Junior* and *Tuzana*. There are 3 excellent leather shoe shops for kids and adults, though with no English names. Bargaining is not so well received in these particular stores but you can try. For more children's clothes try the corner shop towards the main road for good bargains.

Getting There

From McDonald's, follow Haichang Street to A.Best in the direction of Mama's restaurant. Just before the traffic lights, cross to the other side and take a left down the alley (refer to picture previous page.) This is the start of Old Walking Street.

From Expats to Expats
Western Foreign Wholesale Fashion City

THE WESTERN FOREIGN Wholesale Fashion City is as it sounds, a cluster of wholesale outlets looking to sell wholesale quantities, but this does not stop them from selling single pieces. It's time you will need, though, to seek them out.

Fashion City is a group of 4 multi story buildings, with mainly the ground floor levels containing hundreds of small individual shops. The garments can be largely Chinese in style, however once you start looking you will be delighted and amazed at what you find. Prices can be fair and reasonable, and bargaining is not widely accepted in many of these small outlets, though it does not hurt to try.

If its evening wear you seek, then start from the Century Square (see further "Getting There".) They also carry a great variety of formal wear. During summer you can find some basic summer dresses, don't be put off by the Chinese style, you need to have a good look and investigate everywhere. To the left of Century Square is 'JINDU Fashion Wholesale City'. There is a main entrance at the front with escalators straight up, though don't forget to look around the ground floor. Here you have 3 levels of the same little shops presenting you with a variety of casual wear, evening wear and even handbags. Accessories, hats and some gorgeous pashminas can also be found here. Jackets or long winter coats and winter gear are available almost all year round. The best time to start shopping here is about 10h30 in the morning; it's less frantic and you can take your time. Behind Century Square is Sipoly Fashion, the smallest of the group and located on a single level. Some children's wear can be found here, along with much of the same as JINDU Fashion and Century Plaza. This is an eclectic mix of just about everything. If it's vintage you want, try Tairon Fashion across from Sipoly. The single level offers a great variety of everything from evening wear, vintage look, jeans, casual wear and some handbags. The variety is endless.

Getting There

✉ Walking away from Wal-Mart down Nanhai Boulevard, cross diagonally at the first set of traffic lights. This will take you to the Sundan store on the corner. Moving left, you will see the Century Plaza on your right. The 'Foreign Trading Clothes Terminal Market – Century Square' is the first building you will come across. Century Square is on ground level with street side shop fronts and entry into the building can be from any of these small outlets.

From Expats to Expats

by Mary Ann MacCartney

The Shekou Wet Market

NOT LONG AGO, traditional Chinese Wet Markets were the only place to shop for your daily necessities. The Cantonese prefer to have the freshest ingredients. A trip by bicycle to the nearby market was a daily ritual. Nowadays, your average Shenzhener may have a car, and do his/her weekly shopping in a hyper-mart just like you do. Modern supermarkets like Wal-Mart, Carrefour and Ren Ren Le and their ilk have several advantages such as improved hygiene, brighter lighting, air-conditioning and quality control. Still there is something about the wet markets that is colorful, intriguing and exotic.

The Old Shekou Wet Market (老蛇口市场 Lǎo Shékǒu Shì chǎng) is located just off Old Shekou Street (蛇口老街 Shékǒu Lǎo Jiē) on Fishing Village Road (渔村路 on YúCūn Lù). It is open air two story building divided into sections. The left front portion has fresh vegetables (蔬菜 shūcài). The right front has various fresh meats including, pork (猪肉 zhū ròu), beef (牛肉 niú ròu), mutton (羊肉 yang ròu) and dog (狗肉 gǒu ròu)! Thankfully there are no live animals in this section. If you are squeamish, you may want to steer clear as none of the meat is refrigerated. Just behind the meat is the fruit section (水果 shuǐ guǒ) and just beyond that fresh tofu (豆腐 dòufu) in many varieties. My favorite section is the fresh seafood (海鲜 hǎixiān). Being carefully appraised by particular Chinese cooks are buckets and buckets of fresh live seafood. In addition to fish and shellfish, you will find turtles, crabs, eels, snakes, sea cucumbers and plenty of other squirmy creatures. On the back streets surrounding the market, small stalls offer a variety of goods like groceries (杂货店 záhuò diàn), live poultry (家禽店 jiāqín diàn), kitchen utensils (厨具店chújùdiàn), dried seafood, dried noodles (干货店 gānhuòdiàn) and spices (香料 xiāngliào). Upstairs a lackluster supermarket has mainly packaged foods with fixed prices.

One can spend an hour just looking at all the colorful vegetables. Invariably, I pick up something I have never tried before and bring it home to our maid to prepare.

If you are keen to learn more about Asian produce, look for Wendy Hutton's "A Cook's Guide to Asian Vegetables" which is available in Hong Kong book stores. It features a full description with illustrations and recipes in English.

Armed with a few key phrases and the list of food names on the next pages, you will be able to bargain with the best of them. Remember to wear sensible closed toe shoes. They don't call it wet market for nothing.

Did you know?

THE MAIN CHARACTERISTICS of the wet market have traditionally been associated with a place that sells live animals out in the open. The collection may include poultry, fish, reptiles, and pigs. Freshly imported fruits and vegetables are also available.

Wet markets generally combine butcher shops and fish markets in the vicinity. The higher hygiene standards of supermarkets have forced many wet markets to operate indoors.

Getting to the Shekou Wet Market

菜市场

✉ From Seaworld, when facing MacDonald's go left, follow Xinhua Rd., then Haichang Road. At the intersection of Haichang Road and Yuncun Road, turn left. The market is 30 meters away, on your left hand side. On foot, it takes about 20 minutes from McDonald's. By Taxi, it only takes a few minutes.

Food Vocabulary List

Fruit	水果	shuǐ guǒ
Market	市场	shì chǎng
Vegetable	蔬菜	shūcài

Amaranth (Chinese Spinach)	苋菜	xiàncài
Asian lettuce	生菜	shēngcài
Baby corn	小玉米	xiǎoyúmǐ
Bamboo shoots	竹笋	zhúsǔn
Bananas	香蕉	xiāngjiāo
Basil	罗勒	luólè
Black moss	发菜	fàcài
Bok choy	小白菜	xiǎobáicài
Broad beans	蚕豆	cándòu
Broccoli	西兰花	xilanhua
Carrot	胡萝卜	húluóbo
Cauliflower	花菜	huācài
Chayote	佛手瓜	fóshǒuguā
Chestnut	栗子	lìzi
Chick peas	鹰嘴豆	yīngzuǐdòu
Chinese cabbage	大白菜	dàbáicài
Chinese celery	芹菜	qíncài
Chives	青蒜	qīngsuàn
Coriander or cilantro	香菜	xiāngcài
Corn	玉米	yùmǐ
Cucumber	黄瓜	huángguā
Eggplant	茄子	qiézi
Enokitake (golden mushrooms)	金针蘑菇	jīnzhēn mógū
Galangal	良姜	liángjiāng
Garlic	大蒜	dàsuàn
Garlic chives	韭黄	jiǔhuáng
Ginger	姜	jiāng
Green soybeans	青豆	qīngdòu

Hot pepper; chili; capsicum	辣椒	làjiāo
Jicama	豆薯	dòushǔ
Kidney beans	菜豆	càidòu
Kohlrabi	球茎甘蓝	qiújīng gānlán
Leeks	大葱	dàcōng
Lemongrass	柠檬香茅	níngméng xiāngmáo
Lotus	莲藕	lián'ǒu
Mangoes	芒果	mángguǒ
Mung beans	绿豆	lǜdòu
Mung been sprouts	绿豆芽	lǜdòuyá
Onions	洋葱	yángcōng
Papayas	木瓜	mùguā
Peanuts	花生	huāshēng
Peas	豌豆	wāndòu
Plantains	芭蕉	bājiāo
Radish	萝卜	luóbo
Round cabbage	卷心菜	juǎnxīncài
Rutabaga	大头菜	dàtóucài
Shallots	小葱	xiǎocōng
Snow peas	糖荚豌豆	tángjiá wāndòu
Soy bean sprouts	黄豆芽	huángdòuyá
Soy beans	黄豆	huángdòu
Soy milk	豆乳	dòurǔ
Spinach	菠菜	bōcài
Sweet potatoes	甘薯	gānshǔ
Tempeh	印尼豆豉	yìnní dòuchǐ
Tofu	豆腐	dòufu
Water chestnuts	荸荠	bíqi
Watercress	西洋菜	xīyángcài
Watermelon	西瓜	xīguā
Winter melon	冬瓜	dōngguā

From Expats to Expats
Shekou's Hotels

THE NAN HAI Hotel is located in Shenzhen's Shekou area, adjacent to the ferry terminal.

The hotel has 396 comfortably designed guest rooms with non-smoking guest floors, Japanese style guest rooms and Deluxe Executive Floor, all equipped with free ADSL broadband system and International cable TV channels. Wireless Internet service for speedy connection is available in the public areas. The Nan Hai Hotel has Western, Chinese, and Japanese (genuine Japanese Soba) restaurants, a coffee shop, a club, and a bar.

The Nan Hai Hotel is 30 mins away to Shenzhen International Airport, and 40 mins to Luohu Railway Station. Hotel shuttle service also link up with Shenzhen Bay Border and the Overseas Chinese Town metro station (Hua Qiao Cheng). The Nan Hai Hotel is a good choice for business travelers who need to commute to and from Hong Kong, Macao, and Zhuhai. In-town check in counters service available at the Shekou Ferry Terminal.

Nan Hai Hotel (南海酒店)

✉	1, Gong Ye 1st Road, Nanhai Blvd, Shekou, Nanshan District (next to the Shekou Ferry Terminal) 南山区蛇口南海大道工业一路1号
☏	2669 2888, Fax: 2669 2440
🖱	www.nanhai-hotel.com

FRASER PLACE SHEKOU is nestled on the hillside in one of Shekou's upscale residential neighborhoods. Built in 2006, its sleek profile is modern and attractive. The smallest units are one bedroom studios (35 m²), which are a basic hotel room. The beds are unfortunately rock hard. The ferry terminal is a five minute drive while Shenzhen. Airport is 25 minutes away.

The Fraser Place Shekou is geared towards the long term guest If you are going to be in Shenzhen for a long visit this is an option in the area.

Fraser Place Shekou (深圳泰格公寓)

✉	8 Nanhai Road (former Industrial Road), Shekou, Nanshan District 南山区蛇口南海大道8号
✆	2688 3333, Fax: 2688 5706
@	sales.shenzhenshekou@frasershospitality.com
🖱	shekou.frasershospitality.com

THE FUZON HOTEL is a 4-STAR BUSINESS HOTEL, located behind Luna Bar. The hotel has a total of 176 guestrooms, all equipped with air-conditioning, color television, IDD/DDD telephone and refrigerator.

Fuzon Hotel (金銮富众酒店)

✉	1, Kangle Rd., Shekou, Nanshan District 南山区蛇口康乐路1号
✆	2682-7888 , Fax: 2682-7123
🖱	www.fuzonhotel.com (Chinese)

HONLUX APARTMENTS AND the Cruise Inn Hotel are both managed by the same group, the Honlux Hotel Group. Located between the Seaview Plaza and McDonald's at Seaworld Square, the Honlux Apartments is a small hotel with reasonably priced rooms. It is a good choice for businessmen coming to Nanshan/Shekou.

Honlux Apartments (深圳鸿隆公寓)

✉	Taizi Road, Shekou, Nanshan District 南山区蛇口太子路
✆	2681-6666, Fax: 2681-5533
@	reservations@honlux.com
🖰	www.honlux.com

THE MING HUA International Convention Center is nestled on the hillside in one of Shekou's upscale residential neighborhoods. Built in 1992 and renovated in 2006, the Ming Hua Hotel offers clean, comfortable and affordable rooms to people doing business in Shekou/Nanshan and/or need to quickly commute to Hong Kong, Macao or Zhuhai.

Ming Hua Hotel (ICC) (明华国际会议中心)

✉	NO.8, Gui Shan Road, Shekou, Nanshan District 南山区蛇口龟山路8号
✆	2668-9968, Fax: 2667-9615 / www.mhctr.com

Transportation in Shenzhen

General Information

7 BORDERS

Shenzhen has cross-border train and bus connections to Hong Kong. There are also trains to Guangzhou and buses to most nearby cities.

In Shenzhen, there are 7 land border crossings. The following 5 are the most commonly used:

- Shenzhen Bay Bridge 深圳湾口 岸 - 6:30-24:00
- Huanggang 皇岗口岸 24h
- Futian 福田口岸 6:30-24:00
- Luohu 罗湖口岸 - 6:30-24:00
- Shekou (Ferry Terminal) 蛇口 口岸 - 24h

TAXI

Taxis are normally available everywhere on the streets. For taxis registered in the special economic zone (yellow or red taxis), their meters start at 12.5RMB for the first three kilometers. For those registered outside the zone (green ones), the meters start at 7RMB for the first two kilometers.

After 11pm, the taxi fare will include an extra service fee, 30% (for yellow/red taxis) or 20% (for green ones) of the normal charge. The total fare will be automatically calculated by the meter. Taxi fare from Shenzhen Airport to Luohu downtown costs around 100RMB plus 10RMB for toll.

See also "Taxi" on page 262, for more details.

HONG KONG MTR

The MTR East Rail Line commuter train which connects East Tsim Sha Tsui to Luohu and Huanggang (Lok Ma Chau), with several intermediate stops, mainly serves Hong Kong locals. It interchanges with the urban section of the MTR at Kowloon Tong Station and East Tsim Sha Tsui Terminal. For those traveling to or from Hong Kong Island, the Cross Harbor Bus in Hung Hom Station or the Tsuen Wan Line at East Tsim Sha Tsui is recommended.

The journey from East Tsim Sha Tsui to Luohu takes 42 minutes and costs 33-36.5HKD. First class tickets must be purchased prior to boarding, and they are charged double. Trains depart every few minutes, but some short trips are operated in rush hour, so check the destination screen before boarding. The train can be crowded during rush hour as it serves millions of commuters along the line as well. For more details, check www. mtr.com.hk.

See "Hong Kong MTR System Map" on page 277 for a Hong Kong MTR System Map.

Visa

See "Chinese Visa" on page 306.

Getting to Shenzhen

Via Luohu

Hong Kong side

The train from Hong Kong's East Tsim Sha Tsui MTR station to the Luohu and Lok Ma Chau border crossings take 43 minutes and 45 minutes respectively. Trains depart East Tsim Sha Tsui for Luohu every 6-8 minutes from 5:36am to 11:13pm.

Luohu side

Luohu has the only train border connection, and is the most popular crossing. It operates daily from 6h30am until midnight. Be aware that the last few trains do not go to all the way to Luohu. Luohu Station is the last stop of the KCR East Rail train (HK section). East Rail, which connects to downtown Kowloon at East Tsim Sha Tsui, is the only way to reach Luohu. As it is in a restricted area, Luohu Station is only for travelling to Shenzhen or beyond, so a visa or other travel document is required to travel there without being fined.

Via Huanggang

Huanggang (黄岗口岸) border is open 24h. Unlike the other crossings, the distance between the Shenzhen and Hong Kong checkpoints is inconvenient for pedestrians. However, after immigration, then get a taxi to take you to where you want to go. The taxi fare to Shekou (蛇口) from Huanggang is about 60RMB. The bus fare is 6RMB.

Via Futian Checkpoint

From Hong Kong you can take the MTR to Lok Ma Chau, in Hong Kong's New Territories. Lok Ma Chau is also a major pedestrian and border crossing point between Hong Kong and Shenzhen. It is linked directly to the Hong Kong MTR.

The Lok Ma Chau border crossing closes around 10:30. The Lok Ma Chau Trains run at 10 minute intervals.

Once you cross the border, you can take the Shenzhen Metro, starting from Futian Kou'an (福田口岸) line 4, which is located in the same building as the immigration checkpoint.

Via Shenzhen Bay Bridge

If you're using the Hong Kong Metro system, the closest Metro Station is Tin Shui Wai. From there, you can either take a taxi or catch the B2 bus to the Shenzhen Bay Bridge.

From Shenzhen Int'l Airport

Shenzhen International Airport (See eng.szairport.com) has domestic and international flights. It is normally cheaper for people based in Hong Kong to fly to Mainland Chinese destinations from Shenzhen rather than from Hong Kong. It is usually cheaper for those based in southern Mainland China to fly out of Hong Kong to international destinations.

Direct coach 330 (25RMB) connects the airport with downtown with its final stop next to the Kexue Guan Metro Station 科学馆站.

Mini-bus K568 connects the airport with Shenzhen Rail Station in Luohu (7h30am-11h30pm, 10 mins interval, 20RMB), which is within walking distance from the Luohu border with Hong Kong.

To Luohu train station:

Airport bus Line 2, 8am - 10pm, 20RMB, 8 stations.

To Huanggang Border

Airport Bus Line 9, 8am - 9pm, 20RMB, 8 stations.

To Shenzhen Bay Bridge

Airport Bus Line 8, 8am - 9pm, 15RMB, 12 stations.

To Shekou

Airport Bus Line 10, 8am - 9pm, 8RMB, 15 stations.

Other local buses serving the airport include the 10, 327, 355, etc.

FROM HK INT'L AIRPORT
By Bus

From Hong Kong International Airport (HKIA), there are very frequent bus and van services that can take you from the Hong Kong Airport to most hotels in Shenzhen.

China Travel Tours Transportation Development H.K.Ltd. (ctsbus.hkcts.com/routes/air/air_shenzhen.html) provides transportation between Shenzhen and Hong Kong Central/Hong Kong Kowloon/HKIA.

- HKIA (counters A04, A09, C05) to Bao Li Lai International Hotel (next to the Shenzhen International Airport); first bus at 7h05am, last bus at 8h05pm, hourly; HK$180, round trip HK$320, child HK$90.

- HKIA (counters A04, A09, C05) to majors hotels in Shenzhen; 7h05am, last bus at 10h05pm, hourly; HK$180, round trip HK$320, child HK$100.

- HKIA (counters A04, A09, C05) to Shenzhen International Airport; first bus at 7h05am, last bus at 8h05pm, hourly; HK$180, no round trip, child HK$90.

- HKIA (counters A04, A09, C05) to Huanggang Border; first bus at 7h05am, last bus at 8h05pm, hourly; HK$150, round trip HK$230.

By Ferry

To catch the ferry from HKIA to Shekou, you need to buy a SkyPier ticket at the ferry counter and provide them with your luggage tag one hour before the ferry departs. See www.hongkongairport.com/eng/tbu/skypier_to.htm.

The staff will then go and retrieve your luggage from the carousel, and it will be taken to the ferry for you. It is always reassuring to be at the bus departure area (Gate 10) a bit early and actually see they have your luggage (though we have not heard of and missing baggage on this service).

<u>Do not go through Immigration Control</u>, or else you will not be able to get to the ferry as the ticket counter is behind security in the transfer zone. The staff will tell you how to get down to Gate 10.

You are subject to another baggage check here, and the 100ml fluid restriction applies to all hand carry items, even duty free.

See www.xunlongferry.com for latest time table.

HK Airport – Shekou 香港国际机场 - 蛇口客运码	
Fee	$HK200
Time	30 mins
09:00	16:30
10:15	17:30
11:00	18:30
12:30	19:30
13:30	20:30
14:30	21:20
15:30	

From Hong Kong Kowloon

By bus

To Shenzhen Bay Bridge border
深圳湾口岸 蛇口

Hong Kong Kowloon - Shenzhen Bay Port - Guangzhou Downtown - Second Line 香港,九龍 - 深圳灣口岸- 廣州 二線		
Mong Kok CTS Branch 旺角中旅社	07:20 08:20 10:20 12:20	14:20 15:20 16:20 17:20
Prince Edward CTS Branch 太子中旅社	07:30 08:30 10:30 12:30	14:30 15:30 16:30 17:30
Tsuen Wan- Jockey Club Tak Wah Park 荃灣(德華公園)	07:50 08:50 10:50 12:50	14:50 15:50 16:50 17:50
Shenzhen Bay Port 深圳灣口岸	08:45 09:45 11:45 13:45	15:45 16:45 17:45 18:45

By Ferry

Since the opening of the Shenzhen Bay Bridge, there are less and less ferries from Kowloon to Shenzhen/Shekou. At the time of this writing there are 3 ferries a day; 7h45am, 10h15am, 1h15pm. See www.xunlongferry.com for latest time table.

HK Kowlon – Shekou 香港九龙 - 蛇口客运码	
Fee	HK$105 HK$125 night
Time	60 mins

HK Kowlon – Shekou 香港九龙 - 蛇口客运码	
07:45	19:00
10:30	

HK Central – Shekou 香港港澳码头 - 蛇口客运码	
Time	60 mins
07:45	15:15
09:00	18:00
11:30	20:30

FROM HONG KONG CENTRAL

By Bus

To Shenzhen Bay Bridge border
深圳湾口岸蛇口

Hong Kong Island - Shenzhen Bay Port - Guangzhou Downtown - Second Line 香港,港島線 - 深圳灣口岸- 廣州二線		
Metropark Causeway Bay Hotel 銅鑼灣維景酒店	07:20 08:20 10:20 12:20	14:20 15:20 16:20 17:20
WanChai CTS Branch 灣仔中旅社	07:35 08:35 10:35 12:35	14:35 15:35 16:35 17:35
Sheung Wan CTS House 中旅集團大廈	07:45 08:45 10:45 12:45	14:45 15:45 16:45 17:45
Shenzhen Bay Port 深圳灣口岸	08:45 09:45 11:45 13:45	15:45 16:45 17:45 18:45

By Ferry to Shekou

See www.xunlongferry.com for latest time table.

HK Central – Shekou 香港港澳码头 - 蛇口客运码头	
Fee	$HK110 20h30: HK$120 Return: HK$180

FROM ZHUHAI

珠海市 — 深圳市

By Bus

Doumen Changtu Bus Station - Futian 斗门长途汽车站 - 深圳福田	
Fee	53RMB By Taiping 75RMB
First bus 07:10 Last bus 18:50	

Gongbei Changtu Bus Station - Shenzhen 拱北长途汽车站 - 深圳	
Fee	53RMB By Taiping 75RMB
First bus 08:00 Last bus 20:30	

By Ferry

Zhuhai – Shekou 珠海九州港 - 深圳蛇口客运码头	
Fee	85 RMB
Time	60 mins
08:00 - 20:30 Every 30 minutes	

FROM ZHONGSHAN

珠海市 — 深圳市

By Ferry

Zhongshan Changtu Bus Station to Shenzhen Futian Bus Station 中山长途客运站 深圳福田车站	
Fee	Unknown
First bus 08:00 Last bus 21:00	

Zhongshan Qiche Bus Station - Luohu Train Station 中山汽车总站 - 罗湖汽车站	
Fee	Unknown
First bus 06:50 Last bus 20:50	

From Guangzhou

广州市 — 深圳市

By bus

To Futian - 福田区

Jinhan Tianhe Dasha Bus Station - Shenzhen Futian 天河大厦客运站 - 深圳福田	
Fee	50RMB
First bus 06:50 Last bus 20:30	

Tianhe Bus Station - Shenzhen Futian 天河客运站 - 深圳福田	
Fee	55RMB
First bus 07:05 Last bus 20:35	

To Luohu - 罗湖区

锦汉天河大厦客运站 - 深圳罗湖 Jinhan Tianhe Dasha Bus Station - Shenzhen Luohu	
Fee	60RMB
First bus 07:40 Last bus 20:30	

Tianhe Bus Station - Shenzhen Luohu 天河客运站 - 深圳罗湖	
Fee	55RMB
First bus 07:30 Last bus 17:30	

Jiaokou Bus Station - Shenzhen Luohu 窖口客运站 - 深圳罗湖	
Fee	60RMB
First bus 08:00 Last bus 17:00	

Haizhu Bus Station - Shenzhen Luohu 海珠客运站 - 深圳罗湖	
Fee	60RMB
First bus 06:50 Last bus 20:20	

From Macao

By Ferry

Macao Yuetong Matou – Shekou 澳门粤通码头 - 蛇口客运码头	
Fee	HK$135
Time	80 mins
10:00	16:30
12:30	18:15
14:00	20:15

New Macao Ferry to Shekou

Macao New Ferry Terminal – Shekou 澳门新港澳码头 - 蛇口客运码头	
Fee	170 RMB
Time	60 mins
12:00	18:00
15:00	20:45

By Helicopter

There is a helicopter service between the Terminal Marítimo in Macau to Shenzhen airport (and HK). See www.skyshuttlehk.com.

Macau Heliport - To Shenzhen
3/F Macau Maritime Terminal
Avenida da Amizade
Tel: (853) 2872 7288
Operating hours: Mon - Sun 9h45am to 7h45pm
HKD2,400 (day), HKD2,600 (night)

Shenzhen Heliport - To Macau
2/F Terminal B
Shenzhen International Airport 深圳国际机场
Tel: 2777-8333
Operating hours: Mon - Sun 11h45am to 8h30pm
HKD2,490 (day), HKD2,690 (night)

15mins per trip day time 25mins per trip night time Arrive at the passenger lounge at least 15 minutes before the flight time. You can check your flights as early as 28 days in advance through the Telephone Enquiry: (852) 2108 9898, then press 2, 1, 1, or via their website.

Traveling from Shenzhen

To Shenzhen Int'l Airport

Shenzhen International Airport (See eng.szairport.com) has domestic and international flights. It is normally cheaper for people based in Hong Kong to fly to Mainland Chinese destinations from Shenzhen rather than from Hong Kong. It is usually cheaper for those based in southern Mainland China to fly out of Hong Kong to international destinations.

Direct coach 330 (25RMB) connects Kexue Guan Metro Station 科学馆站 to the airport.

Mini-bus K568 connects Shenzhen Rail Station in Luohu (6am-10pm, 10 mins interval, 20RMB), which is within walking distance of the Luohu border with Hong Kong, with the airport.

From Luohu train station

Airport bus Line 2, 6h30am - 8h30pm, 20RMB, 8 stations.

From Huanggang Border

Airport Bus Line 9, 6h30am - 8h30pm, 20RMB, 8 stations.

From Shenzhen Bay Bridge

Airport Bus Line 8, 8am - 9pm, 15RMB, 14 stations.

From Shekou

Airport Bus Line 10, 6h30am - 8h30pm, 8RMB, 15 stations.

Other local buses serving the airport include the 10, 327, 355, etc.

TO HONG KONG

Via Luohu

Luohu is the only port for train connections and the most popular connection. Trains from Luohu to East Tsim Sha Tsui depart every 6-8 minutes from 6:38am to 12:30am.

Luohu can be accessed by Metro (Luohu Station, 罗湖站) and by many busses.

Via Futian Checkpoint

Once you crosss the Futian Kou'an checkpoint (福田口岸), you will be in Hong Kong's New Territories, in Lok Ma Chau. Lok Ma Chau is also a major pedestrian and border crossing point between Hong Kong and Shenzhen.

Via Shenzhen Bay Bridge

From Shekou, take a taxi to the bridge "Shenzhen wan" is what you tell the driver. The cost is roughly 30RMB. There are 3 alternatives; use public transport, buy a bus ticket, or take a taxi.

Bus tickets can be purchased at the blue ticket booths located in front of the immigration building. For 40HKD you can take a bus directly to Kowloon, Kowloon Tong and Prince Edward Metro Stations. They will give you a sticker and a ticket and tell you which bay the bus leaves from. The buses are located on the Hong Kong side of immigration and to the right.

Public transport is very convenient. Once through immigration walk straight by the moving sidewalks. The B2 bus at the end of the walkway goes to Tin Shui Wai Metro Station and costs 8.5HKD. From there the Metro is a cheap and easy way to get around Hong Kong. You can use the Octopus card for the bus and the Metro.

Via Shekou Ferry Terminal

See www.xunlongferry.com for latest time table.

Shekou - HK Airport 蛇口客运码头 - 香港国际机场 (海天码头)	
Fee	250RMB
Time	30 mins
7:45	15:30
8:45	16:30
10:00	17:30
11:15	18:30
12:15	19:30
13:30	20:15
14:30	

From your hotel

Ask the hotel reception. Major hotels have private mini busses to Hong Kong.

To Hong Kong Int'l Airport
By Ferry

The ferry service to the airport is one of the best things around.

If you fly with Cathay Pacific (and some others now), you can check your luggage in at the ferry terminal and collect it at your final destination point. For other airlines you will need to check it in when you get to the ferry terminal at HK airport. This is where you check into the flight and get your boarding pass.

Many passengers are also entitled to claim a refund of their departure tax, and you will be given a small three part voucher to do so. There is a tax claim desk on the left hand side at the rear of the departure lounge. The refund is about 110HKD.

We suggest that you buy your ferry ticket at least one day prior to your flight. This gives you advance warning of any issues that may occur, which is especially useful around holidays. It does get booked out occasionally, but also some airlines have restrictions on which ferry you can catch for their flights.

Most airlines require you to catch a ferry at least three hours prior to their departure time.

If you get to the ferry terminal and are confronted with this situation, you need to take a taxi to the Shenzhen Bay bridge border crossing and then get a bus to the airport.

To Guangzhou
By train

There are more than 40 trains running between the Luohu train station and Guangzhou everyday.

Shenzhen Luohu Train Station – Guangzhou Dong Train Station 深圳罗湖火车站 - 广州东火车站	
Fee	Eco: 96RMB 1st Class: 76RMB
Time	1h10 mins
6:20 - 22:30 Every 10-20 minutes	

By Bus

Nanshan Nanxin Tianqiao – Guangzhou 南山南新天桥 - 广州	
Fee	55RMB
Time	> 2h
6:15 - 19:15 Every 30 mins	

Window of the World – Guangzhou 世界之窗 - 广州	
Fee	60RMB
Time	> 2h
7:15 - 18:45 Every 50 mins	

Shekou Bus Station – Guangzhou 蛇口汽车站 - 广州	
Fee	65RMB
Time	> 2h
6:00 - 20:00 Every 30 mins	

Bao An Bus Station – Guangzhou 宝安汽车站 - 广州	
Fee	55RMB

Bao An Bus Station – Guangzhou 宝安汽车站 - 广州	
Time	> 2h
5:50 - 20:30 Every 20 mins	

To Macao

By Ferry

Shekou - Macao Yuetong Matou 蛇口客运码头 - 澳门粤通码头	
Fee	125RMB
Time	80 mins
8:15	18:05
11:45	18:30
16:45	19:50

To New Macao Ferry

Shekou - Macao New Ferry Terminal 蛇口客运码头 - 澳门新港澳码头	
Fee	170RMB
Time	60 mins
10:00	16:45
13:30	19:15

By Helicopter

There is a helicopter service between Shenzhen airport (and HK) and the Terminal Marítimo in Macau. See www.helihongkong.com.

Macau Heliport
3/F Macau Maritime Terminal
Avenida da Amizade
Tel: (853) 2872 7288
Operating hours: Mon - Sun 8h15am to 11pm

Shenzhen Heliport
2/F Terminal B
Shenzhen International Airport
深圳国际机场
Tel: 2777-8333
Operating hours: Mon - Sun 8h30am to 9h00pm

To Zhuhai
By Ferry

Shekou – Zhuhai 蛇口客运码头 - 珠海九州港	
Fee	85 RMB
Time	60 mins
07:30 - 20:30 Every 30 minutes	

Traveling out by Busses

There are several bus stations in Shenzhen including Luohu Passenger Station (8232-1670), Futian Passenger Station (8370-4526), and Nanshan Passenger Station (2616-2978). Everyday, there are regular coaches setting out to Guangzhou, Shantou, Zhanjiang, Fuzhou, Xiamen, etc. Luohu Passenger Station is in charge of the coaches traveling to major cities inside or outside the Guangdong Province. Luohu Coach Station, which is near East Railway Station, is in charge of the coaches traveling to cities in the Guangdong Province. The first floor of the station is mainly for luxury buses to Guangzhou which depart every 5 minutes. The waiting hall upstairs is for other cities in Guangdong.

Traveling out by Trains

The high-speed train from Shenzhen to Guangzhou departs from both cities at intervals of 15 minutes, and the travel time is one hour. All High-speed trains begin with the letter "D" and leave from the Shenzhen Railway Station.

Shenzhen Railway Station is located in Luohu District. Travelers interested in going to Beijing (23 hrs), Shanghai (17 hrs), Changsha (10 hrs), and Shantou (8 hrs) and other major cities depart from this station. During holidays, travelers are advised to purchase tickets in advance. This station serves as the ticket sales office for both stations with automated ticketing machines available. Tickets are on sale at least five days in advance.

Shenzhen West Railway Station is the largest station in Shenzhen. The station is located in Nanshan District and has trains to Hefei (21 hrs), Huaihua (18 hrs), Yueyang (13 hrs), Dongwan (1.5 hr), and Nanjing (26 hrs).

Travelers can purchase train tickets at ticket agency offices. There are several ticketing offices inside major hotels and around town.

Shenzhen Metro System

LINE 1: LUO HU – AIRPORT

1. Luohu — 罗湖站, to KCR East Rail
2. Guo Mao — 国贸站, Int'l Trade Center
3. Lao Jie — 老街站, Dongmen
4. Da Ju Yuan — 大剧院占, Grand Theater, Diwang & MixC
5. Kexue Guan — 科学馆站, Science Museum
6. Huaqiang Lu — 华强路占, Huaqiang Rd.
7. Gangxia — 港厦站
8. Hui Zhan Zhong Xin — 会展中心站, Exhibition Ctr. & Central Walk
9. Gou Wu Gong Yuan — 购物公园站, Coco Park
10. Xiangmi Hu — 相迷糊站, Honey Lake
11. Che Gongmiao — 车公庙站, Che Gong Temple
12. Zhuzi Lin — 竹子林站, Bamboo Forest
13. Qiao Cheng Dong — 桥成东站
14. Hua Qiao Cheng — 华侨城站, OCT
15. Shi Jie Zhi Chuang — 世界之窗站, Window of the World
16. Bai Shi Zhou — 白石洲站
17. Gaoxin Yuan Gaoxin Yuan — 高新园站, Technology Park
18. Shenda — 深大站, Shenzhen University
19. Tao Yuan — 桃园站
20. Da Xin — 大新站
21. Li Yu Men — 鲤鱼门站
22. Qian Hai Wan — 前海湾站
23. Xin An — 新安站
24. Bao'an Zhong Xin — 宝安中心站
25. Bao Ti — 宝体站
26. Ping Zhou — 坪洲站
27. Xi Xiang — 西乡站
28. Gu Shu — 固戌站
29. Hou Rui — 后瑞站

30. Ji Chang Dong_____ 机场东站, SZ Int'l Airport, not opened yet

LINE 2: SHEKOU – XINXIU

1- Chi Wan_____ 赤湾站
2- She Kou Gang_____ 蛇口湾站
3- Hai Shang Shi Jie_____ 海上世界站
4- Shui Wan_____ 水湾站
5- Dong Jiao Tou_____ 东角头站
6- Wan Xia_____ 湾厦站
7- Hai Yue_____ 海月站
8- Deng Liang_____ 登良站
9- Hou Hai_____ 后海站
10- Ke Yuan_____ 科苑站
11- Hong Shu Wan_____ 红树湾站
12- Shi Jie Zhi Chuang_____ 世界之窗站
13- Shen Kang_____ 侨城北站
14- Qiao Cheng Bei_____ 深康站
15- An Tuo Shang_____ 安托山站
16- Qiao Xiang_____ 侨香站
17- Xiang Mi_____ 香蜜站
18- Xiang Mei Bei_____ 香梅北站
19- Jing Tian_____ 景田站
20- Lian Hua Xi_____ 莲花西站
21- Fu Tian_____ 福田站
22- Shi Min Zhong Xin_____ 市民中心站
23- Gang Xia Bei_____ 岗厦北站
24- Hua Qiang Bei_____ 华强北站
25- Yan Nan_____ 燕南站
26- Da Ju Yuan_____ 大剧院站
27- Dongmen_____ 湖贝站
28- Huang Bei_____ 黄贝岭站
29- Xin Xiu_____ 新秀站

LINE 3: YITIAN – SHUANGLONG

1- Yi Tian_____ 益田站
2- Shi Xia_____ 石厦站
3- Go Wu Gong Yuan_____ 购物公园站
4- Fu Tian_____ 福田站
5- Shao Nian Gong_____ 少年宫站
6- Lian Hua Cun_____ 莲花村站
7- Hua Xin_____ 华新站
8- Tong Xin Ling_____ 通新岭站
9- Hong Lin_____ 红岭站
10- Lao Jie_____ 老街站
11- Shai Bu_____ 晒布站
12- Cui Zhu_____ 翠竹站

13- Tian Bei		田贝站
14- Shui Bei		水贝站
15- Cao Pu		草埔站
16- Bu Ji		布吉站
17- Mu Mian Wan		木棉湾站
18- Da Fen		大芬站
19- Dan Zhu Tou		丹竹头站
20- Liu Yue		六约站
21- Tang Keng		塘坑站
22- Heng Feng		横岗站
23- Yong Hu		永湖站
24- He Ao		荷坳站
25- Da Yun		大运站
26- Ai Lian		爱联站
27- Ji Xiang		吉祥站
28- Long Cheng Guang Chang		龙城广场站
29- Nan Lian		南联站
30- Shuang Long		双龙站

LINE 4: SHENZHEN KOU AN – QING HU

1. Futian Kou'an		福田口岸站
2. Fumin		富民站
3. Hui Zhan Zhong Xin		会展中心站
4. Shi Min Zhong Xin		市民中心站
5. Shaonian Gong		少年宫站
6. Lian Hua Bei		莲花北站
7. Shang Mei Lin		上梅林站
8. Min Le		民乐站
9. Bai Shi Long		白石龙站
10. Shenzhen Bei Zhan		深圳北站
11. Hong Shan		红山站
12. Shang Tang		上塘站
13. Long Sheng		龙胜站
14. Long Hua		龙华站
15. Qing Hu		清湖站

STATIONS/LINES BY NAME

- Cao Pu (草埔站) _____ Line 3
- Che Gong Miao (车公庙站) _____ Line 1
- Chi Wan (赤湾站) _____ Line 2
- Cui Zhu (翠竹站) _____ Line 3
- Da Fen (大芬站) _____ Line 3
- Da Ju Yuan (大剧院占) _____ Lines 1,2
- Da Xin (大新站) _____ Line 1
- Da Yun (大运站) _____ Line 3
- Dan Zhu Tou (丹竹头站) _____ Line 3
- Deng Liang (登良站) _____ Line 2
- Dong Jiao Tou (东角头站) _____ Line 2
- Dongmen (东门) _____ Line 2
- Fu Tian (福田站) _____ Lines 2,3
- Fu Min (富民站) _____ Line 4
- Fu Tian Kou An (福田口岸站) _____ Line 4
- Gang Xia (港厦站) _____ Line 1
- Gang Xia Bei (岗厦北站) _____ Line 2
- Gao Xin Yuan (高新园站) _____ Line 1
- Go Wu Gong Yuan (购物公园站) _____ Line 3
- Gu Shu (固戍站) _____ Line 1
- Guo Mao (国贸站) _____ Line 1
- Hai Shang Shi Jie (海上世界站) _____ Line 2
- Hai Yue (海月站) _____ Line 2
- He Ao (荷坳站) _____ Line 3
- Hong Lin (横岗站) _____ Line 3
- Hong Shan (红岭站) _____ Line 4
- Hong Shu Wan (红山站) _____ Line 2
- Hou Hai (后海站) _____ Line 2
- Hou Rui (后瑞站) _____ Line 1
- Hua Qiang Bei (华强北站) _____ Line 2
- Hua Qiang Lu (华强路占) _____ Line 1
- Hua Qiao Cheng (华侨城站) _____ Line 1
- Hua Xin (华新站) _____ Line 3
- Huang Bei (黄贝岭站) _____ Line 2
- Hui Zhan Zhong Xin (会展中心站) _____ Lines 1,4
- Ji Chang Dong (机场东站) _____ Line 1
- Ji Xiang (吉祥站) _____ Line 3
- Jing Tian (景田站) _____ Line 2
- Ke Yuan (科苑站) _____ Line 2
- Ke Xue Guan (科学馆站) _____ Line 1
- Lao Jie (老街站) _____ Lines 1,3
- Li Yu Men (鲤鱼门站) _____ Line 1
- Lian Hua Bei (莲花北站) _____ Line 4
- Lian Hua Cun (莲花村站) _____ Line 3

- Lian Hua Xi (莲花西站) _____ Line 2
- Liu Yue (六约站) _____ Line 3
- Long Cheng Guang Chang (龙城广场站) _____ Line 3
- Long Hua (龙华站) _____ Line 4
- Long Sheng (龙胜站) _____ Line 4
- Luo Hu (罗湖站) _____ Line 1
- Min Le (民乐站) _____ Line 4
- Mu Mian Wan (木棉湾站) _____ Line 3
- Nan Lian (南联站) _____ Line 3
- Ping Zhou (坪洲站) _____ Line 1
- Qian Hai Wan (前海湾站) _____ Line 1
- Qiao Cheng Bei (深康站) _____ Line 2
- Qiao Cheng Dong (桥成东站) _____ Line 1
- Qiao Xiang (侨香站) _____ Line 2
- Qing Hu (清湖站) _____ Line 4
- Shai Bu (晒布站) _____ Line 3
- Shang Mei Lin (上梅林站) _____ Line 4
- Shang Tang (上塘站) _____ Line 4
- Shao Nian Gong (少年宫站) _____ Lines 3,4
- She Kou Gang (蛇口湾站) _____ Line 2
- Shen Da (深大站) _____ Line 1
- Shen Kang (侨城北站) _____ Line 2
- Shenzhen Bei Zhan (深圳北站) _____ Line 4
- Shi Jie Zhi Chuang (世界之窗站) _____ Lines 1,2
- Shi Min Zhongxin (市民中心站) _____ Lines 2,4
- Shi Xia (石厦站) _____ Line 3
- Shuang Long (双龙站) _____ Line 3
- Shui Bei (水贝站) _____ Line 3
- Shui Wan (水湾站) _____ Line 2
- Song Hai (松海站) _____ Line 3
- Tang Keng (塘坑站) _____ Line 3
- Tao Yuan (桃园站) _____ Line 1
- Tian Bei (田贝站) _____ Line 3
- Tong Xin Ling (通新岭站) _____ Line 3
- Wan Xia (湾厦站) _____ Line 2
- Xi Xiang (西乡站) _____ Line 1
- Xiang Mei Bei (香梅北站) _____ Line 2
- Xiang Mi (香蜜站) _____ Line 2
- Xiang Mi Hu (相迷糊站) _____ Line 1
- Xin An (新安站) _____ Line 1
- Xin Xiu (新秀站) _____ Line 2
- Yan Nan (燕南站) _____ Line 2
- Yi Tian (益田站) _____ Line 3
- Yin Hai (银海站) _____ Line 3
- Zhuzi Lin (竹子林站) _____ Line 1

Traveling Shenzhen by Bus

THERE ARE MANY buses in the city and all connections are good, but bus signs are only in Chinese (no pinyin). Without a good map of Shenzhen or without speaking Chinese, it can be quite difficult to travel by bus. Buses are often overcrowded during rush hours. Depending on the type of bus (new air-conditioning buses are most expensive) and the distance, it costs between 1 and 6RMB.

It is possible to use a transport card (Shenzhen Tong). They are available for sale in Metro Stations. The deposit is 40RMB, refundable. You then need to top it up with at least 50RMB. The Shenzhen Tong Card card be topped up at many stores throught Shenzhen (7/11, pharmacies, shops, etc).

There are two classes of busses.

1. Some busses have a fixed fare rate. In those busses you need to flash your card at the reader located in the front of the bus, next to the driver.

2. All other busses have variable rates. The ticket lady will ask you where you want to go. Make sure you know the name of the stop in Chinese. She will use a card reader to deduct credits from your card, according to the distance.

If there is no ticket seller, and you don't have the Shenzhen Tong card, remember to bring some coins or small notes as the bus driver will not return you the change.

The official Shenzhen bus website (www.szbus.com.cn) is not available in English.

MAJOR BUS STATIONS

Yinhu Bus Station: The Yinhu Bus Station has the most long-distance bus lines, with busses departing to Guangxi, Hunan, Fujian, Zhejiang, Jiangxi, Jiangsu, Hubei, Anhui, Hainan, Sichuan, and other cities of Guangdong Province. Regular bus No.222 can take you to the Yinhu station.

Futian Bus Station: Located in

Futian District, it has buses to some cities of Guangdong and Guangxi provinces.

Luohu Bus Station: Most of the buses from Luohu Bus Station depart to cities in Guangdong Province. There are also some that go to Fujian Province. Buses 1, 7, 12, 17, 25, 38, 101, 102, 106, 205, 215, 302, K302 and 352 can be used to get to Luohu Bus Station.

SIGHTSEEING AND SHOPPING LINES
Sightseeing line

It departs from Window of the World, Happy Valley, Splendid China, and other popular tourist sites.

Bus number:

Tourist Line 1 - 观光巴士1.

Note that the bus "1" and "1" Tourist Line" are two different lines, the latter is a double-decker.

Price:

The whole tour is 8RMB

Running hours:

7am - 9pm

Line:

Window of the World - OCT East 未来时代 - 东部华侨城总站

Stops:

Window of the World 世界之窗 - Hexiang Ming Art Museum 何香凝美术馆 - Splendid China 锦绣中华 - 康佳集团 - Shenzhen Press Group 特区报社 - 投资大厦 - Gangxia 岗厦 - 田面 - Huaqiang Bei 上海宾馆西 - 兴华宾馆西 - 市委 - Diwang Sightseeing Building 地王大厦 - 门诊部 - 广深宾馆 - 京鹏大厦 - 冶金大厦 - 新秀立交 - Huangbei Hill 黄贝岭 - Shenzhen Luohu Gymnasium 罗湖体育馆 - 西岭下 - 聚宝路口 - 莲塘 - 畔山花园 - 长岭 - 盐田防疫大楼 - 新一佳 - Yantian Government Building 盐田区政府 - Yantian Bus Station - 盐田汽车站 - 沙头角保税区 - 海港大厦 - 西山吓 - 海滨浴场 - Dameisha 大梅沙 - OCT East 东部华侨城总站

Shopping line

This line brings you to some famous shopping centers such as Women's

World, Mao Ye Department Store, Buji Free Market, etc.

Bus number:

Tourist Line 2 观光巴士2.

Note that the bus number "2" and "2 Tourist Line" are two different lines, the latter is a double-decker.

Price:

3RMB

Running hours:

7:30am - 10:30pm

Line:

Buji Lianjian Station - Futian Nongpi Market

布吉联检站 - 福田农批市场

Stops:

Buji Lianjian Station 布吉联检站 - Buji Nongmao Market 布吉农贸市场 - Honghu Lake Park 洪湖公园 - Honghu Lake Wal-Mart 洪湖沃尔玛 - Dongmen Center 东门中 - Dongmen Center 东门 - Dongmen Center Shopping Streets 东门老街 - 门诊部 - 人民桥 - Shenzhen Book City 深圳书城 - 经济大厦 - 华强中 - Huaqiang Bei electronic Market 华强北 - 市二医院 - 莲花一村 - 公交大厦 - 彩田村 - 北大医院 - Xiameilin Market 下梅林市场 - Futian Nongpi Market 福田农批市场

Hong Kong, Macao, Shenzhen, Zhuhai Ferry Map

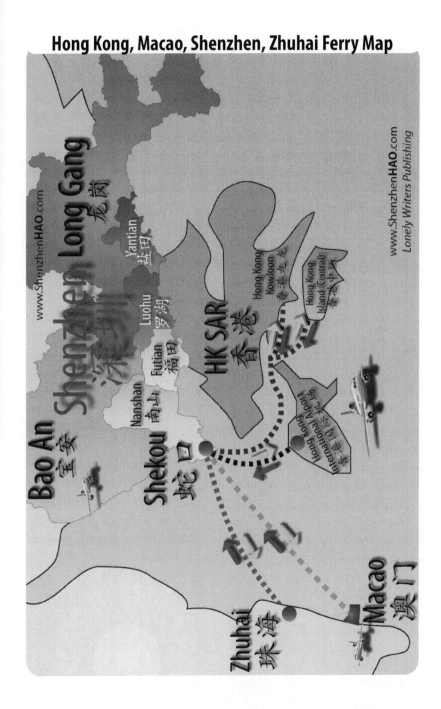

Hong Kong MTR System Map

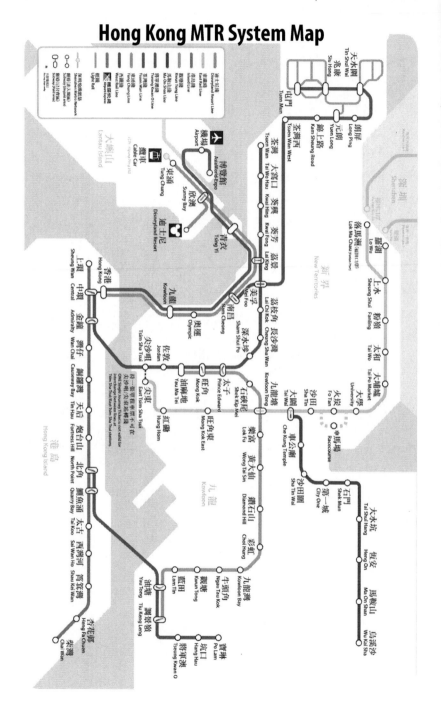

Guangzhou Metro System Map

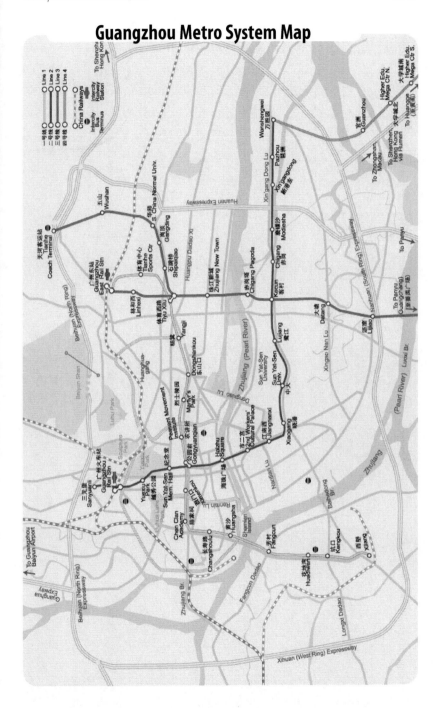

Chinese Corner & Transportation

Airplane	飞机	fēi jī
Airport	机场	jī chǎng
Airport check-in	机场签	jī chǎng qiān
Airport counter	机场柜台	jī chǎng guì tái
Airport lounge	机场贵宾室	jī chǎng guì bīn shì
Bicycle	自行车	zì xíng chē
Bill	买单	mǎi chán
Boarding pass	登机卡	dēng jī kǎ
Boat	船	chuán
Booking	预订	yù dìng
Bus	巴士	bā shì
Button	按钮	àn niǔ
Cancel	取消	qǔ xiāo
Cash	现金	xiàn jīn
City	城市	chéng shì
Credit card	信用卡	xìn yòng kǎ
Departure	出发	chū fā
District	市区	shì qū
Door	门	mén
Economy	经济	jīng jì
Exit	出口	chū kǒu
Ferry terminal	码头	mǎ tóu
First class	头等	tóu děng
Gate	门	mén
Lake	湖	hú
Late	晚	wǎn
Metro	地铁	dì tiě
Money	钱	qián
Number	号	háo
Order	点	diǎn
Park	公园	gōng yuán
Passport	护照	hù zhào
Plane pilot	飞机驾驶员	fēi jī jià shǐ yuán
Plane ticket	飞机票	fēi jī piào

Please take me to	请带我去 ...	qǐng dài wǒ qù ...
Port	港口	gǎng kǒu
Price	价格	jià gé
Road	路	lù
Seat	座位	zuò wèi
Stewardess	空中小姐	kōng zhōng xiǎo jie
Ticket	机票	jī piào
Too expensive	太贵了	tài guì le
Train	火车	huǒ chē
Transportation	交通运输	jiāo tōng yùn shū
Vegetarian	吃素的	chī sù de
Wait	请稍等	qǐng shāo děng
What time?	什么时间?	shén me shí jiān?

Useful Information about Shenzhen

Chinese Visa

GETTING A CHINESE VISA

I N MOST CASES, a visa should be obtained from a Chinese embassy or consulate before arriving anywhere in China. Chinese visa procedures tightened up quite a bit before the Beijing Olympics. Towards the end of 2008, the Chinese government loosened the rules but not yet completely. You may have to show airline ticket and hotel accommodation in China before your visa is granted, and it will be only single entry for 30 days. This may apply to all foreigners. It is now a major issue for anyone trying to do business in China.

Certain nationalities visiting from Hong Kong can obtain a single-entry five-day Special Economic Zone Tourism Visa on arrival for costs ranging from 160 to around 1,000RMB, depending on your nationality. The office is located in Luohu, upstairs after clearing Hong Kong immigration and customs. Currently, the Hong Kong immigration only ac-

cepts RMB as payment. Be sure to obtain sufficient cash in advance. The office can be reached at tel. +86 755 8232-7700. Visas on arrival are reported to be available for Canadian, New Zealand, and British passport holders, but often unavailable for United States passports. At the time of this writing, visas for US citizens cost 130USD for each visa for 1.5 days visit. There is no visa-on-arrival office at Lok Ma Chau (Huangang checkpoint).

Getting a tourist visa in Hong Kong now takes 3-4 days and costs HK$150-1100. The old approach of arriving in Hong Kong and immediately applying for a visa is no longer worth the cost, as you may be forced to pay expensive hotel bills in Hong Kong until your visa is granted. Macau's visa office is less crowded and the hotels a bit cheaper, but it takes just as long. In general, only single and double entry visas are granted to visitors without Hong Kong ID cards, although foreigners with previous entries into the mainland or Hong Kong student and work visas have been known to be approved for multiple entries.

Once in Shenzhen, if you need further information about visas, residence permits and working permits, you can contact the Shenzhen Municipal Public Security Bureau (深圳市公安局出入境管理处), tel: 9500-0100, Add: 4018 Jiefang Road, Luohu District (罗湖区解放路4018号).

VISA OVERVIEW

- G visa: transit
- L visa: tourism
- F visa: business trips, internships, short study

- Z visa: working
- X visa: study more than 6 months

LOSS OF VISA/PASSPORT

1. Go to the local public security bureau (当地公安局) to report the loss, you will be given a receipt.
2. Take the receipt to the second floor of the Shenzhen Public Security Bureau (深圳公安局, it's near Diwang Building 地王大厦, address: Shenzhen Public Security Bureau, 4018, Jiefang Rd. 深圳市解放路4018号中共深圳市公安局) to apply for a one-entry visa, if you want to apply for a long-stay visa, go to the Chinese embassy.

Important Phone Numbers

Accident & Emergency	120
Fire Department	119
Police	110
Traffic Accident	122
ADSL Customer Service	8370-0112
Air Ticket Reservations	8320-7888
Bank Of China, Shenzhen Branch	8228-8288

Consumer Complaints	8210-1315
C-trip	021 3406-4888
DHL China	800-810-8000
Directory Enquiries	114
Express Post Delivery	185

Fedex China	800-830-2338		Shenzhen Radio Station	2541-0011
Hong Kong Ferry	2669-5597		Shenzhen Railway Station	8232-8647
Information Service	160		Shenzhen Special Zone Daily	8351-8888
Municipal Government	8210-0000		Shenzhen TV Station	2516-0630
On-call Taxi Service #1	8393-8000		Telecomm Service Complaints	180
On-call Taxi Service #2	96511		Theater tickets	11185
Shenzhen Cable TV	(Topway) 8306-6888		Time Check	117
			Tourist Complaints	8322-1397
Shenzhen Economic Daily	8390-0011		Transport Complaints	8322-8111
Shenzhen People's Hospital	2553-1387		UPS China	800-820-8388
Shenzhen Post Office	8223-8466		Weather Information	121

Police Stations

Nanshan

Nantou Police Station
2674-6110
No.168, Zhongshan Yuan Rd, Nanshan District

Nanshan Police Station
2664-0284
No.1155,Nanshan Rd, Nanshan District

Shekou Police Station
2668-5111
No.68,Shekou Huaguo Rd, Nanshan District

Xili Police Station
2662-0723
Xili Wenxin Rd, Nanshan District

Futian

Nanyuan Police Station
8363-8110
No.123, Nanyuan Rd, Futian District

Futian Police Station
8338-8110
No.1001, Shenzhen Nan Rd, Futian District

Yuanling Police Station
8210-0222
No.1010, Shangbu Mid Rd,Futian District

Meilin Police Station
8331-8110
No.38, Meilin Rd, Futian District

Xiangmihu Police Station
8370-2115
The 6th Zizhu Rd, Zhuzilin, Futian District

Luohu
Dongmen Police Station
8223-7352
No 3002, Renmin North Rd, Luohu District

Nanhu Police Station
8223-9119
No.2009, Nanhu Rd, Luohu District

Guiyuan Police Station
2559-5314
No.28, Songyuan Rd, Luohu District

Huangbei Police Station
2540-1471
No.1065, Huali Rd, Luohu District

Cuizhu Police Station
2553-0840
No.30, Shuitian 1st street, Tianbei 4th Rd,
Luohu District

Sungang Police Station
8243-2263
No.213, Baogang Rd, Luohu District

Donghu Police Station
2551-1808
No.1128, Taibai Rd, Luohu District

Liantang Police Station
2570-8907
No.198, Liantang Rd, Luohu District

Yantian
Shatoujiao Police Station
2555-0659
No.110, Shensha Rd, Yantian District

Yantian Police Station
2520-0059
No.43, Yanheng Rd, Yantian District

Meisha Police Station
2506-1202
No.9, Jinsha Street, Dameisha

Bao'an
Zhen nan Police Station
2778-8547
No.91, Xinghua Rd, the 19th Area of Bao'an
District

Baomin Police Station
2781-3110
No.1, Yu'an 2nd Rd, Bao'an

Fanshen Police Station
2758-7110
No.88, Shangchuan Rd, Bao'an District

Xixiang Police Station
2795-6108
No.1, Le Yuan Street, Xixiang Town, Bao'an
District

Huangtian Police Station
2751-0234
Huangtian Village, Xixiang Town, Bao'an
District

Fuyong Police Station
2739-5110
Fuyong Town, Bao'an District

Shajing Police Station
2772-9110
No.492, Xinsha Rd, Shajing Town, Bao'an
District

Songgang Police Station
2706-4110

Hongxing Ganglian Industrial Area, Songgang Town, Bao'an District

Gongming Police Station
2710-0110
No.296, Minsheng Rd, Gongming Town, Bao'an District

Shiyan Police Station
2776-0209
No.411, Baoshi East Rd, Shiyan Town, Bao'an District

Longhua Police Station
2813-6110
No.17, Longguang West Rd, Longhua Town, Bao'an District

Fumin Police Station
2802-2353
Baochang Rd, Fumin Village, Guanlan Town, Bao'an District

Niuhu Police Station
2808-4110
No.87, Golf Rd, Guanlan Town, Bao'an District

Guangming Police Station
2740-9110
Guangming Street, Guangming Town, Bao'an District

Longgang
Buji Police Station
2887-1099
No.117, Jihua Rd, Buji Town, Longgang District

Bantian Police Station
8419-3123
No.610, Bulong Rd, Bantian Village, Buji Town, Longgang District

Pinghu Police Station
2884-3110
No.532, Pinghu Rd, Pinghu Town, Longgang District

Henggang Police Station
2886-3299
No.852, Shenhui Rd, Henggang Town, Longgang District

Longgang Police Station
2883-3220
No.468, Longyuan Rd, Longgang Town, Longgang District

Tongle Police Station
8489-5110
No.48, Dakang Rd, Longgang Town, Longgang District

Pingdi Police Station
8409-2296
No.390, Shenhui Rd, Pingdi Town, Longgang District

Pingshan Police Station
2882-6282
No.348, Dongzhong Rd, Pingshan Town, Longgang District

Kengzhi Police Station
8413-4541
No.1, Renmin West Rd, Kengzhi Town, Longgang District

Kuichong Police Station
8420-7357
No.57, Kuiping North Rd, Kuichong Town, Longgang District

Dapeng Police Station
8430-2110
No.28, Yingbin South Rd, Dapeng Town, Longgang District

Nan'ao Police Station
8440-2110
No.138, Fumin Rd, Town, Longgang District

Dongshen
Dongshen Police Station
2541-0562
No.10, Donghu 2nd Rd, Reservoir

Airport Police Station
2777-6031
Commercial Street, Airport 6th Rd

Dayawan
Shuishang Police Station
8447-3928
Dayawan Nuclear Power Station

Consulates in Guangdong

Canada	Room 801, China Hotel, 120 Liuhua Road, Guangzhou	86660569
Denmark	Room 1578,China Hotel, 120 Liuhua Road, Guangzhou	86660353 86660795
France	Room 803, GITIC Plaza, 339 Huan Shi Dong Road,Guangzhou	83303405
Germany	GITIC Plaza, 339 Huan Shi Dong Road, Guangzhou	8330653
Holland	Room 5304, GITIC Plaza, 339 Huan Shi Dong Road, Guangzhou	83302067 83302824
Italy	CITIC Plaza, 233, Tian He Bei Road, Guangzhou	38770556
Japan	Garden Hotel, 368 Huan Shi Dong Road, Guangzhou	83343009
Kampuchea	Garden Hotel, 368 Huan Shi Dong Road, Guangzhou	83879005
Republic of Korea	18F West Tower, Guangzhou International Commercial Center, No.122, Tiyu Road East, Tianhe District, Guangzhou	3887-0555
Malaysia	CITIC Plaza, 233 Tian He Bei Road, Guangzhou	87395660
Philippines	GITIC Plaza, 339 Huan Shi Dong Road,Guangzhou	83311461 83310996
Poland	Room 1401, GITIC Plaza, 339 Huan Shi Dong Road, Guangzhou	83350909
Thailand	Third Floor, White Swan Hotel, 1, Sha Mian Nan Jie, Guangzhou	81886968-3303
U.S.A.	White Swan Hotel, 1, Sha Mian Nan Jie, Guangzhou	81888911
United Kingdom	2nd Floor, GITIC Plaza, 339 Huan Shi Dong Road, Guangzhou	83331354
Vietnam	Suite B, HuaXia Hotel, No.8, Qiaoguang Road	83305910

INDEX

Discovery Publisher LTD (探索出版社有限公司)

Suite 902, Wing On Central Building

26, Des Voeux Road

Hong Kong SAR, China

Phone :	(+852) 2421-1498
Website :	www.discoverypublisher.com
Email :	contact@discoverypublisher.com
Facebook :	facebook.com/DiscoveryPublisher
Twitter :	twitter.com/DiscoveryPB

ISBN 978-988-15257-3-4

Second Edition, March 2014

DISCOVERY PUBLISHER

NEVER SEEN BEFORE • NEVER BEEN BEFORE

Printed in Great Britain
by Amazon.co.uk, Ltd.,
Marston Gate.